YELLOW WOLF
Photograph taken in 1908.

I am telling you true! I will die, you will die! This story will be for the people who come after us. For them to see and know what was done here.
—YELLOW WOLF

Yellow Wolf:

His Own Story

By

LUCULLUS VIRGIL McWHORTER

Photographs are reproduced from originals in the L. V. McWhorter
Collection, Washington State University Libraries,
Pullman, Washington.

REVISED AND ENLARGED EDITION

The CAXTON PRINTERS, Ltd.
Caldwell, Idaho
1995

First printing December, 1940
Second printing March, 1948
Third printing August, 1983
Fourth printing January, 1986
Fifth printing July, 1991
Sixth printing April, 1996

Library of Congress Cataloging in Publication Data

Yellow Wolf, 1855–1935.
    Yellow Wolf, his own story.

    Bibliography: p.
    1. Nez Percé Indians — Wars, 1877 — Personal narratives.
2. Yellow Wolf, 1855–1935. I. McWhorter, Lucullus Virgil,
1860–1944. II. Title.
E83.77.Y4   1986   973.8′092′4   85-16659
ISBN 0-87004-317-X
ISBN 0-87004-315-3 (pbk.)

Printed, lithographed, and bound in the United States of America by
The CAXTON PRINTERS, Ltd.
Caldwell, Idaho
160989

YELLOW WOLF:
His Own Story

❁

DEDICATION

TO THE shades of patriotic warriors, heroic women, feeble age, and helpless infancy—sacrificed on the gold-weighted altars of Mammon and political chicanery, 1863-77, are these pages most fervently inscribed.

YELLOW WOLF:
His Own Story

☸

ACKNOWLEDGMENTS

I WISH to express my appreciation to the following Nez Perce interpreters, named in the order of service. Their willingness and perseverance have helped to clear many a thorn from the path of interpretation:

THOMAS HART	MANY WOUNDS
RALPH ARMSTRONG	CHARLEY WHITE
SILAS WHITMAN	HENRY WILSON
MISS SOPHIA KAMIAKUN	THOMAS BRONCHEAU
THOMAS WATERS	ALBERT SPENCER
BILLY YELLOW WOLF	MISS ADELINE ANDREWS
STAR J. MAXWELL	CAMILLE WILLIAMS

PAUL AMBRO

To many other persons I am much indebted for encouragement and assistance. In particular I wish to express my gratitude to Alonzo V. Lewis and Emil Kopac for photographs; to W. P. Bonney, secretary, Washington State Historical Society; O. G. Libby, secretary, North Dakota State Historical Society; Mrs. Anna Connell, assistant librarian, Historical Society of Montana; and the staffs of the State Historical societies of Idaho and Washington for invaluable aid. My appreciation is also extended to the following for services of varied nature: W. D. Vincent; Major General R. H. Fletcher, military attaché, Spanish Embassy; H. Dean Guie; J. H. Horner; O. H. Lipps, superintendent, Nez Perce Indian Reservation; Joseph G. Masters; J. P. MacLean; Harvey K. Myer, superintendent, Colville Indian Reservation; John Rooke; Carl Schurra; and J. L. Sharon; to Nipo Strongheart, for research in the War Department archives, Washington, D. C.; and to my brother Judge J. C. McWhorter; my sons O. T. and V. O. McWhorter; and my granddaughter, Miss Judy McWhorter, for innumerable favors.

YELLOW WOLF:
His Own Story

✪

CONTENTS

Part One: *The War and the Warrior*

CONTENTS

YELLOW WOLF:
His Own Story

&

ILLUSTRATIONS

ILLUSTRATIONS

PART ONE:
The War and the Warrior

✦

YELLOW WOLF:

His Own Story

❦

INTRODUCTION

IN THE mellow glow of an October sunset in the year 1907, a strange Indian, of strikingly strong physique, rode into the lane leading from the highway to the author's residence, driving before him a saddle horse limping from a severe wire cut. After a formal greeting, he pointed to the ragged wound and, in a soft, modulated tone of broken English, asked inquiringly:

"Sick! Hoss stay here?"

Receiving an affirmative response, the Indian turned and rode away, revealing neither name nor tribal affiliation. It was ten months later that he appeared with four other tribesmen, and asked for his horse. I released it, in accordance with tribal ethics, free of charge.

Such was my introduction to Heinmot Hihhih, "White Thunder" or "White Lightning," better known as Hemene Moxmox, "Yellow Wolf," Nez Perce warrior of 1877. It was the beginning of a friendship which proved inductive of this volume. With his wife, small son, and other members of the Chief Joseph band of exiles, he was at this time on the annual "trek" to the Yakima Valley hop fields.

At the close of hop picking of this second year (1908) the band encamped on the riverbank at my place for several days. It was during this time that I obtained the first portions of Yellow Wolf's war narrative, which were added to annually for the ensuing twenty-four

13

years, or until the aging warrior was no longer physically able to appear at the hopyards. His last contribution was in May, 1935, at his home on the Colville Indian Reservation, Washington, at which time he contributed many more details to the narrative.

If Yellow Wolf was resentful of ill treatment, he was equally reciprocal to kindness and just dealing. It was in the evening gloaming preceding the breaking of the Nez Perce camp at my place in October, 1909, that, standing on the riverbank, he spoke through interpreter Whitman:

> "This is the last night I will be with you, and I would like you to understand. I have been here with you for a few suns. I am glad we get along so well. It is the way I have been with everybody who treats me right. I like good people! I will never forget you and your family. I will remember while I live. How is your heart? What do you think about it?"

On that occasion, in acordance with tribal rites, I named Yellow Wolf to take the place of a brother of earlier years, thus sealing a sacred friendship for all time.

At the time that I first became acquainted with Yellow Wolf (October, 1908), he stood 5 feet 10½ inches in his moccasins, and his weight was 187½ pounds. Well built, he had been very athletic, and was quick and accurate in movement. Tragedy was written in every lineament of his face; his laughter was infrequent, and was never more than a soft, scarcely audible chuckle.

As his land allotment was not provided with irrigation, his rifle and fish spear were long the principal means of supplying the home larder with meat, until old age and failing vitality precluded such activity. It is

YELLOW WOLF AND THE AUTHOR

Left to right: Thomas Hart, interpreter; Yellow Wolf; L. V. McWhorter.
October, 1908.

NEZ PERCE CAMP
On L. V. McWhorter's ranch, Yakima, Washington, October, 1908.

AYATOOTONMI AND JASPER
Yellow Wolf's wife and younger son, 1908.

gratifying to know that under the later regime of the Indian Department, the old warrior was the recipient of marked aid during his declining years.

Of his war record, Yellow Wolf was justly proud. His war name, as he explains in Chapter 1, was Heinmot Hihhih—White Thunder, or White Lightning *(Heinmot* meaning either). As a combatant, he could boast possessing not only the irresistible force of thunder, but also of the adroit circumspection and fierce fighting qualities of the timber wolf.

As the wolf is the greatest hunter among all the wilderness denizens, so Yellow Wolf excelled as a hunter.

As the wolf is unsurpassed in the sense of smell, so Yellow Wolf, like the famed "Deaf" Smith, of Texas, and the renowned Jesse Hughes, of the Monongahela border, could detect the presence of an enemy at a considerable distance by the olfactory sense alone.

As the wolf is the only forest dweller of which the mighty grizzly bear stands in dread, so Yellow Wolf reveled in combating the grizzly.

Yellow Wolf, in his younger days, was renowned for his wonderful horsemanship. Even when past middle age, he once tamed a vicious range horse of man-killing propensities. After corralling and roping the animal, and meeting with no success at friendly overtures, Yellow Wolf sprang to its back, where he stuck and hung until it was brought into submission. If the enraged animal resorted to rolling in order to dislodge its tormentor, it regained its feet only to find Yellow Wolf again on its back—and all the time the Indian had no hold but a rope looped about the animal's head.

Yellow Wolf later received a lasting injury when a fractious horse, rearing, fell backwards, and the rider failed to get clear. The impact was on his right breast, which was ever afterwards "sick," as he termed it. The injury caused a slight droop to his shoulders.

To obviate a possible misconception because of a name, it is well to mention that the following item which appeared in the Yakima press in September, 1910, does not refer to the Yellow Wolf of war fame:

> Yellow Wolf, an Indian arrested here by Deputy Monroe of Lewiston, Idaho, was returned to Lewiston to face a charge of murder. Yellow Wolf was described by Monroe as a horsethief, gambler and bad character.

At the time of this arrest, Yellow Wolf and his wife, with their small son, were all picking hops in the Yakima field and at the end of the season camped for a few days at the writer's place, adding to his narrative, as was our wont each year. He returned to his home the latter part of October. The man arrested was also known among his tribesmen as Wolf Shirt-on.

In the winter of 1916-17, Yellow Wolf headed a tribal petition praying for state legislative protection from the blighting inroads of the bootleggers. This "Macedonian cry" was read at a morning session of the state senate preliminary to its being referred to the Committee of Public Morals—never to be further heard from.

Of a sensitive nature, Yellow Wolf felt his isolation keenly during his latter years, when the last of his war mates was gone. The younger generation held no particular interest in the lonely old hero of a "lost cause." But there was an occasional cheery flash athwart his gloomy horizon, and such was his meeting with the late Major General Hugh Lenox Scott, of which he never tired of speaking. Major General Scott was at the Colville Indian Agency in the earlier twenties, and hearing of

Yellow Wolf as a warrior, had the superintendent send for him. There was no interpreter, the conversation being wholly in the Indian sign language, at which they both excelled. Of their meeting, Yellow Wolf related the following:

We met. General Scott threw me the words, "I come from away off. I am glad to meet you. We will talk a few words before I ask you about some very important business."

I answered him, "All right. We will talk. You came a long distance. My heart and your heart are like shaking hands."

"You ever been in war?"

"You see I am nearly old man."

"How old are you?"

"Come near seventy. Over sixty. Will be seventy very soon."

"You remember the war?"

"Yes."

"I am glad you tell me you were in war. Tell me why you people travel rough lands, through timber."

"Yes. I know all about this mountain traveling. That was decided by the chiefs. They decided for this purpose. If they went over rough mountains, the big cannon could not follow. It was safest way."

"That was why General Howard failed to overtake you."

"Yes."

Then General Scott spoke to the agent in English. "Are there other warriors around here in Nespelem?"

The agent pointed to Red Star [Willie Andrews] and answered, "Ask him. He is chief and knows."

I had never reported to the agent that I was higher [referring to his warrior record] than Red Star. The General and agent talked. He asked the agent if Andrews fought in war and was told no. The General then said, "I won't make conversation with him. Only one I talk to is warrior when I have chance. I do not care for others not in the fight."

This was the first time the agent looked at me. From that moment he respected me. General Scott now threw me the words, "It is nearly noon. We will eat dinner together because you are alive and I am alive. If I had been in the fight where you were fighting, I think you would have killed me with war club and not the gun. As result of that war was bloody water, bloody eating. It was like

17

drinking blood. Bloody hands, suffering. For that reason we are going to eat together. In fact, we are good friends. I realize we are friends."

General Scott and I were of same mind, same feeling. I answered, "I am glad to hear you speak of eating dinner. That food gives us strength and life. Gives strength that hostile feelings are past."

"We are like brothers. If I had got to the surrender in lead, I could have done something for you. I was not there."

That was General Scott's last word of the war. That was all we talked about the war. We parted, and I never saw him again.

During one of our interviews in 1931, Yellow Wolf made the following remarks, which may be taken as a just summary of his feelings about the long-suppressed truths of the Nez Perce War:

"The story I gave you long ago—if people do not like it, I would tell it anyway. I am not strong, and do not expect to be better any time. I would like finishing it as truth, not as lie.

"We have worked together a long time. You always helped me from first time we met. I am aging where I can not do much more.

"White people, aided by Government, are smothering my Indian rights. The young generation behind me, for them I tell the story. It is for them! I want next generation of whites to know and treat the Indian as themselves.

"We came from no country, as have the whites. We were always here. Nature placed us in this land of ours— land that has been taken from us. I am telling my story that all may know why the war we did not want. War is made to take something not your own."

Yellow Wolf, patriot of a lost cause, died at his home on the Colville Indian Reservation, August 21, 1935, aged seventy-nine years. His son, Homas—inherited name of his maternal great-grandsire—cared for his

HOMER L. MORRISON

"THERE THEY ARE! DO YOU NOT SEE THEM?"

The weed-grown mound in the foreground is Yellow Wolf's grave in Colville Indian Reservation cemetery. The headstone is merely a rough, unlettered field stone.

father during his last illness. Of the closing scene this son, who is better known as Billy, gave the following brief depiction:

"My father grew very weak and thin. Not weighing over sixty-five pounds, I could easily carry him about. The evening before his death he said to me:

" 'I am going in the morning when the sun *eetetolokt* [pauses on the horizon's edge]. It is then that I will leave you and all others. You, my only son, and my daughters gone, were only loaned to me. Loaned by Ahkunkenekoo [God, Deity]. You are my brother, they, my sisters. I will go with the new sun.'

"Next morning just as the sun rested on the edge of the horizon, although he could not see it, he said to all of us:

" 'I am now going! My old friends have come for me! They are here! Do you not see them? There stands Eshawis [Crow Blanket], and there Peopeo Howisthowit [Curlew], and Diskoskow [Sun Faded]. They have come to take me to Ahkunkenekoo [Land Above; Happy Hereafter].'

"Those were my father's last words."

Yellow Wolf was buried at Nespelem (Wash.). His grave is near that of his renowned chief and leader, Joseph, Heinmot Tooyalakekt (Thunder Traveling to Loftier [Mountain] Heights), whom he loved so well.

It seems ironical that these two, and others of their comrade warriors—votaries of an ancestral Dreamer faith never understood by the whites—should sleep in the very shadows of a Christian church, beneath the echoes of its chiming bell, when it was to the institutional tenets of the religion that they attributed their downfall, through the bogus "treaty" of 1863.

The multiplicity of names borne by certain warriors proved most confusing in hearing Yellow Wolf's narrative, as in the capture of the howitzer at the battle of the Big Hole, and in the leadership of the night raid on General Howard's night camp at Camas Meadows, and the seizing of Lieutenant Jerome at the last battle. Practically every warrior was known by two names, and many by a half dozen—although some of them were "pet," or "fun," nicknames.

Names were sometimes pronounced variantly by different interpreters. For instance, Spowyeyas, Sepowyes, Espawyas, and Powyes all allude to one person, and all are interpreted as "Light in the Mountain."

Therefore, throughout Yellow Wolf's narrative all Indians will be designated by the names by which they were known during the war, so far as can be ascertained. Their surplus names will be found, with definitions, when known, in the Glossary at the end of this volume.

Painstaking care was observed in obtaining these ofttimes intricate definitions, in spite of the disconcerting diversity of interpreters. In the midst of one such ordeal interpreter Hart explained:

"There is a lot in our language that bothers me, the same as in yours. When Yellow Wolf was ready to pull out from camp at your place the other day, he said that you had told him you wanted his story. He did not know how he could do this, since he speaks only a few English words. He tried one boy for interpreter who told him to find somebody who better understands. Yellow Wolf learned where I was and came to me and said, 'I need you!'

"I answered him, and he said to me again, 'I am going to say things, and I need you! I need you!'

" 'Yes, I will come with you,' I told him.

" 'I will tell of my war story; of facts that I have seen,' he said.

" 'Any hard words I can not pronounce in our language,' I answered him, 'I will make them nearest that I can.'

"This warrior says tell you, 'It is hard work for me—this talking. Like the heaviest lifting, it buzzes in my head! Too heavy lifting every day!'"

On one occasion an interpreter wrote out for me the following definition of a name which I had requested: "Teeweeyownah: Over the Point—it means like I send you over point of hill somewhere, or like you sit down and then scoot over something in that way; so you can make that out you self."

Such were some of the difficulties encountered. Thomas Hart, ex-private of the Fourth U. S. Cavalry, who saw service in the Philippines, was conscientious in his endeavor to give honest renditions. The more satisfactory interpreters were, like him, those who had but a fair English education, for such Indians retained to a greater degree the native ideas, assuring a clearer rendition of the narrator's speech and thought. In this respect a Carlisle graduate proved the least satisfactory, for his manifest proneness to modifications tended to suppress the native point of view and make it conform with the general white (and Christian Indian) contention that the war upon the Nez Perces was, in its essence, a just and righteous cause.

This point is well illustrated in the attitude shown by members of Chief Lawyer's family. When approached on the topic of the proposed chronicling, one of them vehemently protested:

"We want no such history written of that war! The blame was all with Chief Joseph! He was the cause of the trouble, and he got a lot of people killed. His land was not being taken from him. The Government would not do such a thing! We owe all that we are to the

Church, and we want to hear nothing more about any such history writing."

When the Chief Joseph Memorial Association proposed a colossus to the memory of the Nez Perce patriots, one of the Lawyer faction again remonstrated:

"If you want to honor anybody, why don't you put up a monument of that kind for my grandfather, Chief Lawyer? He did more for this country and for the white man than any other Indian!"

It is scarcely strange that whites were found equally bitter, and displaying about the same degree of logic; but it is doubly strange that this brand of invidious opposition should rear its baleful visage amidst the younger members of the fast-diminishing Chief Joseph band itself. One of them, whose paternal grandparents were both killed in the Big Hole shambles, openly declared to the writer: "Yellow Wolf has made a blanked fool of himself working with you. There will be a history written of that war, and it will be done right! The Indian boys will do it themselves."

None of the "Indian boys" has as yet come forward with a study of the causes and course of the Nez Perce conflict. In the meantime, it has been my high privilege to be the instrument for recording and bringing to publication the verified and corroborated narrative of Yellow Wolf as set forth in the following chapters.

SPECIAL NOTE ON THE WORD "NEZ PERCE"

Throughout this volume—except in quoting written authorities —the absurdly useless accent on the final *e* of Perce, as still used by most writers and as still given in Webster's *New International Dictionary*, will be omitted. This tribe of Indians call themselves Nĕz Per-cĕs (singular, Nĕz Pers), and have so pronounced it probably ever since the vast influx of American citizens in the gold rushes to Washington and Idaho in 1859-60. This tribe was originally given its French appellation by the French trappers who came with the Hudson's Bay Company brigades in the decades from 1810 to 1850, but even during this early period the French pronunciation of the tribal name was corrupted in usage among the equally omnipresent British and American fur traders. There is therefore not the slightest reason for retaining a totally obsolete accent mark and a misleading spelling in this word. In thirty years' experience I have *never* heard the Indians call themselves Nā Per-sā.

In Idaho there is a county named Nez Perce, also a town called Nezperce (written as one word). Both are locally pronounced in the American fashion—to rhyme with "verse." It is an interesting fact that the U. S. Geographic Board, the final arbiter in all geographical spellings, approves this usage, and ignores the accent mark. It is to be hoped that our leading dictionaries will eventually adopt this common-sense decision in regard to the name of that tribe which occupies so important a place in our Western history.

L. V. McW.

YELLOW WOLF:
His Own Story

✿

Youth of the Warrior

Hoping to incorporate something of Yellow Wolf's earlier life as a prelude to his war career, I broached the subject to him at our last interview at his home in May, 1935. The effort was futile. His native pride and modesty proved aversive to the measure. "I am now getting old," he protested. "I had seen twenty-one snows when the war was fought. It is not right for me to tell of my own growing-up life. That does not belong to history. Would not look well in this history we are writing. I do not want to hurt, to spoil what I did in the war. Only that should go in my story of the war. The other would not be well placed."

Insistence was not to be thought of. It was only by an assemblage of items gleaned from our previous interviews, covering more than a quarter of a century, that the meager glimpse of his early career as set forth in this chapter could be constructed.

I WAS born in the Wallowa Valley, Oregon,[1] long the home of Nez Perces. Our name for that river is Kahmuenem, named for a trailing vine growing at places along its banks and sands. There is where I grew up.

My father, Seekumses Kunnin [Horse Blanket][2], was rich in horses and cattle. A true horseman himself, he raised me among horses. Lived part of time east of Lapwai,[3] Idaho, but mostly in the Wallowa Valley.

I was with my father until well grown. Hunting,

---

[1] Legend places Yellow Wolf's birthplace in Idaho. This is an error, arising from the fact that the family lived there at one time—which, however, was subsequent to the date of his birth (1855).

[2] He was also known as Seekomgets Kanee (Using His Horse for Blanket).

[3] In 1926, Many Wounds said to me: "I will show you the true name of Lapwai." Leading the way to a partially dried-up quagmire lying between the Spalding Mission site and the mouth of Lapwai Creek, he pointed to the myriads of butterflies settled on the black mud, and demonstrating with his hands the slow fanning of their wings, explained: "That winging is *laplap*. The Indians knew this spot by that name. The whites changed it to 'Lapwai,' and so called the entire creek."

sporting of all kinds known to Indians. We would go to Wallowa in spring for salmon. Stay there all summer and until late fall. Plenty of game. It was easy to get our winter's food.

We often wintered in the Imnaha Valley, and most Indians wintered there always. The Imnaha was warmer than the Wallowa.

I was told that in early days my father was in battle near Walla Walla, fighting for the soldiers. With another man whose wife was with him, they were chased for their lives by Chief Kamiakun's warriors. They saw, and fled to a bunch of soldiers who received them kindly. The two joined the soldiers in a fight against the enemies.

Kamiakun's warriors rode swift circles about the camp, shooting arrows and bullets from horseback. But they were stood off and night drew on. In the darkness my father and companion guided the soldiers out from there. All escaped. It may have been other Indians than those of Chief Kamiakun, the Yakima. I do not know.

My name as a boy can not be translated. Too deep! You can not write it down. One inherited name was Inneecheekoostin.[4]

My mother Yiyik Wasumwah [Swan Woman; Swans Lighting on Water] was a sister [first cousin] to Chief Joseph. It was this way. The mother of "Old" Chief Joseph, and my grandfather on my mother's side were full brother and sister. This was why I belonged to Young Joseph's band. Joseph's people held strong to blood kinship.

---

[4] As common among Indians, especially warriors, Yellow Wolf had a multiplicity of names. No interpretation for Inneecheekoostin was found. Another of his early names was Pahkar Tamkikeechet (Five Times Looking Through, or Fifteen Lightnings).

My great grandfather [maternal], Seeloo Wahyakt [Eye Necklace], was a great war chief. He was killed in battle with the Pokatellas, fighting for possession of Wallowa Valley. Became separated from his band and outnumbered. His arrows exhausted, he was captured. His arms and legs were cut off before he was killed.

My grandfather [maternal], Homas, son of Seeloo Wahyakt, died on a buffalo hunt in Yellowstone Park. I am not mistaken! It was at Sokolinim [Antelope] where he was buried. This is north of some hot springs. Not over or beyond any big mountain, but is above where two rivers meet. Names of larger river Pahniah Koos [Tongue Water]. A smaller river above there is Wiyukea Koos [Elk Water]. There were Indians living around there somewhere. We hunted there, for the Sioux [Assiniboins] attacked us if we went on south side of the big mountain.

We knew that Park country, no difference what white people say! And when retreating from soldiers we went up the river and crossed where are two big rocks. The trail there is called Pitou Kisnit, meaning Narrow Solid Rock Pass. This is on south side of Pahniah Koos. We did not enter the Park by our old trail when on war retreat.

I grew up among warriors, and since old enough to take notice, I made defending myself a study. The whites call me Yellow Wolf, but I take that as a nickname. My true name is different, and is after the Spirit which gave me promise of its power as a warrior.

I am Heinmot Hihhih, which means White Thunder. Yellow Wolf is not my own chosen name.

Upon being asked how he came by the designation of Yellow Wolf, the warrior discoursed earnestly for some moments with interpreter Hart, and then gave this explanation:

I was a boy of about thirteen snows when my parents sent me away into the hills. It was to find my *Wyakin*.[5] I saw something—not on the ground, but about four feet up in the air.

I took my bow and shot an arrow.

It was in moon you call May when my parents again sent me out. This time it was to the wildest part of the mountains. To a place beyond Kemei Koois. Gave me one blanket, but no food. I might go fifteen, maybe twenty, suns with nothing to eat. But could drink water aplenty. Only trees for shelter, and fir brush to sleep on. I might stay in one place three nights, maybe five nights, then go somewhere else. Nobody around, just myself. No weapons, for nothing would hurt me. No children ever get hurt when out on such business.

After going so many suns without food I was sleeping. It was just like dreaming, what I saw. A form stood in the air fronting me. It talked to me in plain language, telling me:

"My boy, look at me! You do as I am telling you, and you will be as I am. Take a good look at me! I will give you my power; what I have got. You may think I am nothing! You may think I am only bones! But I am alive! You can see me! I am talking to you! I am Hemene Moxmox [Yellow Wolf]."

It was a Spirit of a wolf that appeared to me. Yellow-like in color, it sort of floated in the air. Like a human being it talked to me, and gave me its power.

---

[5] Yellow Wolf had a strong belief in *Wyakin*, as will appear throughout. For an explanation of this supernatural force, see Appendix A, end of volume.

I did not say anything back to the Spirit talking to me. I was asleep [in a trance]! I was not scared. Was just as I am now. Nothing was there to hurt me.

After I saw this wolf-thing, after I heard the Spirit-voice, I awoke and started for home. When near to maybe quarter mile of home, I dropped down, supposed dead. Someone, man or woman, came and brought me to the tepee. They had seen me, had watched for me. It was good for the one finding me.

That was how I got named Yellow Wolf. Named for that vision-wolf appearing to me. It was yellow-colored, and gave me the power of the wolf.

The name of thunder is to kill as it strikes and rolls along. My *kopluts* [war club] I made when a boy, by directions of the Spirit that gave me promise of warrior power. It has the same killing strength as thunder.[6]

I have had different spirit guidance. I was not full-grown when we were hunting, moving into Montana, near falls in the river. It was dark night and freezing cold. The chiefs told me to watch the horses. So cold I did not know all the time what I was doing. Horseback, I was doubled over, eyes closed. I went sound asleep. Did not know anything. I must have been near death. I felt something lightly touch and shake my thigh. Felt it about three times. Then I heard a voice speaking, "What are you doing? Wake up! You are dead! Go home!"

I awoke, numb with cold. I could see no one. But the way that Spirit directed, I drove the horses. I moved them the direction that Spirit guided. I was afraid enemy Indians would take the herd. I was scared. About two miles I must have gone when I heard a voice calling, "Where are you going? Come this way!"

---

[6] See Appendix B, "Yellow Wolf's War Club," end of volume.

I awoke again, came to myself. I turned that way where my people were calling. I was freezing! A wild northeast wind was blowing. Coldest of all winds, it kills quickly!

I would have died had not that Spirit guided me where I could hear my people calling. They heard the horses passing.

Always after that night I could smell an enemy anywhere for a long distance away. This Spirit at that time gave me such power. I could then tell if enemies were around watching to take our horses or attack our camp.

This Spirit told me never to be mean. Never hurt a dog without cause. To do nothing violent only as had to be done. When in war, this Spirit wanted me to be alone. For this reason did I scout mostly alone on our retreat. Sometimes I never ate for three or four days. Only drank water. Water is medicine for everything.

What I am giving you is from my heart. I could have been dead many times only for this Spirit protection. For all this I am thankful. Happy for it all.

Another way I feel now. All my people are dead. I am alone. My heart is heavy because of way I am treated by whites. In early days my parents were to the whites as brothers. Why should I be badly treated by whites? Why is it they do not want to pay me for my land? They robbed us of all our country, our homes. We got nothing but bullets. I am now old. I feel worried about my grandchildren, what may become of them. It can not be for them as with me, when growing up hunting buffaloes.

In Montana my uncle traded a yearling horse to some miners for a magazine rifle. It was like one I carried through the war [1866 repeating Winchester]. With it

I hunted buffaloes until somebody stole it. I killed year-lings mostly. It was robes we were after more than meat.

You had to be a good horseman when running buffa-loes. Sometimes they chased you, horned your horse. If a man was thrown to the ground, best that he lie still. The buffalo would then lick his face raw, but he could thereby escape.[7]

At times the Nez Perces hunted goats, bighorns, deer, and elk. All kinds of game in that country. We knew that country well before passing through there in 1877. The hot smoking springs and the high-shooting water were nothing new to us.

Once I returned from hunting in the Yellowstone country, to Idaho. From there I went to Wallowa by stage. One snow from that time war broke out.

My age was then twenty-one snows. A strong young man, I was never sickly.

One time I was out hunting with other Indians. We separated. Snow was about ankle-deep. I came onto a bear's trail, and tracked him to his home in a rock cliff. I jumped off my horse, went to the door, and looked in. I saw two eyes just like fire. If you see animal eyes in darkness, they always shine as coals of fire. I leveled my gun and fired, aiming at center between those eyes.

I stood in the doorway, listening. I heard him knock-ing against the walls of his house. Soon the knocks stopped. Then I knew that bear was dead.

I got the lariat from my saddle and crawled in where the bear lay. Slipped the loop over his head, drawing it tight. Then I backed out and tried to pull him from his house. Only got him part way. I brought my horse, and

---

[7] It is reported that on occasion a buffalo would be attracted by the saliferous moisture on the perspiring face of a fallen hunter.

fastening the rope to saddlehorn, soon had that bear outside.

I now went to top of a ridge and gave the signal yell. The other hunters not too far away understood. They came and helped skin and get the meat to camp. I always had good luck hunting bears.

One other time I met a bear at his home. There were three of us horseback. I dismounted and went to the opening in the rocks. I peeked in. Yes, that bear was there, all right. I called in to the bear, "Come out! I want you!"

My partners were afraid, and stayed off a distance. I told them to come closer, but they would not mind me at all. One was afraid the bear might get hold of him. He stayed on his horse about thirty steps away. The other man was maybe forty steps from the bear's ground lodge. He dismounted and stood behind a big pine tree. His name was Jesse. I told them again to come closer, but they said "No!"

Those two Indians were scared at nothing.

I now put my head in at the bear's doorway and told him, "I want you! I have come for you. You must come out!"

But that bear would not come. He only growled and talked to himself. I now yelled a sharp command and struck him with a stone. That bear made a bad noise with his mouth, and started out. I took three steps back. That bear came out of his doorway, mad. Just as he made to jump, I shot him through the head. I now called to my partners, "Come over!" They said, "No!" Told me to examine if the bear was dead.

I laughed at them. I put my rifle down and gripped the bear's head. They now said, "We were afraid to come close. We thought that bear might put up a bad fight."

They laughed, seeing the bear dead. I told them, "The bear is nothing to me. He is just like a dog to me. I can kill him with a club."

I was hunting deer in the mountains. I was alone. I heard a voice coming from the east. From some place among the big rocks. I thought it was a true voice of a person. I listened good! Yes, it was there all right.

I ran, and came near where the voice had sounded. No human voice whatever. Only the voice of *itsiyiyi* [coyote]. That *itsiyiyi* was crying, "Quit that! Quit that!" A bear was trying to catch that *itsiyiyi*, and I thought to shoot him. I shot just as he reared up, and the bullet struck his right paw.

I ran to get closer to that bear, but he saw and came at me. Getting close, I shot him in the head.

After killing that bear, I discovered a dead deer. A fresh-killed deer. That bear had been fighting *itsiyiyi* from eating the deer.

It is a strange story I am now telling you. I had hunted two suns and seen nothing. In camp all morning, I went out in the afternoon. There was a good snow. I found no tracks. I wondered what was wrong. I have never felt as I did that time. I sat down to think. Sun shining, nice day. The way I was looking, I saw a deer about fifty steps away. It was reaching up, eating the long moss from lower limbs of a tree. It was the kind of moss we cook in the ground ovens for food. The same kind you liked at our camp dinner. Yes, it was a deer standing broadside to me. I raised my rifle and fired.

That deer continued to eat the hanging moss. I thought, "What is wrong?" I fired again, aiming good.

Eeh! That deer did not move. Just kept eating moss. I did not hurry as I fired a third time.

That deer remained in same place, still filling on moss. Paid no attention to what was being done to it. I thought, "Maybe gun sight not good?" I put my eye to rifle sight and back again quickly. *Eeh!* That deer was gone. My rifle sight was nothing wrong.

I went over where that deer had stood. No tracks whatever. I looked up. A long lodgepole could not reach that moss—that high it was above the ground! I must have been shooting *atemis* [dead] deer. A spirit deer, maybe from out the ground. I never saw such any other time. I thought about it for many long snows. I have never forgotten it. I returned to camp, hunting no more that sun.

YELLOW WOLF:
His Own Story

❂

CHAPTER 2

General Howard "Shows the Rifle"

The primal facts contained in this chapter were secured during my first interviews with Yellow Wolf; but it is well to bear in mind that a few additional facts were added from various interviews until as late as the narrator's death in 1935.

The first interviews were to be at my house, and on the morning of the appointment I was surprised to see Yellow Wolf and interpreter Hart walking up from the river, accompanied by Two Moons, Roaring Eagle, and Chief David Williams, all of the Joseph band. These men came and sat through each day's session, mostly in silence, but there was an occasional short conference held in their own language. It was not until afterwards that I learned it was customary to have witnesses to what was said. The listeners, should they detect error—intentional or otherwise, in statements—were not only privileged but honor bound to make corrections. These three witnesses had been through the great retreat, the first two as warriors, the last named as a boy large enough to carry water to the warriors during the Clearwater battle.

In this chapter Yellow Wolf gives a short review of a contented and prosperous tribal life destroyed by armed enforcement of a treaty to which the Nez Perces had not given assent. He tells how they were "shown the rifle." He depicts the excitement throughout the Indian encampment as they learn of the outbreak of hostilities; Looking Glass's hurried retreat with his followers to their old home in a futile effort to avoid war; the retreat of the remaining bands to White Bird Canyon; the night warning of the approach of Captain Perry's troops, and the silent massing of the warriors to meet the soldiers in battle.

IT WAS our custom for the old people to instruct the children. That was not like the learning of today, but was what we needed for living in this world.

I paid attention to what the old people said. I have always told the truth. I am telling the truth now.

We had a good country until the white people came and crowded us. Now they have us to the brush. My fathers had property in lands, horses, and goods. Just as you have what belongs to you in town or in country. My ancestors were glad to see the white strangers come. My people made no trouble. Never thought about making trouble. Never held anything against the white race. I am telling you, my people made no trouble, although the whites killed many of them! Only when they wanted to put us in one small place, taking from us our home country, trouble started.

We were raising horses and cattle—fast race horses and many cattle. We had fine lodges, good clothes, plenty to eat, enough of everything. We were living well. Then General Howard and Agent Monteith came to bother us.

I had seen twenty-one snows when they came. They told us we had to give up our homes and move to another part of the reservation. That we had to give up our part of the reservation to the white people. Told us we must move in with the Nez Perces turned Christians, called Upper Nez Perces by the whites. All of same tribe, but it would be hard to live together. Our religions different, it would be hard. To leave our homes would be hard. It was these Christian Nez Perces who made with the Government a *thief* treaty [1863]. Sold to the Government all this land. Sold what did not belong to them. We got nothing for our country. None of *our* chiefs signed that land-stealing treaty. None was at that lie-talk council. Only Christian Indians and Government men.[1]

---

[1] Contrary to Yellow Wolf's assertion, the name of at least one Lower Nez Perce, Waptastamana, appears as the twenty-seventh signer to the treaty of 1863. (Charles

Trouble began in the councils. First was a council at Umatilla. Ollokot[2] and others went there to meet General Howard. But General Howard was not there. He sent a boy [Lieutenant Boyle] in his place. Ollokot did not like this. He, a chief, could not talk to a boy. Nothing was done. No agreement made.

Next council was at Walla Walla. All chiefs were instructed to be there. A call went out for Heinmot Tooyalakekt [Thunder Traveling to Loftier (Mountain) Heights], known as Joseph; also for Ollokot; for Peopeo Hihhih [White Bird]; for Toohoolhoolzote[3]; for Looking Glass; and for Hahtalekin.[4]

Joseph was my uncle [first cousin to Yellow Wolf's mother]. He did not go to Walla Walla. Ollokot said to him, "You stay here. I will go see what is wanted."

J. Kappler, *Indian Affairs, Laws and Treaties.* Government Printing Office, Washington, D. C., 1904. Vol. II, p. 848.) "Wahtasstummannee" is also the fifty-fifth signer to the 1855 treaty. *(Idem,* p. 706.) These two names represent one and the same party: "Black Feather," a medicine man.

Waptastamana was "well off, rich, and never signed anything in 1863. Never knew how his name was put to that 'steal treaty.' He knew it was bad and refused to sign."

Another Lower Nez Perce, Hahhahstoortee, more correctly Wahwahsteestee (Bear on Top), appears as the twentieth signer to the 1855 treaty. *(Idem,* p. 705.) He is reputed to have signed the 1863 treaty also. This he did, it is said, "about ten o'clock at night, and he was given a good saddle for his name." If such was the case, an unidentified alias was used, for no name similar to that of 1855 is in evidence. Bear on Top is said to have been "not very well off" financially, and "did not understand just what he was signing."

[2] While spellings and pronunciations vary, preference is given, from the best interpretations obtained, to the form Ollokot, which will be adhered to throughout this volume. It is seemingly a Cayuse word, and probably means "frog." Tewetakis, an old, unidentified word, was Ollokot's earlier name.

[3] Toohoolhoolzote—variously spelled—signifies "noise," or "sound," such as is produced by striking any vibrant timber or metal with a hard substance. A scarcely discernible legato in the last syllable—*tzote*—will not be used in these pages.

This noted chieftain, sadly maligned by partisan writers, was dubbed by a white pioneer, a veritable "fighter from hell." As a Dreamer prophet and medicine man, he had a pronounced influence over the patriot bands, but reliable evidence is lacking that from the first he counseled war. Every warrior interviewed on the subject testified to his advocacy for peace; but after the irretrievable step had been taken, he promptly took up the rifle.

[4] The first syllable of this name was variously pronounced: Ah—, Nah—, or Hah—, preference being given to the latter. No English rendition has been found. He was reckoned a buffalo hunter and a warrior of ability. He was killed at the Big Hole, his first engagement of the war. He was one of the six nontreaty chiefs (*i.e.,* a Lower Nez Perce), but has been accorded no place in the annals. His band, the Waiwaiwai Paloos, the smallest of the war bands, joined the war party at Weippe, after the Clearwater battle. It was to this band that the Dreamer priest, Husishus Kute (Naked Head), belonged. Because of his oratorical ability, Husis was chosen by the Nez Perces as a speaker at the councils called by General Howard, who, mistaking him for the head of his band, dubbed him "a wily *chieftain,* about the age of Young Joseph." (Howard, *Nez Perce Joseph,* p. 19.) He thus unconsciously usurped the chieftainly renown that rightfully belonged to Hahtalekin. It is doubtful if either of them ever realized the mistake.

"All right! You go," Joseph told him.

I was surprised, my uncle saying that. But he was not feeling well, was why Ollokot spoke to go.[5]

Ollokot was gone nearly one week. When it was morning, we heard a horse running, and soon Ollokot came into the tepee. After eating and smoking, he said to Joseph:

"Government wants all Indians put in one place. If you say, 'Yes,' I will bring in the stock and we will go there. If the white officers ask what you will do, you answer, 'Nothing to talk about. Ollokot has settled everything.' "

Soon after this came report that General Howard and soldiers had come to Lapwai. Our camp-village was on Asotain [Eel Creek] about where Asotin now stands. Not many miles from Lapwai. We wondered why they were at the fort. Then followed word for all the chiefs to meet General Howard and Agent Monteith there in council. The chiefs who could go went with their followers, and I, Yellow Wolf, went with Chief Joseph's band. But Peopeo Hihhih and Toohoolhoolzote of Salmon River country were not there. Slippery trails and mountain snowbanks held them back. They arrived later.

The soldier guardhouse was close to the council place. Indians stood all around—a lot of Indians. A soldier was there with only one good arm. Right arm mostly gone. Left arm sound. This soldier was General Howard. After they had a prayer-talk, he asked, "Where is Chief Joseph?"

"There he is," the interpreter said, pointing to my

---

[5] "Ollicut put in an appearance about six P. M. (April 19).... These Indians came to the western gate and Ollicut gave in an excuse in the most gentlemanly manner for not having been at the fort sooner, and stated that the chief, his brother Joseph, was not at that time well; otherwise he would have been there himself to meet me...." (Howard, *Nez Perce Joseph*, p. 42.)

uncle. General Howard asked Joseph if he had anything to say. Joseph answered, "I will hear what you
have to tell the chiefs. My brother and I came to listen.
You must not hurry. White Bird and Toohoolhoolzote
will be here tomorrow."

But General Howard would not wait. He talked short.
Said the Indians would have to do as ordered. Agent
Monteith read a paper and said we had to go on a small
reservation.

Ollokot made a short talk. He wanted to wait for the
Salmon River chiefs before anything was done.

General Howard now said, "If you do not come on
the reservation, my soldiers will put you there!"

This hurt the Indians. They said no more in that sun's
council. But there was talk in camp that night. Many
wondered what would happen.

With morning came Chiefs White Bird and Toohoolhoolzote. The council met. General Howard had one
Christian Nez Perce speak a prayer. Agent Monteith
made his same talk, telling us we had to move to the small
reservation. General Howard told us again if we refused orders, soldiers would drive us on that reservation.
He asked for Toohoolhoolzote and was told, "He is here."
This chief was our speaker. General Howard shook
hands with him, but would let him talk only a little.
They quarreled some, then agreed to rest, to finish the
talk three suns later.

During this delay, more Indians came in and more
soldiers were seen to arrive. It was Sapalwit [Sunday]
evening when this announcement was made all through
the camp, "Tomorrow morning everybody be at the
soldier council camp."

All went. I, Yellow Wolf, went. I wanted to hear

what was talked. I did hear what was said. I saw what was done. In after snows I listened to my boy read in white people's history things not true about that council. The Indians were *not* armed! General Howard broke friendship. The council was held in front of the guardhouse, maybe 150 steps away.

Agent Monteith made his same talk again. How we must obey orders or soldiers would be sent against us. General Howard got up and shook hands with the chiefs. He told them they could talk, but they had to come on the reservation.

Chief Toohoolhoolzote stood up to talk for the Indians. He told how the land always belonged to the Indians, how it came down to us from our fathers. How the earth was a great law, how everything must remain as fixed by the Earth-Chief. How the land must not be sold! That we came from the earth, and our bodies must go back to earth, our mother. General Howard stopped the chief.

He ordered, "I do not want to hear you say anything more like that. I am telling you! Thirty days you have to get on the reservation."

"You ask me to talk, then tell me to say no more," Toohoolhoolzote replied. "I am chief! I ask no man to come and tell me anything what I must do. I am chief here!"

General Howard answered sharp. "Yes, you are chief. I am telling you! Thirty days you have to move in!"

"Yes, picking your own count!" our chief said. "Go back to your own country! Tell them you are chief there. I am chief here."

General Howard was showing mad. He spoke sharply,

"If you do not mind me, if you say, 'No,' soldiers will come to your place. You will be tied up and your stock taken from you."

Toohoolhoolzote answered, "I am telling you! I am a chief! Who can tell me what I must do in my own country?"

General Howard was now strong mad. He spoke in loud voice, "*I* am the man to tell you what you must do! You will come on the reservation within time I tell you. If not, soldiers will put you there or shoot you down!"

Chief Toohoolhoolzote did not become afraid. His words were strong as he replied, "I hear you! I have *simiakia*, that which belongs to a man! I am a man, and will not go! I will not leave my home, the land where I grew up!"

General Howard now called a soldier to come forward. He pointed to Toohoolhoolzote and ordered, "Take him to the guardhouse."

The chief turned around, and the soldier thought he was coming with him, but he was not. The soldier then shoved him over some Indians sitting on the ground close together. They called out, "Come get him!"

The soldier did not come, and the other chiefs advised Toohoolhoolzote, "Go! We do not think they will do much to you."

The chief then stepped forward to the soldier. General Howard went with them to the jail, and there he again asked Toohoolhoolzote, "Have you decided to go on the reservation?"

The chief, a prisoner, made quick reply. "Have you no ears? I said NO! I am a chief! Raised here by my father! No one tells me anything what I am to do!"

"No more talk here now," General Howard said. "You study and decide if you come in or not."

To all of us General Howard now spoke, "If you do not mind me, I will take my soldiers and *drive* you on the reservation."

Again, Agent Monteith told us, "You must understand from this day you are going on the reservation. If you do not do as told, soldiers will put you there."

All that hurt us. In peace councils, force must not be talked. It was the same as showing us the rifle. General Howard was just pricking with needles. That was not suited for the Indians.

Toohoolhoolzote was kept in the guardhouse several suns, like a thief.

That was what brought war, the arrest of this chief and showing us the rifle!

Some young men talked secretly among themselves. To one another they said, "General Howard has shown us the rifle. We answer 'Yes.' We will stir up a fight for him. We will start his war!"

The chiefs were not talking war. After the Lapwai council they gave orders, "Everyone get ready to move to our new home. Round up horses and cattle, as many as can be found."

That was done. Cattle were rounded up and herded south of Salmon River. Water was too high and swift for their crossing. All the young calves—there were many—would be drowned. So would the old cows. While this was being done the people assembled at Tepahlewam, our old camping grounds at Tolo Lake.[6] There were about six hundred people in camp. Many old men, many

---

[6] See Appendix I, this chapter.

women and children The women dug camas which grew thick on the prairie, while men and boys had good times gambling and racing horses. I was with Chief Joseph. I slept in his lodge.

None of the chiefs wanted war. They held many councils to hear what the older warriors had to say. Some of these said, "We will wait for those returning from buffalo hunting in Montana. Then will be decided what to do if war breaks."

There were six leading chiefs. Joseph, Ollokot, White Bird, Toohoolhoolzote, Looking Glass, and Hahtalekin. This last chief had the smallest band, the Paloos. He did not want war. No chief talked or wanted war. Looking Glass was strong against fighting. I am telling you about three times,[7] no chief wanted war.

When informed that the Nez Perces are accused in history of having cavalry drills, and of training for the war before fighting broke out, Yellow Wolf replied earnestly:

Not true! There was no training with horses, no practicing with rifles for that war. True, we rode concealed on side of horses as did all buffalo-hunting Indians. There was always likely to be fighting with enemy tribes. We had learned, had done that riding from child days. We did it in Wallowa Valley for sport. Some of us would ride by where friends were standing or sitting and fire at them under our horse's neck, but not hit them. I have done that myself in play.

We were not expecting war with the whites. But when we did get into war, we used those tactics in battle.

---

[7] According to Nez Perce custom, two equivocations could be indulged in without reflecting upon the narrator's veracity, but to repeat the same equivocation a third time was to forfeit self-respect and the respect of fellow tribesmen. Allusions to thrice-told statements will come to the reader's notice throughout the course of this volume.

We did this at White Bird Canyon, Cottonwood, and Clearwater fights. It was our privilege, our right to do so.

Of men to fight should war come, there were less than 120. This was counting full-aged men not too old and young men of war age. No boys under seventeen snows did fighting. And those who proved actual fighters numbered less than fifty. I can give you names of all.[8]

To Chief Joseph's wife a baby was to come. It was because of this that Joseph, Ollokot, and a few men and two women crossed Mahsamyetteen [Buzzard Mountain] to the White Bird for beef. As I have said, all our cattle were south of Salmon River, which Joseph and party boated.

It was then, while they were gone, that war started.

Many of our people had been killed by white men on our reservation. But at no time was anything done to punish them. The discovery of gold on our reservation [1860] brought thousands of white men. That was the beginning of our trouble. Those white killers were never bothered from living on our lands. They were still there. Still robbing and shooting or hanging Indians.

One of those who had been killed was Chief Tipyahlanah Siskon [Eagle Robe]. His home had been at the same place on Salmon River for many snows. A white man came to him who wanted land. The chief gave him some land. The man built a house and raised crops. Then he took more land, a part of Eagle Robe's garden. When

---

[8] It is a source of regret that a compilation of the Nez Perce warriors was not made with Yellow Wolf's assistance. The bands assembled in camp at Tolo Lake contained between six and seven hundred men, women, and children. Many of the families were polygamous, resulting in a preponderance of women. From this largely feminine aggregation, General Howard miraculously conjured "over three hundred warriors," including "a substantial reserve" composed of women. (Howard, *Nez Perce Joseph*, p. 166; also *Report of Secretary of War*, 1877-88, Vol. I, p. 124.)

G. O. Shields, *Battle of the Big Hole*, p. 16, visioned them at "about 400 warriors and 150 women and children."

the chief tried to stop him from plowing, he drew his six-shooter and shot Tipyahlanah, who was unarmed. He lived only a short time. When dying, he spoke to his son, Wahlitits,[9] a boy, but almost grown.

He said, "Do not bother the white man for what he has done to me. Let him live his life!"

That was about two snows before the war. Now [1877] Wahlitits was grown strong of body, sound and quick of mind. He had two near-brothers [first cousins], Sarpsis Ilppilp [Red Moccasin Tops], and Wetyetmas Wahyakt [Swan Necklace]. Wetyetmas was youngest of the three.[10] The two older men made their minds to kill that white man. They talked this way, "General Howard spoke the rifle in a peace council. He made prisoner our speaker, Chief Toohoolhoolzote. We will stir up a fight for him. We will kill the white man who killed Tipyahlanah Siskon!"

The three went to the Salmon, but could not find the killer of Tipyahlanah. Becoming scared, he had run away to Florence mines. He put on Chinamen clothes and worked with the Chinamen, washing gold.

The young men now killed another man who had badly treated the Indians. They took a good horse be-

---

[9] Wahlitits is spelled variously. One interpreter, an intelligent, educated young man, explained: "Wahlitits is Nez Perce for 'Springtime ice along the river banks which permits one to walk on it while the water is flowing down the open center of the stream.'" Another rendition is "Crossing," with no particular connotation.

[10] The youngest of the avenging trio, Wetyetmas Wahyakt (Swan Necklace), was also known as Young Swan Necklace, the prefix distinguishing him from his father, who bore the same name. Silas Whitman, a recognized authority, explained: "The first three syllables mean 'Fictitious Bird.' The last two syllables, 'Neckwear.'"

The only one of the three to survive the war, his identity was never known to the whites. It was kept concealed by those who knew him until after his death, which occurred in the late twenties. At the time of the Salmon River killing, in which he had no actual part, he was but seventeen years old. His name then was Heyoom Tililpkaun (Red Sun-rayed Grizzly), which, as Yellow Wolf expressed it, was "put away"—not used thereafter. To the whites he became known only as John Minthon, no one suspecting his connection with the starting of the war. It was by that name that Yellow Wolf and other of the veterans referred to him during his life, not wanting him to "get into any trouble."

WETYETMAS WAHYAKT (SWAN NECKLACE)

Although he was implicated in precipitating the Nez Perce War, his identity was never revealed by his fellow warriors. Under the name of John Minthon he lived for years on the Nez Perce Reservation, where he died in the early thirties.

CHIEF OLLOKOT (LEFT)

Right: Wetyetmas Likleinen, relative of Ollokot. Photograph taken in Walla Walla, Washington, 1876, the year before the outbreak of war.

CHIEF JOSEPH
From an old photograph in the collection of Joseph Sherburne, Sr., made during
the exile in Indian Territory.

LEPEET HESSEMDOOKS (TWO MOONS)
The warrior who rode out to meet Joseph and Ollokot to inform them of the hostilities that had broken out in their absence.

longing to him and returned home.[11] They arrived at camp late at night.[12]

With Joseph and Ollokot away killing beef, four chiefs were at Tolo Lake. These four and some old men were holding council in one tepee. Not wanting war, they talked what to do about General Howard's orders.

Someone called to them from a near-by tepee, "You poor people are talking for nothing! Three boys have already started war! They killed a white man on Salmon and brought his horse here to this camp. It is already war!"

That stopped the council. There was lots of excitement.

Next morning Lepeet Hessemdooks [Two Moons] rode out to meet Chief Joseph and Ollokot. He told them what had been done. Leaving the women to bring the pack horses loaded with meat, the men rode fast to camp. They found most tepees already down, the people moving from there. They tried to stop them, but no use. All left but Joseph and his band and about thirty-five other men. These stayed to guard against any enemy surprise, but some were afraid Joseph and Ollokot might desert the other Indians. The bands that moved away went to Sapachesap [Drive In], a cave on Cottonwood Creek.

---

[11] The first white man killed—on June 13, 1877—as narrated by Yellow Wolf, was Richard Devine, an old man, who lived alone on Salmon River, eight miles above Slate Creek. The man primarily sought by the three avengers was Larry Ott, who had murdered the father of Wahlitits on the first day of March, 1875. Ott, taking alarm, fled to the Florence mines, where he was seen disguised as a Celestial engaged in placer mining, by Many Wounds. The latter described Ott as having red hair reaching to his shoulders. Balked of their prey, the trio turned their attention to Devine, who, according to reputable Indians and early settlers, had won for himself an unsavory reputation with the tribesmen. An interloper on the Nez Perce domain, he would curse the Indians and set his vicious dogs on them when they passed his place, and he imposed on them in other ways.

General Howard *(Nez Perce Joseph,* p. 103) mentions a "Moxmox" as a party to the killing, but there was no Indian of that name mixed in it. There is evidence, however, that Chuslum Moxmox (Yellow Bull) figured in the Salmon River forays during the next two days, June 14 and 15.

[12] Be it said to the credit of the three avengers that no charge of mistreatment of women and children has ever been placed against them. Subsequent outrages of that nature are traceable directly to a superabundance of "fire water"—barrels of it—found in Benedict's saloon at the mouth of the White Bird. See Note 14.

This same sun the three young men—Wahlitits and his near-brothers—returned to the Salmon. With them went several warriors. They killed a few more whites, all bad men. One of these, a mean man, liked by nobody, had killed Dakoopin, who was lame. Hungry, he had gone to this white man's house to ask for food. The man had shot him. Now this sun, the two sons of Dakoopin went to the white man and asked, "What you mean, killing our father?"

The man drew his six-shooter and fired at them, but missed. Then the older boy jumped off his horse and with one rifleshot killed the man.[13]

The war now came on fast.

That night I was in Chief Joseph's tepee. We had no timepieces in those days, but it must have been about two hours before midnight when I heard the sound of horses approaching and a white man's voice. Then a gun sounded. A bullet came through the tepee, but hit nobody.

I grabbed a magazine rifle and stepped through the doorway. Out a way I could see shadow forms of mounted men.

Chuslum Lapitkif Hotswal [Bull Second Boy] called in our tongue, "Shoot him!"

The men must have seen as I drew up my rifle. They whirled and galloped swiftly away. I fired, but missed.

From that time, the Nez Perces had no more rest. No more soft pillows for the head.

As the sun was dawning, I heard a gun report. Its sound was like a two-mile distance. Shortly, full sun-

---

[13] Owing to Yellow Wolf's inability to give the offending settler's name, it was not possible to determine the identity of the murderer of Dakoopin. He was described as a trader who never returned to an Indian any change due him or her in a transaction.

light came, and Chief Joseph said, "We must pack and go to Sapachesap, where the other chiefs are."

We packed quickly and started. We had gone about a mile and a half when I heard someone say, "They have killed one white man. They have taken two wagons from some white men." I learned later there was whisky in those wagons.[14]

Before the capture of these wagons, General Howard said, "I do not want war. If the chiefs will give up the three Indians who did the killing, I will hang them and let the others go."

But Ad Chapman, a white man living on White Bird Creek with a Umatilla wife, declared, "I can whip the Injuns alone. They are cowardly."

That was what we were told.

Yellow Wolf paused and, as if addressing General Howard and Indian Agent Monteith, said, "You can see now for yourselves, General Howard and Agent Monteith, why the killing of those white men. It was your own fault!"

Then, steadily regarding the recorder of this narrative, he earnestly continued, "You and I are best of friends. We have been good to each other. There will be no trouble about this business?" Assured that he need entertain no fear of trouble because of his statements of where the blame of the war should be placed—assurance sealed with a handclasp—he resumed:

It was during these first suns of trouble that an Indian and a white man were killed near Mount Idaho. Three Indians traveled from White Bird Canyon. They were Pahka Alyanakt [Five Winters], Henawit [Going Fast], and Jyeloo, also named Pykat.

---

[14] The late Elias Darr, a blacksmith in Grangeville, who saw local service as a volunteer, informed the writer that the whisky—three or four barrels of it—was, with other freight, being hauled by Lue (or Lew) Wilmot and a man named "Ready" (possibly Pete Reddy), from Lewiston to Mount Idaho. Each wagon, with a trailer, was drawn by a four-horse team. The Indians came upon them while they were crossing Camas Meadows at night. The teamsters escaped on their fastest horses, the Indians making no marked effort to capture them.

They came to three buildings, the home of a white man. These buildings must have been a dwelling and outhouses. It was early morning, about breakfast time, when they arrived. Nobody was there. I understood the three were drinking, or had been drinking. Tired, they rested in the house. They slept a short while. When ready to leave, Henawit took a swift chestnut-colored racer belonging to Jyeloo and went to bring the other two horses. Pretty quick he came running the horses and called, "We are attacked!"

Pahka Alyanakt jumped on his horse. The white men, a bunch of them, were coming fast. The two mounted Indians could not wait for Jyeloo. He had a lame leg, and his back was weak from an old wound. He moved slowly. Maybe was part drunk. The horse left by Henawit walked away, and he had to run after it. Because they left him, the two Indians gave him the only gun among them, an old 45-70 with but one cartridge. They forgot to give him the belt of ammunition.

Jyeloo finally got on the horse, a poor runner. His partners were now some distance away, the white men fast gaining on him. Coming to a fence, Jyeloo had to dismount. He was no longer young, and had gone through many hardships. Slow moving, he was soon cornered and killed.[15]

The whites did not try to catch Pahka Alyanakt and Henawit. The two came to our camp at Sapachesap and told what had happened.

Thirty of us quickly mounted and hurried with them to where the attack was made, where Jyeloo had been

---

[15] Jyeloo had the usual multiplicity of names. Red Wolf, warrior, states in his brief narrative: "One man named Piah was killed near Grangeville during the early trouble. He was drunk at the time." Pykat and Piah may be different pronunciations of the same name. The killing of this Indian is verified by both Volunteers Darr and Rowton, participants in that affair.

killed. We spread out, searching the tall grass for Jyeloo. We found him. I saw his body myself, all covered with blood. He had many gunshot wounds on his body and legs—eleven in all. His head, crushed, was all over blood. Blood on the ground. I saw he had drawn his sheath knife. It was in the grass not far from him—must have been shot from his hand. We did not find the rifle.

With only one cartridge and side knife in a running fight, Jyeloo could do nothing against so many enemies. But he was hard to kill.

His body was taken back over the trail while fifteen of us went to the house where the three had been attacked. We wanted to see, and remained there for a time. Then one of us saw a white man approaching. He seemed coming to the house, so we lay concealed. We wondered why he was coming, but he had no chance to explain. When he got close, we made for him. We chased him toward a steep hill.

Pahkatos Watyekit [Five Times Looking Up] had a bow and arrows. He rode close to the man's side and drew an arrow on the bow. The man grabbed the arrow and nearly jerked Pahkatos from his horse. Six of us overtook him. Kosooyeen [Going Alone] was ahead. He shot the man from his horse while fast running; but he got up. He was then shot and brought down for good.

Nothing more happened, and we went no farther. The man killed was young. He had a six-shooter, but did not fire it. We thought maybe he owned the house and was returning for something left there.[16]

We now rode back to camp where was great excitement. All knew trouble was ahead. The chiefs held

---

[16] The white man killed by the Nez Perces was Charley Horton, a young single man, who was returning to the Salmon River. His body was found four to six days later by John Adkinson.

council what to do. It was a short council. Soon they made announcement: "We will move to Lahmotta!"[17]

Chief Looking Glass and his band, the Asotains, felt differently. They left for their old home on Clearwater River. The women had gardens planted there. The Asotains wanted no war. Looking Glass, strong against war, went with his people.

This left five chiefs, five bands, if fighting broke.

We packed up and started. Going about three miles, we saw a troop of soldiers [probably citizen scouts]. They stopped when they saw us, and we crossed Buzzard Mountain to Lahmotta.

After supper three men went back on the trail to watch if soldiers followed. One went to the top of the mountain, two stopped on the side of the canyon. One of these two had been a bad Indian, a thief. He was not a Nez Perce. Before coming to us, he was a slave. For stealing, his master put steel traps on his wrists and ankles, then placed him outside the tepee in a winter night. He must have been left out too long. Both feet and one hand died and came off. We called him Seeskoomkee [No Feet].[18]

In after part of night I heard Seeskoomkee shouting, "Soldiers coming this way! Soldiers coming this way!"

The people heard and ran out of the tepees. When I got out I saw Seeskoomkee sitting on his horse still calling, "Soldiers coming this way! Soldiers coming this way!"

No more sleep that night. All five chiefs gave orders

---

[17] The Nez Perce designation for the White Bird Canyon is Lahmotta. How the name originated and why applied to the district, no one knows. There are two distinct interpretations of the name; the first is "Wishing for More," "Wanting More"; the second, "Bothered," "Tired," "Weary," or "Restless." The vast reaches of fine range in the Canyon, its milder winters, its natural products, and its fisheries, might well induct the first interpretation; while the long, tedious trail leading into and out of the Canyon on the north could as readily engender the latter.

[18] See Appendix II, this chapter.

to bring horses in close. When that was done, we caught and tied best ones up. The others were herded.

Sunlight breaking, the other two scouts galloped in and reported, "Soldiers coming close! Big bunch of them!"

At this announcement, warriors quickly stripped and armed for war. I saw them going out, one by one, to meet the soldiers. Most of them kept to the left [west], back of buttes near base of the mountain.

Four of us went up the creek, along edge of brush and timber. We wanted to get on other side of the soldiers. I had only hunting bow and arrows.[19] My rifle was with my mother in Chief Looking Glass's camp at their gardens. We stopped at nearest of the two Cemetery Buttes, where some great Nez Perce chiefs are buried.[20] We sat down on a low swell on south side of the butte. A young fellow took our horses back of the upper butte to hold for us, there hidden from our enemies.

Soon came lighter sun. I raised up and looked north. Something seemed moving away up country. I watched closely. Yes, there came the soldiers a good distance off. We all lay flat and watched.

---

[19] A near-replica of his bow that Yellow Wolf made for the author measures three feet, four and a half inches in length. Of yew wood and strung with a splendid sinew cord, it is slightly decorated with red and dark-green paint. The four arrows accompanying the bow measure slightly over two feet in length, all winged with hawk and other wild bird feathers. Two are tipped with short hoop-iron points, the other two are barbless, the shafts merely trimmed to blunt cone points. All in all it appears a pitifully inadequate weapon when compared with the Springfield rifles with which the soldiers were armed.

[20] These two notable buttes, on the summits of which are to be seen the desecrated graves of some of the most renowned chiefs and warriors of the earlier Nez Perces, are just to the right (traveling south) of U. S. Highway 95 from White Bird, Idaho. They are those designated by Captain Perry as "two round knowls of considerable height" flanking the left of his advance. (C. T. Brady, *Northwestern Fights and Fighters*, p. 114.) Perry's force, however, never reached a point so far south, never arrived anywhere near opposite them. These buttes are landmarks of historic importance and should be designated by a monumental marker. See photographs in next chapter.

APPENDIX I

Tolo Lake, made historic through local events in 1877, originally had no special Nez Perce name. Ewatam, meaning a small body of water, either lake or pond, was all the name it could boast.

Tepahlewam, variously defined as "Deep Cuts," "Cracked Rocks," and "Split Rocks," an impressive, cavernous gorge about a mile west of the lake, imposed its name on the immediate surroundings, including the lake. The great annual campgrounds of the Nez Perces not only covered the area between the gorge and the lake, but also extended across the ravine at the head of the gorge.

The lake was named "Tolo" by the whites to honor a Nez Perce woman who carried the news of the Nez Perce outbreak to the Florence mines. A noted poker player, acknowledged champion of the Nez Perce bands, she was called by her associates Tulekats Chikchamit. The name, interpreted, means: Tulekats: "Placing Money on Betting Cards"; Chikchamit: "Dealing Cards." Her name was shortened to "Tule," and corrupted to "Tolo" by the whites.

For a sketch of the Indian woman for whom the whites named Tolo Lake, see C. J. Brosnan, *History of the State of Idaho,* pp. 207-08. For a poetic description of the Lake, see R. Ross Arnold, *Indian Wars of Idaho,* pp. 107-08, 114.

APPENDIX II

Seeskoomkee, sometimes pronounced Eskoomskee or Askoomskee, has also been defined as "Cut Off." His tribal origin was uncertain. All that is known of his prewar life was given to the author by the late Chief Tomio Kamiakun, son of the famous Yakima war chief, Kamiakun. Chief Tomio spoke in Nez Perce.

"My father," said Chief Tomio, "often traded with the tribes to the southwest, sometimes going as far as California. On one of these distant trips he purchased No Feet, who was a slave captive. I do not know his tribe. His true name was Attween; I do not know the English meaning. Maybe it has none. Many Indian names, as with white names, have no real meaning. A still earlier name was Kepgavants Wewowwow.

"Askoomskee would steal. One winter while we were living at Tekam ["Falls," at Spokane, Wash.], my father, to punish him—after he had been warned repeatedly to reform—one night put steel traps, not heavy ones, on his ankles and wrists, and put him outside the lodge. My father left him there too long in the freezing cold, and that caused the loss of both feet and one hand. It cured him of theft.

"A law among the tribes was that after a purchased slave had served his owner sufficiently to repay the cost of his purchase he was given his freedom. So when three visiting Nez Perces were to return home, my father gave them some cattle and sent Askoomskee along to drive them. My father told him that he need not return unless he chose to, that he was now free to go wherever he wished. Askoomskee remained with the Lower Nez Perces. Though crippled, he was a splendid horseman, and made his living breaking wild horses."

No Feet was treated well during his stay with the Nez Perces, the interpreter explained, and added, "He was furnished blankets for bedding, but could not take them away. He was required to leave them where used."

When the Nez Perce camp was attacked at the Big Hole, No Feet escaped from the thick of the confusion by alternately hobbling on his one hand and knees, and rolling, until he gained a shallow depression on the eastern boundary of the camp.

No Feet is the Indian spoken of by J. B. M. Genin, missionary apostolic, in picturing the pitiful plight of the Nez Perce refugees from the last battlefield, as they fled toward Chief Sitting Bull's camp in Canada. The missionary saw them as they passed through the villages of the Milk River half-breeds, and says: "So great was the fear of the Indians of being hanged that I saw one pass on horseback with only one hand. He himself had cut off the other and both his feet to free himself from his chains." *(Collections of the State Historical Society of North Dakota, 1906, Vol. I, p. 276.)*

Reaching Sitting Bull's village, No Feet remained ever afterward with the Sioux. He was "given a good horse, blankets and clothing," and eventually married into the tribe.

The Nez Perces later understood that No Feet, in an altercation with the son of a Sioux chief, fatally stabbed the young man. The latter, before dying, exonerated No Feet from blame, and successfully importuned his father not to hold the deed against him.

It has been averred—without verification, however—that No Feet was never at any time a slave, and that he came from the Lower Snake River country. The account given by Chief Tomio presumably is correct, as Tomio was a most reliable informant, and his statement is corroborated by Black Eagle, son of Wottolen.

Battle of the White Bird Canyon

In this chapter Yellow Wolf chiefly narrates the engagement in White Bird Canyon, June 17, 1877. After this battle the Indians withdrew to the other side of the Salmon River, and we see the arrival of General Howard with more soldiers on June 25-26.

In July and August, 1930, the writer, accompanied by Yellow Wolf, Peopeo Tholekt, and interpreter Many Wounds, made a tour of the White Bird battlefield and of the sites of the ensuing skirmishes. Yellow Wolf's story of events is largely a transcription of observations made on this tour.

We walked to the more southern of the two Cemetery Buttes, where, in the preceding chapter, we saw the Indians gathered. The climb to its summit so taxed the old warrior's strength that he was compelled to take a short rest. Then for several minutes he stood silently gazing over the broken country to the west. Pointing across to the southern base of the highest ridgelike butte, he took up the trend of his narrative as follows:

IT WAS there under that rock-ridge that I saw the first enemies. Five warriors, led by Wettiwetti Houlis [Mean Person, known to the whites as John Boyd] had been sent out from the other [west] side of the valley as a peace party to meet the soldiers. These warriors had instructions from the chiefs not to fire unless fired upon. Of course they carried a white flag. Peace might be made without fighting.

Yellow Wolf paused, scanning the west buttes which hid the canyon paralleling White Bird Creek. It was up this west-side canyon that the Nez Perce peace embassy was dispatched. Not satisfied with the outlook, Yellow Wolf signified that we should go to the other, the more northern, Cemetery Butte, only a few rods away. The

CHELLOOYEEN (BOW AND ARROW CASE)

Chellooyeen, later known as Phillip Evans, was wounded on the White Bird battle-field while grappling with a soldier. Photograph taken in 1932.

NORTHERNMOST CEMETERY BUTTE

From the two Cemetery Buttes an excellent view of the White Bird battlefield is to be had. Note solitary tree at left of picture and compare with panoramic view on next page.

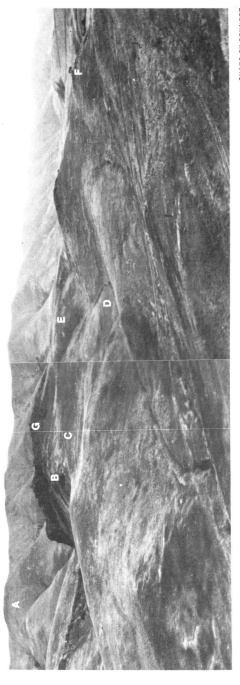

PANORAMIC VIEW OF WHITE BIRD BATTLEFIELD

A, loaf-shaped butte behind which Ollokot and fifty warriors were lying in wait. B, where Bugler Jones was killed by a long-distance shot. C, flat where Chapman was seen. D, draw up which Yellow Wolf and other warriors rode in a flanking movement. E, smoother ground on which occurred the first fierce clash of battle. F, the low butte where the volunteers tried to stop the Indians' flanking advance. G, highest point adjacent to battlefield.

SOUTH END OF WHITE BIRD BATTLEFIELD

Nearer view of features seen in preceding photograph. Compare sites marked with corresponding letters. In this composite photograph there is a certain amount of distortion in the center.

Still closer view of highest point of battlefield (G in panoramic views). Legend declares the Nez Perces manned this ridge. The soldiers, however, failed to advance so far south, and the Nez Perces had no occasion to use this ridge for strategic purposes.

On the low rock-crowned butte in the foreground (F in preceding views), the volunteers tried to stem the flanking movement of the Nez Perces. Their attempt failed and from here the retreat became a rout of panic.

transfer was not accomplished without difficulty. The smooth, rounded knoll, coated with dead midsummer range grass, rendered the climb most laborious for the once strong warrior, now weakened by a life of hardships and penury and by old age. After a few moments of rest on the summit, Yellow Wolf called attention to the largest, loaf-shaped butte in the distance. The fires of other days lit his restless eyes, as with outstretched arm he resumed his story:

Back of that largest butte, near fifty warriors were waiting. From around its southern point I saw a tall warrior, wearing a commander's sash, ride out on a fine, cream-colored horse. All knew that easy rider, Chief Ollokot. Slowly—not hurriedly—as if reconnoitering, he loped northward to midway the butte. Just then, at that time, that moment, broke the *Qoh! Qoh!* of a raven. Ollokot turned back and disappeared where we first saw him. The warning came from an Indian lying close on top of the butte. It reached across to where we were watching. It told, "Soldiers close approaching!"

From the north echoed a rifle report, and right away a white man on a white horse came riding swiftly south. He crossed that bench-flat along the foot of the rockline crowning the ridge. He did not look like a soldier. A big white hat, he was dressed more like a citizen. When he came closer, we knew him. Yes, he had the big-four hat [sombrero]. A *big* hat! It was Chapman, called by the whites a squaw man! Having an Indian wife was why we had been friends. He and my uncle, Old Yellow Wolf, had lived in the same house, just as brothers. Now he was first enemy we see. Changed, and trying to kill each other. It was he who fired the first shot we had just heard. Fired on our peace party.

The chiefs' peace offer was not respected.

About twenty soldiers[1] charging after Chapman were

---

[1] The "soldiers" consisted both of regulars under Captain Perry and of an uncertain number of volunteers. Yellow Wolf and other warriors interviewed

not firing. When Chapman got closer, he fired across at us. Then the soldiers began shooting. That was how the battle started. Chapman made first two shots.

The three men with me now began shooting. A long distance! I, with only bow and arrows, could do nothing.[2] The soldier bugler rode close to the brink of that rounded cliff, north edge of the gorge.

Twelve other warriors joined us. One, an old man, Otstotpoo [Fire Body], made a good shot and killed the bugler.[3] When the bugler fell from his horse, Chapman rode swiftly out from there. His soldiers went with him. We did not try to stop them.

We ran to our horses. Mounting, we rode at swift gallop up that draw you see, leading north. The low, broad ridge on our left hid us from the soldiers. We came out on higher, more level ground which we cannot see from here. It was there the real battle was fought.

Three days later we motored to where Yellow Wolf and his war mates had rushed to join in the defeat of Captain Perry's numerically superior and far better armed force. Selecting his spot of observation, Yellow Wolf cast a rapid glance south to the rock-crowned ridge already mentioned, at the northern foot of which the Nez Perce peace embassy of six had been fired upon by "Ad" I. Chapman, captain of the volunteers. It has been shown that it was along the eastern base of the rocks topping this ridge that Captain Chapman,

seldom made any distinction between the two. Captain Perry reported that there were eight volunteers at this skirmish. (Brady, *op. cit.*, p. 114.) General Howard in his official report specified that Perry was "assisted by eleven volunteers from Mount Idaho." ("Report of the General of the Army," in *Report of the Secretary of War: Messages and Documents*, Vol. I, 1877. N. B.: Subsequent citations from Howard's annual report will be given under abridged caption, "Report of the General of the Army," with date thereof. Field dispatches, however, will be from a different edition of the same report, with different pagination.) A recent historian gives the number of volunteers with Perry as fifty. (G. W. Fuller, *History of the Pacific Northwest*, p. 226.)

[2] The hitherto undisputed claim that the Nez Perces were well armed at the outbreak of the war must now give way to actual facts. Several warriors, among them Yellow Wolf, went into the White Bird Canyon fight armed only with bows and arrows, while many others carried muzzle-loaders, mostly of the musket type. Tipyahlanah Elassanin (Roaring—or Thundering—Eagle) had such a gun, but in the hurry and excitement he left the ramrod behind in camp.

[3] Trumpeter John Jones, First Cavalry—"Johnnie Jonesy," as fondly dubbed by his comrades.

leading his company and some regulars, had disappeared, and it was there that Trumpeter John Jones, First Cavalry, was the first man to fall. Seemingly content with his survey in that direction, Yellow Wolf turned to the northwest and stood for some minutes in silent reverie. It was easy to imagine that he visioned the stirring scene there enacted half a century before. His story was now resumed.

When our party rushed to where we now stand, everything could be seen. We were on the soldiers' left flank. Their right flank was in that low saddle ground over there, where our peace party had been fired upon by Chapman.

The warriors charging up the west canyon struck that flank hard. Hanging on the side of their horses where not seen, they gave the soldiers a storm of bullets. Warriors dismounted, and from hiding dropped soldiers from their saddles.[4]

No wild horses were in this battle, as you say claimed in white man's history. Every horse carried a rider. In all there were not as many as seventy Indians in that fight.

In the meantime, our smaller party, sixteen in number, attacked the enemy's left flank. It was just like two bulldogs meeting. Those soldiers did not hold their position ten minutes. Some soldiers [citizen volunteers] on that low, rock-topped butte you see ahead there, were quickly on the run. Then the entire enemy force[5] gave way.

---

[4] Among the daring horsemen were three who wore coats of the same pattern made of red woolen blankets owned by Chief Yellow Bull. Of this trio, known as the "Three Red Coats," Wahlitits and Sarpsis Ilppilp will be remembered as two of the young men who started hostilities on the Salmon by the murder of Devine. They, together with Strong Eagle, the third Red Coat, have been praised by Two Moons and other warriors for their danger-challenging ability to fight as a unit in the thick of the fray.

[5] In regard to the number of participants in this battle, the numerical superiority attributed to the Nez Perces is fictional. For instance, a recent historian gives their strength as "over 300 Indian warriors." (Brosnan, *History of Idaho*, 1935, p. 206.) In actuality they were outnumbered two to one. For against Captain Perry's command, consisting of troops F and H, First Cavalry, totaling ninety-one enlisted men with their accompaniment of commissioned officers and civilian auxiliaries, the Indians threw fewer than seventy warriors, according to Yellow Wolf. This is corroborated by Chief Joseph, who in his *Own Story* says: "We numbered in that battle sixty men." These figures have further been substantiated by surviving

We nearly headed them off. We mixed them up. I did some bow shooting. Two of my arrows struck soldiers only five steps away—one in the shoulder, the other in the breast. We did not stop to fight the wounded. We chased hard after the others.

Wanting to bring out some latent phases of this first battle of the war, I asked Yellow Wolf, while he was relating the quick defeat of the soldiers, if either side had occupied the rock-crowned ridge where Captain Chapman was first seen, to which he replied:

When Chapman and soldiers ran away, no more soldiers got that far south. No Indians were on that butte.

Asked if he thought the soldiers might have won had they gained possession of that butte—since it commanded the entire field —he explained:

Had the soldiers gained that far south and divided their army at north end of the butte, one division fighting on west side, the other division taking that small, rocky butte off northeast there, they could have put up a stronger fight. But the soldiers could not do that. They were stopped too quick. Had they gone on that high butte, we could have starved them for water. Fighting makes bad thirst. The wounded die of thirst.

About a mile from the main battleground, five soldiers dismounted and took shelter among rocks. I did not know. I had not seen them go in there. As I drew near and dismounted, I heard a voice—somebody calling, "Heinmot Hihhih! Get to the rock! You will be shot!"

I saw and became mad. I ran to strike one soldier with

warriors who participated in the battle. Incidentally, the Nez Perce forces were reduced by the fact that many of them lay in camp at the time, drunk on whisky that had been brought in by a small band of raiders.

Lieutenant Parnell speaks of "White Bird with about seventy warriors" being frustrated in a "flanking" movement by a "few well directed vollies" from Captain Perry's men. (Brady, *op. cit.*, p. 107.) Chief White Bird, however, was not even on the battlefield, let alone leading such a force as described.

For the Army's description of this defeat, see Appendix I, this chapter.

my bow. I leaped and struck him as he put a cartridge to his gun. I grabbed the gun and shoved hard. The soldier went over backward, but he was not hurt. I wrenched the gun from him, and at same time a warrior back of me killed him. That was the Nez Perce way of war.

I now jumped down a bank where was another soldier. About a seven-foot jump. My feet slipped, and I slid in front of him. He was on one knee, pointing his rifle. The bullet passed over my shoulder. I grabbed the barrel of his gun. While we wrestled, a Nez Perce fired from the bank, and the soldier fell dead. I had the gun, and I took the belt of ammunition.

I was partly winded. I glanced around. A soldier was pointing his rifle at me. In that I saw danger. I jumped and ran, springing from side to side. I did not look back. Before the soldier got sights on me, a warrior threw a rock. It struck the soldier above the ear and killed him.

Farther on, we came upon two white men, dismounted. They hardly slowed us. They did not last any time.

Keeping after the runaway soldiers, we made a stop to fight seven or eight who had dismounted. Their horses were played out. They were in a ravine where grew thornbushes. Those soldiers put up a fight.

I saw Moositsa [Salish for Four Blankets], about my age, riding on opposite side of the soldiers. He had no gun. Was not fighting. He rode too close. Someone called, "Moositsa! Dangerous there!"

Just then a soldier fired. Moositsa fell off his horse, but was only slightly hurt. The bullet cut across his thigh, a light wound. It did not lay him up. He went through the war, to the last battle, and was among those exiled to Eeikish Pah [Hot Place; *i.e.*, Indian Territory], where he died.

Those seven or eight soldiers in the ravine were wiped out.[6]

We chased the remaining soldiers. Fought them running for several miles. We drove them back across the mountain, down to near the town they came from [Mount Idaho]. Then some of the chiefs commanded, "Let the soldiers go! We have done them enough! No Indian killed!"

The warriors have to mind what the chiefs say, so all stopped. Not one Indian killed! But three wounded.[7] Moositsa's hurt was small. Chellooyeen [Bow and Arrow Case; afterwards known as Phillip Evans] was shot through the right side while wresting a gun from a soldier. Auskehwush was shot in the belly when he reached for a gun held by a wounded soldier. That soldier played as dead. Auskehwush's mother sang medicine songs over him, and he recovered.

About eleven soldiers escaped from where I last saw them retreating.

---

[6] In describing the retreat from the White Bird, W. R. Parnell, who was a lieutenant in Captain Perry's command, says, in part: "The Indians dared not approach too closely, yet at one time they were near enough for my last pistol cartridge to hit one of them in the thigh." (Brady, *op. cit.*, p. 105.) It would be easy to imagine that onlooker Moositsa was the recipient of Lieutenant Parnell's last shot, except that Parnell could hardly have been among the seven or eight doomed troopers hemmed within the thorn-thicket ravine, none of whom escaped. The incident of which Parnell speaks must have been farther towards the mountain summit; but his "last pistol cartridge" was wasted. No thigh or other part of Indian anatomy was touched by it.

[7] In Indian accounts there is a slight discrepancy as to the number of their wounded in the White Bird fight. Yellow Wolf and Raven Spy say there were three, while Phillip Evans and Phillip Williams (Lahpeealoot) make the number but two. The difference hinges on Moositsa. Williams says:

"I heard announcement made by a warrior after the fight, as he rode about our camp, 'Auskehwush and Chellooyeen are wounded!' Moositsa, two others, and myself, none of us having guns, rode to where the seven soldiers were ambushed. We were warned by the warriors not to go to a certain spot, as dangerous. Make a good target for soldier bullets. But Moositsa, whose horse did not keep even with ours, disregarded the warning. When he was a few rods from us, he was shot at by the soldiers. The bullet must have passed close to his head, for he fell backwards and struck his wrist on a sharp rock. Blood flowed, and the cut was thought to be a gun wound. But when close examined, it showed differently. I saw not any wound on his thigh. Besides the two I have mentioned, I do not know any one else being gun-wounded in that battle."

(Phillip Williams died at his home near Kamiah, Idaho, December 2, 1938.)

We returned to the main battlefield. There we counted thirty-three dead soldiers. We did no scalping. We did not strip them naked. This may be in white man's history, but it is not true. We did not hurt the dead. Only let them lie.[8]

I heard that one hundred soldiers and twelve of General Howard's Christian Indians fought in the battle. Those Nez Perces were fighting against their own people. Three of them were captured. They begged not to be killed. They cried, holding up both hands. One man said, "Do not kill them. We will take them before the chiefs. Whatever they say will be done to them."

The chiefs held council just below our village.[9] They took pity on the three Indian prisoners and said, "These three Christian Indians! Poor fellows! They are crying about what they are doing to us. Let them go home."

The three were told, "If you help the soldiers again, if we catch you again, we will whip you! We will take hazel switches and beat you good!"[10]

Then the chiefs said, "Bring all guns you take from the soldiers."

The guns were brought, and one man appointed to count them. He counted and reported, "Sixty-three guns!"

---

[8] The charge, so often made, that the Nez Perces scalped and mutilated the dead on the White Bird field has no foundation in truth. A typical example of this accusation is the following:

"On arrival at the White Bird Canyon it was found that although more than a week had elapsed, the dead was still unburied and that disagreeable task was performed by the volunteers. The squaws had badly mutilated the bodies, as were their custom, making the duty a most gruesome one to perform." ("The Nez Perce Campaign," MS. by Eugene T. Wilson, first lieutenant with Captain (later Colonel) Edward McConville's volunteers. The MS. is on file with Washington State Historical Society.)

In reply to an inquiry on the subject, Colonel C. E. S. Wood, who, as a lieutenant in the Twenty-first Infantry and a member of General Howard's staff, helped bury the dead, states that he saw no evidence of either mutilation or scalping. The fact that often the hair loosens and slips on an unburied corpse, leaving the cranium smooth and bare, might have suggested, he adds, the scalping story. Colonel Wood also states that the dead were not stripped.

[9] This council site, as located by Yellow Wolf when on the grounds in 1930, was just within the corporate limits of the village of White Bird, on the side toward the battlefield along U. S. Highway 95.

[10] See Appendix II, this chapter.

There were not so many pistols, and not much account taken of them. They were picked up mostly by women. I took one, a six-shot, off a dead soldier.

We stayed two suns at Lahmotta camp near the battle-field. It was at Lahmotta that Pahkatos Owyeen [Five Wounds], Wahchumyus [Rainbow], and a few other buffalo hunters joined us. They were just from Montana. Buffalo hunters were the best warriors, bravest fighters.

Then we moved to south side of Salmon River, crossing at Horseshoe Bend. You have asked me how we crossed the Salmon and other deep, swift streams with our families and goods. I will tell you all, how done. Owning that country, the Nez Perces knew all such streams. Crossed them often without difficulty. They understood to manage.

At this crossing was only one canoe. But we had plenty of buffalo skins. With them we made hide boats. In making such boat, the hide, hair side up, was spread flat on the ground. Across the hide were laid green willow or other limber poles about the thickness of your thumb. The hide and poles were bent up and lashed to other bent poles forming a long circled rim. This rim was on outside. That was all.[11] Such boats carried big loads, and children and old people rode on top of the packs. Everything—tepee covers, cooking pots, pans, blankets—all were ferried in these boats. No paddles used. Boats were hauled by ponies guided by men. Two, maybe three or four, ponies to a boat. Two men swam at the sides to steady it.

---

[11] While Yellow Wolf was not questioned on the subject, subsequent inquiry of several of the warriors, and of the older women who did all the tanning, disclosed that the regular dressed buffalo robes were used for these boats. Rawhide and hides tanned as domestic buckskin, being permeable by water, could not have been used.

In a strange country Indians might have trouble cross-ing bad streams. We knew, and we had no trouble with water during the war.

You asked if we were trying to go to Imnaha and Wallowa country. When we crossed the Salmon we had no intention of going to either of those places. The chiefs planned to cross the Salmon only. If soldiers followed, we would cross back and go to the Clearwater. Just to get soldiers out of way, did we cross the Salmon.

All the people, old people, children, everybody, crossed the Salmon, except thirty warriors. I was one of the thirty. We turned back to Tepahlewam to scout the country, to watch for soldiers.

One evening we were riding along in the dark. Our leader, Teeweawea, stopped suddenly. He pointed to-wards the White Bird trail. There we saw lights moving, as if carried by men. Must be soldiers!

Kosooyeen [Going Alone][12] and I were sent to spy. Whatever we learned we must carry to the chiefs across the Salmon. We rode away in the darkness, in the direc-tion where the lights had been seen. We could see noth-ing. But soon we heard a gun report up the mountain trail. We went that way to see who made the shot.

Sure enough! Soldiers traveling the trail to Lahmotta.

We crossed the mountain by another way, and hurried toward the Salmon. It was morning when we reached the river about two miles below mouth of White Bird Creek.

---

[12] This intrepid young man's prewar name was Wewass Pahkalatkeikt (Five Sun-rayed Bile). It is contended by some Nez Perces that the proper spelling is Kosooyoom, but since Yellow Wolf and other contemporaries pronounced the name as first spelled, that form will be adhered to. Kosooyeen was reputed by his compatriots a brave warrior and adroit scout. A fine-looking young man, he resembled in many respects Chief Ollokot; both were general favorites with the people. He belonged to Chief Hahtalekin's Paloos, but was more often with Chief Joseph's band, because of his sister's marriage to one of its members. At the last battle Kosooyeen escaped to join Sitting Bull, but, returning with other refugees, he was arrested at Pendleton, Oregon, and banished to Indian Territory. He died on the Nez Perce Reservation in the early thirties. The writer knew him only as Luke Andrews.

On the opposite side of the river was a boat belonging to a Chinaman. Kosooyeen had a good swimming horse, so he crossed and brought the boat. I got in with Kosooyeen and towed my horse with a rope. Landing, we went up the river a few miles to a butte overlooking the Nez Perce camp, pitched near Deer Creek.

From the butte we waved a blanket, "Soldiers coming!"

Of course, guards were out on the hills, and the camp was not much excited. The next sun, scouts brought word, "Soldiers on both sides of the White Bird and Skookum Chuck."[13]

This was true. But it was another sun before they came in sight of our camp. They came over the mountain, opposite side of the river—a great string of soldiers. Some thought there must be a thousand—cavalry, walking soldiers, and big guns on wheels.[14] With them were a few Indians, General Howard's Christians. Chief Lawyer, Chief Timothy, Chief Jason, Chief Levi, and other headmen of the Upper Nez Perces had sold our homes. Sold our country which they did not own. This stayed in our minds, and now their followers were helping soldiers take all from us.

---

[13] General Howard in "Report of the General of the Army," 1877, p. 120, describes the approach of the military:

"The 25th [June] I moved my command by two routes to Jackson's ranch, some 4 miles from the head of White Bird Cañon. The 26th with my whole force I made a reconnaissance into the cañon and beyond Captain Perry's battle-field.

"Captain Page, with some twenty volunteers from Walla Walla, that had joined me at Lapwai, moved along the crest of the mountain-ridge on the right of White Bird Cañon, till he came in sight of the country beyond the Salmon."

[14] General Howard reports that at this stage he had "in all an effective force of 400 men." ("Report of the General of the Army," 1877, p. 120.) This force, at a liberal accounting, outnumbered by more than three to one the Nez Perce fighting strength. According to Eugene T. Wilson, there were "about 400 regulars and 100 volunteers," the latter taking the advance after crossing the Salmon. (MS., "The Nez Perce Campaign.")

BATTLE OF THE WHITE BIRD CANYON

APPENDIX I

General Howard in his official report says, "The Indians turn the left flank of the command, and with more than double Perry's numbers force him to retire from his position and return fighting all the way to Grangeville [Mount Idaho]. His losses are 33 enlisted men and one commissioned officer, Lieutenant Theller, killed." ("Report of the General of the Army," 1877, p. 120.)

The same author, later: "Perry and Trimble seemed to be together for the moment. Their left flank was suddenly turned. Two of the citizens at the Butte were wounded; then their companions gave way and began to fly. Some of the cavalrymen, too, had already taken the trail to the rear, at a run." (Howard, *Nez Perce Joseph*, p. 116.)

Still later, the same authority says: "At this decisive juncture of a fierce battle Perry saw that the Indians had at least three to one against him, and that both his flanks were turned." (Howard, *My Life and Experiences among Our Hostile Indians*, p. 285.)

APPENDIX II

Two of the captured "Christian Indians," Joe Albert and Robinson Minthon, subsequently joined Chief Joseph's band. At the battle of the Clearwater, hearing of the death of his father, the only warrior killed in the Cottonwood fighting, Albert, who had accompanied the troops to this point, deserted to the Nez Perces. In his mounted dash across the field, his uniform drew the fire of the warriors and he was wounded. A bullet passed through his thigh, which obliged him "to ride on one leg" in the retreat over the Lolo Trail. Another version has it that he was wounded by the soldiers, who, divining his intention, fired upon him.

Minthon did not remain long with the war party. He left it at Nahush [Fishtrap]—the Clearwater crossing at Kamiah, and returned to Lapwai. Later he took an allotment on the Umatilla Reservation, Oregon, where he died in 1926. The warriors regarded him as a deserter from both sides.

The third scout captured, Yuwishakaikt, states in his testimony establishing his services as a scout, that he was at the White Bird fight, was captured by Joseph and held two days, was freed, and in returning to Fort Lapwai, "rode a horse to death." ("Claims of the Nez Perce Indians," *House Document* No. 552, pp. 93-100; found also in *Report of the Secretary of the Interior*, 1900.)

Of the Nez Perce scouts who accompanied Captain Perry's command into White Bird Canyon, General Howard says: "The Indian scouts were for the most part unarmed, and fortunately were not taken down into the dangerous part of the White Bird Canyon." (*Nez Perce Joseph*, p. 122.)

CHAPTER 4

Annihilation of Rains's Scouting Party

For the narration of the events of July 3, our party took up a position one mile from the mouth of White Bird Canyon. Having thoroughly scanned the mountain slope, Yellow Wolf waved his hand toward the heights to the north, and spoke with grave earnestness:

UP THERE the soldiers appeared on top of the mountain. The families, the entire camp, had crossed the Salmon at Horseshoe Bend. They were camped on Deer Creek. This stream joins the Salmon about two miles above here. Our scouts had kept close watch on movements of the soldiers. From our hiding place across the river we were watching. The cavalry came first, strung from top of mountain to more than halfway to the river. As they came closer, we rode out from buttes and ridges, out from canyons and gulches. Forming, we galloped down the slopes toward the Salmon, yelling as we charged. Some enemies were so near we heard orders given.

James Reuben,[1] one of General Howard's Christian Nez Perce scouts, called to us, "You cowardly people! come over here. We will have it—a war!"

Lakochets Kunnin [Rattle on Blanket] shook his rifle at him and yelled, "You call us cowards when we fight for our homes, our women, our children! You are the coward! You sit on side of Government, strong with soldiers! Come over. We will scalp you!"

---

[1] James Reuben, Jr., was the son of the James Reuben who later succeeded Chief Lawyer.

Reuben made no answer. Another man called to him, "Cross the Salmon yourself! You are the fellows starting this war! Come on if you want to! You are ready mounted for riding the water! Do not be scared like a woman! You are growing fat, eating Government food!"

Chapman was there to interpret to soldiers what was said. When the warriors made that answer, the cavalry showed mad.[2] They fired at us across the river. Then we saw one ridge behind the cavalry covered with walking soldiers. We saw big guns on wagons, hurrying down. We dashed about on horses, playing war, doing a little shooting. We wasted only a few cartridges, and let the soldiers do most of the shooting. Their bullets did not hurt us. The chiefs now ordered, "We will give them this road. Do not bother them. Let them come across the Salmon. We do not have to cross to them. We are not after them. They are after us. If they come to our side, we can fight them if we want."

The women could not sleep when soldiers were so near, so we moved camp high into the mountains. Up to the country of the *pottoosway*, the medicine tree. Its branches are good for perfuming tepee homes. It keeps bugs [moths] from furs and robes.

But the warriors remained behind, hiding among ridges, waiting for soldiers to cross. Waited until the

---

[2] Of this scene, General Howard says, in part: "They were shouting back and forth. We could hear the voices of Indians giving their orders. While we were preparing a ferry, by collecting boats and crossing a cable, the Indians suddenly started from the hill-tops and ravines, and rushed towards our position. Paige [Captain of the Walla Walla volunteers] and I were sitting near the right of our line, on the bluff overlooking the White Bird. . . . Paige became more and more resolute, shouting loudly to the approaching foe, firing his rifle rapidly, while other rifles were coming. Some shots appeared to whistle among them as they drew nigh the river. Away they turned, and down the river they ran, like wild cattle just loose from the corral; and in fifteen minutes they had disappeared. Surely all was ready for them had they swam the swift river. It was partly a ruse, and intended to make me think that they designed to turn my flank at Rocky Canyon crossing, and partly the usual bravado of Indians, who, by their wildness of movement and defiant yelling, hope to inspire surprise and terror." (Howard, *Nez Perce Joseph*, pp. 147-48.)

sun went down, and the darkness came. Then we all went home, to the camp.

Came the morning, and when some of us scouted back we saw the soldiers still on north side of the Salmon. They were making to cross. A white man had a boat there— not a regular ferry. We had not bothered that boat. General Howard could use it if he wanted to. We waited half a sun for the soldiers, but none crossed. Then the chiefs said, "We will move out of their way."

Scouts remained to watch, and the families packed up and moved about twenty miles down the Salmon and camped.[3] In the afternoon we had seen two boats drifting down the Salmon. They may have broken loose, or maybe set adrift by General Howard after using them for crossing.

Next morning scouts brought word the soldiers were on our side of the Salmon. This was good. We immediately crossed back to the north side. We used the skin boats to carry our packs, the old people, and the children, as when we crossed before.

To the inquiry as to why this hasty return, came the reply:

It was from first so fixed. We intended turning back if soldiers followed us south. That was how the war was planned to be carried out. The chiefs wanted the soldiers out of the way. The two great warriors, Pahkatos Owyeen and Wahchumyus, counseled that trick. Counseled it while in Lahmotta camp.

Leaving the Salmon, we moved to Aipadass, a flat

---

[3] The wonderful mobility of the Nez Perces is attested in this march of twenty miles through a mountainous, broken country, encumbered as they were with their families and their herd of between 2,500 and 3,500 horses; they later recrossed the raging, flood-swollen Salmon—all this within thirty-eight hours, and before the enemy had discovered the direction of their flight.

where the women dig *kous* [an edible root]. All desert land. The ridge there is called Tepahlewam. It is not far from Split Rocks, and that is why the same name. We camped there that night.[4]

When morning came, I heard a gun report and the echo of a song.[5] I saw a warrior on a horse and Indians all about him. I took my gun and hurried there to see what enemy had been killed. Seeyakoon Ilppilp [Red Spy or Red Scout], the mounted warrior,[6] said, "Some white men almost kill me. I suppose scouts—two white men coming this way. They didn't look like soldiers."

The white men had seen him, Seeyakoon told us, as he was watching on guard away off from camp. They made for him. Seeyakoon jumped from his horse and dodged behind rocks. They fired at him. When they did that, he ran toward them, keeping hid by rock protection. He was not afraid! He killed one of them, shot him through the head. The other man got away.[7]

That was what I heard Seeyakoon telling, and he

---

[4] The camp was at Craigs Ferry, known to the Indians as "Luke's Place." It was here that General Howard, lacking a boat to pursue the Nez Perces, constructed "from the timbers of a cabin near the ferry" a raft which was lost when launched upon the torrential current. ("Report of the General of the Army," 1877, p. 121.) The cabin was doubtless that of Pahka Yatwekin, called Luke Billy, as in his claim for pay as scout for General Howard he testified that his house, "a lot of apples," and about four hundred head of horses and cattle were lost, and that white men took his place and kept it, all an entire loss. ("Claims of the Nez Perce Indians," p. 109.)

[5] The "echo of a song," as it is described by Yellow Wolf, was a peculiarly intoned chant, signifying that the enemy had been met and one of them killed. This chant was the "scalp halloo" characteristically used among Eastern tribes by victorious returning war parties.

[6] Seeyakoon is reputed to have killed single-handed two of General Howard's scouts on the breaks of Salmon River, and later, one of the General's Indian scouts (John Levi) near Weippe, at the Lolo ambuscade. Seeyakoon was killed *during* the last battle of the war, but not *in* the battle. With others he had sought refuge in a near-by Assiniboin village, but was treacherously killed by them after surrendering his rifle. Other refugee Nez Perces were also killed at the same time, the Assiniboins acting under orders from Colonel Nelson A. Miles.

[7] This pair was Charles Blewett and William Foster, the latter a half blood. Blewett was the one killed by Red Scout, while Foster escaped, carrying the news to Captain Whipple. There has been considerable romancing about Blewett, to the effect that his body was never found, and even that he was not killed. However, Colonel McConville of the volunteers gave the following report to Governor Mason Brayman, of Idaho Territory:

"Aug. 22. Went on Scout with Capt. Winters Company 'E' 1st Cav. found the added, "I tell you, furthermore, soldiers are now close upon us."

"Yes," answered the chiefs. "What are the soldiers doing? Moving or camping?"

"Camping," said Seeyakoon. "Soldiers are ready for the battle. They have embankments and dugout hollows fixed up. All ready for war."[8]

Some said, "Let us go see," and they went.

After they had gone, I followed alone. In a draw I saw my friends gathered together. When I got where I could see them better, they made a left swerve. I looked in this new direction, and saw a blanket waving, a signal of war. I ran my horse that way and, reaching a small hump, I saw about twelve soldiers.[9] When they saw the warriors they became scared and tried to escape.

My friends went after those soldiers, and I overtook them. There was shooting, and one soldier fell from his horse. Then another went down a little way from us. Soon a third fell; and another and another, not far apart, went to the ground. Some distance on, a man—maybe wounded—got down from his horse and was killed. I will not hide anything. That part of the fight was not long. Those six soldiers did not get up.

The remaining six soldiers ran their horses up a hill, maybe one half mile. Then they jumped off and lay among some rocks, and began shooting.

---

body of Bluett, returned to Camp and buried the body at Cottonwood House close to the grave of the Gallant Lieut Raines who lost his life while going to rescue Bluett, Distance traveled twenty (20) miles." *(Fifteenth Biennial Report of the State Historical Society of Idaho,* 1936, p. 72.)

[8] Captain Whipple hastily constructed rifle pits on an eminence near the Norton Tavern—"Cottonwood House"—on the old stage road. (Howard, *Nez Perce Joseph,* pp. 152-53.)

[9] This was Second Lieutenant S. M. Rains's ill-fated scouting party, sent out by Captain Whipple on July 5 in an endeavor to locate the Indians. Foster acted as guide for the lieutenant and his "ten picked men," riding blithely to swift destruction. For a more detailed description of this tragedy, see Brady, *Northwestern Fights and Fighters,* pp. 123-24.

We proceeded to an impressive group of large isolated boulders (on land now owned by Vincent Duman) which has become recognized locally as the scene of the wiping out of Rains's detachment. John L. Rooke, postmaster of Cottonwood, informed the writer that as a boy he played about this boulder formation, and that he saw bullet marks in many places. It would seem that such scars should still be discernible, yet the most searching examination by our party failed to reveal the slightest trace whatever. Yellow Wolf animatedly resumed his narrative:

Not true that this place is where the soldiers stopped. They did not pass by here, but struck more to the right.[10] We were not crowding them very close, and had they kept on they might have gained the timber, although Indian scouts were ahead, watching to catch mail carriers [Army couriers] going either way. The soldiers may have seen those scouts. It was Tipyahlanah Kapskaps [Strong Eagle] they began shooting at. He was what you call a decoy, guarding the road. He let the soldiers see him behind a small dead pine.

Those soldiers were trapped. They had no show. When they began shooting, it was just like their calling, "Come on! Come on! Come on!" A calling to death.

Our leader, Pahkatos, threw up his hand, and we stopped. The soldiers were shooting at Tipyahlanah in the canyon on their left. We dropped back out of sight, then circled the hill to the right. A little beyond the soldiers we dismounted. Some men stayed with the horses, and the others crawled toward the soldiers. I was one of the crawlers. The soldiers were still firing, but not at us. They did not see us, and we got close to them. I will not hide it. Those soldiers were killed!

---

[10] But bullet scars were plainly visible on a group of rocks about 160 rods farther north, on land owned by Carl Schurra, where Yellow Wolf declared the last stand actually was made. The alignment of the bullet scars substantiated Yellow Wolf's designation of the direction from which the attack was launched. As this group of rocks was obviously inadequate for protection, the mounts of the troopers must have been exhausted, else they would not have halted here.

CHUSLUM MOXMOX (YELLOW BULL)
One of the outstanding Nez Perce warriors. He was prominent in the White Bird
engagement and participated in subsequent engagements.

THE LAST STAND OF LIEUTENANT RAINS

Above: the group of boulders which legend declares was the site of the doomed troopers' last stand.

Below: another rock formation near by, identified by Yellow Wolf as the true spot where Lieutenant Rains and his companions were killed.

I was soon there with the others. One soldier was sitting up, leaning against a rock. He was shot in the forehead, almost level with the eyes. He had two other shots, through the breast, and he still lived. He washed his face with his own blood, and looked around. He made a clucking noise, a sound like that of a chicken. The Indians, hearing, wondered! They asked one another, "What about him? He must be more like us!"

From that day the warriors who are left remember what they saw and heard. All stood around that soldier, many of them saying, "He can not live. His body is too bad hurt."

But one man thought differently and he said, "He can live if he wants to!"[11]

"He is too many times shot," answered one. "Head too bad shot!"

Then one oldlike man named Dookiyoon [Smoker], who had a gun with flint to set the powder afire, spoke, "We shall not leave him like that. He will be too long dying."

With those words, Smoker raised his gun and shot the soldier in the breast. The bullet knocked him over, but he raised up again. He sat there, still calling to his Power. Calling with that same clucking. He washed his face again with his running blood, and still looked around.

The warriors, all silent, said nothing. Then some of them taunted Smoker about his gun, that it was not strong. Smoker reloaded and shot once more, but it did no good! The soldier still sat against the rock, still making the clucking of the hen.

[11] Deeply impressed by the wounded trooper's vitality, the warriors applied their own philosophical deductions, and attributed to him a "Power" corresponding to their own belief and practice.

While the warriors stood silent and wondering, one man stepped forward and knocked the soldier over with his *kopluts* [war club]. Others spoke to save him, but our leader said to us, "We have no doctor. Poor fellow! He is suffering. We better put him out of trouble."

When our leader made this talk, we all became one-minded. I then helped with my *kopluts*.

We started for where the other soldiers were camped, the camp that Seeyakoon had told us about. But the chiefs commanded the warriors to stop. "Let's not go farther," they said. "This sun we have killed thirteen enemies, and none of us hurt. It is good to quit now."

The warriors stopped, for they had to listen to the chief's orders. We all went back to camp. We wanted to see where Seeyakoon killed the white man that morning, so we went that way. I saw him lying where he fell some hours before, shot in the head. He was killed in a draw west of where we killed the last six soldiers in the rocks. I do not know the distance, but it was not far. There was timber scattered in and about the draw.

I heard, too, that Pahkatos Owyeen [Five Wounds] killed a white man, thought to be a scout, that same morning.[12] All white people were spies for the soldiers. Five Wounds was with us in that running fight with the soldiers. He was our leader.

---

[12] While it is not known that Pahkatos did kill a white man the morning of that momentous day, the reputed finding of a human skeleton in that region long afterwards indicates that such may have been the case.

Fight with Captain Randall's Volunteers and Its Sequel

At the outbreak of hostilities all the white women and children from the surrounding countryside had gathered at the little town of Mount Idaho for protection. Only twenty miles away, at Cottonwood, General Howard had left a few soldiers to maintain a supply base, but these troops were practically under a state of siege, for the Nez Perces had scouts or raiding parties watching all the roads. Thinking it advisable to join forces with the troops, D. B. Randall organized a company of sixteen armed volunteers, and on the morning of July 5 they rode out of Mount Idaho toward Cottonwood. When about two miles from their destination the volunteers unexpectedly encountered the Indians.

In this skirmish Yellow Wolf had his first experience of actual sharpshooting. Grim exultation may be sensed in his later depiction of the besieging of the volunteers on "Mount Misery," and of the recapture of the Indian ponies stolen some days previously from Chief Looking Glass's village when it was ruthlessly destroyed and plundered by the whites.

W E HELD our old camp, going nowhere. But next sun the families moved to a spring, Piswah Ilppilp Pah [Place of Red Rock]. While this was doing, a small bunch of young warriors went separately. No old men among us. Coming to the wagon road, we looked in direction of the ferry [Craigs Ferry]. We saw them— about twenty armed horsemen. Not uniformed soldiers, but more like citizens.[1] Not riding a close company, but strung out along the road. When they saw us, they bunched and came a little faster. Came straight towards us! Seemed to me they cared not for us. Drawing closer,

---

[1] Captain D. B. Randall's volunteers, numbering seventeen men in all.

they appeared mail carriers [couriers]. We now knew there was to be a fight.

Then those men made for us. We were lined across their path. As they charged we gave way—let them go through. We then struck after them, racing to flank both sides. The shooting became faster, and soon those whites stopped and dismounted. The fighting was from about half-past ten o'clock to middle of afternoon. We did not know why the soldiers in their dugout rifle pits did not come to the fighting. We could see them where they were on higher ground. They seemed a little afraid.

One young white man among those fighting us was brave. I did not recognize him, but some said he had been raised right among the Indians—that his father was Cooks, or Crooks;[2] I do not know. But his father was a friend to us. Had always been our friend.

When we were mixing close, this boy killed the horse of Weësculatat. Then this same young man shot Weësculatat in the leg below the knee. He then shot him through the breast and again a little lower down. But the bullets did not go through his body.

Scattered, the warriors were on every side of the enemies. Plenty of shooting. We gradually crowded in on them. Some of those whites must have been killed.[3] The sun was halfway down the afternoon sky when, looking back, we saw soldiers coming, their big gun in the lead.

The chiefs now called out, "Let us quit for a while!" Hearing that order, we left the fighting, taking

---

[2] The writer was told by an old-timer that in one of the earlier fights a son of one Crooks, a noted friend of the Nez Perces, was recognized by them, and one of the warriors was heard to call out, "You, Charley Crooks! Take your father's horses and go home!" It is not certain that the elder Crooks referred to is the J. M. Crooks, of Grangeville, spoken of by General Howard as riding to Joseph's camp at Rocky Canyon and asking the Indians if they intended to fight: "They told Crooks that they would not fight the settlers provided they would not help the soldiers." (Howard, *Nez Perce Joseph*, p. 103.)

[3] Those killed were Captain D. B. Randall and Volunteer Ben F. Evans: two others were wounded. See Appendix I, this chapter, for full eyewitness account.

Weësculatat with us. Three times wounded at beginning of fight, he lived until about dark. With two bad wounds, he could not hold his life. Not old, about middle-aged, he was first warrior killed. We lost a good fighter.[4]

Next morning, a funeral was held for Weësculatat. It was not what you call a Christian funeral. He was wrapped in blankets with some weapons and a few objects sacred to him. He was buried at Piswah Ilppilp, and his grave was hidden from finding.

After we buried Weësculatat, we packed up and moved to the Clearwater River bottom, a place called Peeta Auüwa (Peeta [at] Mouth of Canyon). An Indian, an old man named Peeta, lived there. That was how the place was named. It is not far from present Kooskia, on the same river. We camped above where town of Stites has been built.

That same sun we got in camp nearly one hundred of us went down to Kamiah. We made James Lawyer, son of old Chief Lawyer, who was leader in helping steal our lands and homes, ferry us across the Clearwater. Had he refused, we would have cut his boat loose. We were going to a Dreamer religious meeting at the camp of some Lapwai Indians just returned from Montana. Those people who wanted to join us went up to our camp afterwards.

Chief Looking Glass joined us here. All his band came at same time. My mother was with them. She was with Looking Glass's family when soldiers attacked his village. His tepee was burned, but my mother escaped with the

---

[4] Weësculatat was the first Nez Perce to fall in actual conflict, in contrast to the forty-six men already lost, up to July 5, on the opposite side. And, ironically, he fell at the hands of one whom, as the son of a well-proved friend, the warriors had refrained from shooting.

Sewattis Hihhih (White Cloud), a half brother of Two Moons and a man of small stature but a brave warrior, was wounded in the right thigh during the Cottonwood fighting, presumably in the Randall skirmish. He was among those who surrendered at the Bear's Paw field. He survived the ordeal of exile and died at Nespelem, Colville Indian Reservation, about four years after the return of the war prisoners.

others. She remembered to save my rifle. Took it apart and hid it in her pack from being seen by whites. I was glad to see my rifle. My parents had bought it for me with one good horse. I now had my own sixteen-shot rifle for rest of the war.

My mother could use the gun against soldiers if they bothered her. She could ride any wild horse and shoot straight. She could shoot the buffalo and was not afraid of the grizzly bear.

My stepfather, Tommimo, three-quarters French, was not at Chief Looking Glass's camp at time of attack. Herding horses near Lewiston, he was arrested and jailed to keep him from joining in the war. He belonged to Chief Joseph's band.

Wanting to obtain the Nez Perce version of the status of Chief Looking Glass at the outbreak of hostilities, I interposed, "General Howard states that some of Looking Glass's men had joined Chief Joseph's band before this time, either before you crossed the Salmon or while you were south of that river." To this came the quick response:

Not true! None of Chief Looking Glass's people joined us until coming to our camp on Clearwater. Looking Glass refused joining with the other five chiefs. He moved to his own camp to get away from war. The soldiers drove him to us when they attacked his village. Those Indians then had gardens planted on the Clearwater.[5]

At this time we heard of soldiers on the hill called

---

[5] General Howard in his official report wrote that Looking Glass had "furnished at least twenty warriors" to the hostiles before the attack by Captain Whipple. ("Report of the General of the Army," 1877, p. 121.) Four years later he wrote in his *Nez Perce Joseph* (pp. 148-49) that "forty bucks" had left Looking Glass to join Joseph. All this while both Joseph and Howard were *south of the Salmon!* There can be no doubt but that the peaceably inclined Chief Looking Glass was driven to war. He possessed a place of long standing at the forks of the Clearwater. Peopeo Tholekt, warrior of Looking Glass's band, declared to the writer: "Gardens had been plowed, planted, and everything growing when we were attacked. We had plenty for our living. One man had ten milk cows, and others had cows and beef cattle. All, everything, was lost. Only about twenty men and boys—some boys small—had guns; part of them shotguns and light rifles. None of us wanted war; nobody expected war."

Possossona [Water Passing], near Kamiah. We went back over the hill to where they were. It was to be a battle about the middle of afternoon. We surrounded those soldiers. There was fighting until sundown. Near dusk we quit and returned home to camp.

It must have been about nine o'clock that same night when somebody said, "Let us go where the soldiers herd their horses!" A small bunch of us went. When the soldier-herders heard us coming, they ran away. Left their horses. We took them all, except a few we did not want. They were no good for us.

We had those soldiers surrounded, and they kept firing.[6] We skirmished awhile. It was just like fireworks cutting the darkness. It was about middle of night when our leader called out, "Let's quit! We have got horses."

We then went home, taking the horses with us.[7] They were horses stolen by soldiers. Good horses taken from Looking Glass when soldiers came and attacked his village. We returned them to warriors who claimed them.

Next morning some of us—I do not know how many —went back to where the soldiers were. We would make another war. We found no officers, nobody there. We thought we must have killed or wounded some of them.

---

[6] The hill on which the soldiers were encamped was that which was afterwards designated as Mount Misery. Eugene T. Wilson, participant, gives the following account of the events of that night in his MS., "The Nez Perce Campaign":

"In the meantime, Joseph discovered the proximity of the volunteers and, as a fight was imminent, Colonel McConville ordered his men to take a position upon the summit of a hill, afterwards designated as 'Mount Misery,' and to begin digging rifle pits at once, using their knives and tin cups for the purpose. With such implements, it was slow work, but by nightfall the hill top was fairly well fortified. The men did not have to wait long for an attack. By ten o'clock the fight was on and the bullets flying thick and fast. Time after time the Indians charged the hill, only to be met with a fire so deadly as to compell them to fall back. The night was so dark that it was only by the flashes from the guns that the savages could be seen, and firing on both sides was mostly at random. Just before dawn, the enemy withdrew, and a sigh of relief went up from within the rifle pits. None of the volunteers received serious injury, the location of the improvised forts being such that the fire of the Indians was too high to do much damage. Empty cartridge shells were found next morning within fifteen feet of some of the rifle pits, and when an account of stock was taken, it was discovered that forty-five head of horses were missing."

[7] See Appendix II, this chapter.

They had lain close in dugout trenches, but we had crept within a few steps of them. No time did we see any of them. We had fired at close range, and they knew where to find us. But they would not raise up to shoot. Nobody there now to fight. We returned to camp. We stayed here three suns.

* * *

APPENDIX I

The following description was written by Second Lieutenant Luther Wilmot, participant, for the late W. D. Vincent, of Spokane, Washington, through whose courtesy it is here published for the first time.

CAPTAIN RANDALL'S FIGHT WITH THE NEZ PERCES

When Randall returned from Salmon River, the volunteers elected him captain, Jim Curley, first lieutenant, Lew Wilmot, second lieutenant, Frank Fenn, sergeant. There had been rumors of the Indians having recrossed the Salmon River and that they were making their way to join Looking Glass at the mouth of the South Fork of the Clearwater.

It was early in the morning Capt. Randall said to me, "Lew, will you take ten men and go over toward Lawyer's Canyon on the old plowed trail and see if you can locate the Indians on their trail?" I called for the men and it took us probably one hour to get everything ready and we started. We had gone not one quarter of a mile when we met Dan Crooks. He said, "Lew, where are you boys going?" I told him my orders.

Will said, "The Indians are camped on Craig's Mountain, and day before yesterday they killed Lieutenant Rains, Billy Foster, Blewett, and ten soldiers at the foot of the mountain above Cottonwood, and yesterday they came down and fired a good many shots at the soldiers."

I turned around and with Dan and the boys we rode back to the hotel and reported to Capt. Randall, to whom Dan told what he had told us. Capt. Randall then called for twenty-five volunteers to go to the assistance of the soldiers at Cottonwood. Seventeen was all that could go.

We got ready as quick as we could. One young man, Ben Evans, came to me and said, "I would like to go, but I have no horse." I had been told by a friend who owned one of the best horses on the prairie that when I wanted to go out for a scouting I could have his horse. I told Ben he could have my horse, and I would go get the horse.

We started. Quite a number of the boys regarded the trip more as a picnic than the serious job it really was. I know I felt very serious about it. I was leaving my wife and a two-day-old baby, three other girls, and an aged father. I had been in a number of Indian skirmishes, and I was afraid we would meet the Indians in full force, and I thought there was quite a number of our boys who I knew were not good shots and as they had never been under fire, the chances were decidedly in favor of the Indians, who up to this time had cleaned up every command that had been sent against them.

It was ten miles to the Cottonwood House. We traveled as fast as we dared to not to exhaust our horses. When we had got about two thirds of the distance we could see large bodies of horsemen and many thousands of stock being driven down the mountain, and they were Indians, I was certain. Some one had a small field glass. This I took and got down from my horse and I could plainly see the Indians. I could see the soldiers around their rifle pits. I rode up to the Company and told Randall and asked him to call a halt, which was done for a few minutes. I tried all of my persuasive powers to get the Company to retreat. This we could have done without any loss. But they said no. "Well, then," said I, "let's go on to the little mound near by and let the Indians attack us." This mound we could have held, as it commanded the prairie.

This they refused to do. Randall said, "Lew, if you want to go back, you can go. I and the rest of the boys have started to Cottonwood and we are going." I said, "Randall, you know I am not going back unless the rest go. You know we have nearly all the arms of the settlers and you can see we have the Indians between us and Cottonwood to fight, and they outnumber us ten to one." "Well," said he, "if you are afraid, you can get behind me." I said, "Randall, this is too serious a situation to be made a joke of and I can stand it if the rest can. But the best thing we can do is to go back before it is too late." For a short distance we rode in silence. The Indians had run their stock, women, and children off toward Rocky Canyon. All of the warriors were drawn up in a line extending one half mile long, directly across our road.

I then broke the silence by asking Randall what he proposed to do.

81

He said, "We are going to charge the Indians." "Well," said I, "you want to have some understanding what we are to do in case of someone's being shot or some horse being killed from under one of the boys." So we agreed that if anyone was killed or his horse killed, someone must stop and pick him up.

The Indians quietly awaited us. Some were horseback, some were standing by their horses. I saw a few without guns. Soon as they saw we intended to charge them they broke and ran. When we passed through their lines they fell in behind and chased us. Frank Vansise's horse was killed. Henry Johnson (who lives at Opportunity) stopped and took him up behind him. Randall, Jim Curley, Abe Bartlett, Frank Fenn, Charlie Johnson, and Ben Evans were a little to my left. I had stopped a couple of times to shoot and was a short distance from Randall. When his horse was shot he hollered, "Boys, don't run, let's fight 'em." I kept on, as Randall and the other boys mentioned were all down in a small depression. I stopped on a little mound which commanded a view of the surrounding country. I jumped from my horse and began shooting at every Indian in sight.

When the boys came up I asked them to get off. Soon D. H. Houser rode up and said he was wounded. I told Geo. Riggins to go with Houser to a fence not very far away. Eph. Brunker asked if he could not go on to the Cottonwood House for assistance and Jim Buchanan wanted to go with him. "Cash" Day I sent down to cover our left flank. That left on the little mound Charley Case, Peter Bemen, Henry Johnson, and myself. From the time Randall's horse was shot there was but six of us to defend our position. We held the position unaided from eleven A. M. to nearly three P. M., notwithstanding that our two men had gone to the soldiers at the rifle pits, who had been eyewitnesses to the fight. Perry, the commander, said a number of times we were all killed and he did not want to expose his men. Finally he gave permission for Captain Winters to take his company of cavalry and go to our assistance. It was after they had got about halfway to us that Geo. Shearer came on ahead, and at that time there was no possible danger, except from a long-range shot.

The Indians had drawn off about one and one-half miles and occasionally fired a shot. Shearer rode up and I told him to get off. He said, "There is no danger now. Get the boys and let's go to the Cottonwood House." Just then I saw smoke from an Indian rifle and soon a bullet passed through the withers of the horse and Shearer dismounted. Capt. Winters sent his bugler down and asked me to get our boys and we would return to the Cottonwood House.

I got up and called to the boy laying in the depression. When Curley said, "Ben Evans is killed and Randall is wounded," I ran down to where Randall was lying by his dead horse. He said, "Lew, I am mortally wounded. I want some water." I hollered to the soldiers and one brought his canteen. I lifted Randall's head and he said, "Tell my wife—" I gave him a drink. This he threw up, and died without finishing what he wanted to say.

Soon several civilians came down, and Capt. Winters became impatient and wanted us to go. I told Pete Ready to take my horse and with his go to Cottonwood House and get a wagon and come and we would take our dead and wounded. Capt. Winters said we could carry the wounded on horseback and the dead could be removed later. I told him I would wait until Ready returned, so Capt. Winters waited. It was after four P. M. when we got to the Cottonwood House. Hunter and the volunteers came in after dark, where he met a hearty welcome from the officers, and we were glad he came. It was arranged for him to accompany us across the prairie. Perry was court-martialed but was exonerated on the ground that to have come to our assistance would have endangered his base of supplies. After the charge by Capt. Randall we were between Perry's supplies and the Indians.

Lieutenant Wilmot is reputed to have fired seventy-six shots in this battle. The volunteers "estimated the number of killed and wounded at 25 to 30 of the Indians." (Fifteenth Biennial Report, State Historical Society of Idaho, p. 57.)

Consult Howard, Nez Perce Joseph, pp. 152-54, for an exculpatory résumé of this affair; also Brady, Northwestern Fights and Fighters, p. 125, where Colonel Perry in seven sentences disposes of the charges for which he was court-martialed with a memory so defective that the "casualties" suffered by the "home guards," as he dubbed the volunteers, could not be recalled.

APPENDIX II

Colonel McConville in his report to Governor Brayman claims that during the siege of "Fort Misery" a body of Indians, in attempting to flank a company of volunteer re-enforcements, was frustrated by Lieutenant Wilmot's "firing and killing the leading Indian and shooting the horse of the second." (Fifteenth Biennial Report, State Historical Society of Idaho, pp. 66-67.) The truth is that the only Indian hurt during the entire attack was Paktilek (an uninterpreted Salish name), whose right-hand forefinger was shot off while he was

83

leading away two of the horses captured from the beleaguered volunteers. A heavy ring saved his index finger and possibly others. Paktilek was an uncle of Camille Williams. The latter writes:

"My uncle has often told me about his adventure. He did not know that his finger was gone until several minutes afterwards. He was told by others of his hurt, but he answered, 'No.' Finally he felt his horse's mane all wet with blood, and then knew.

"This was after the skirmish with McConville. The killing of an Indian, and killing the horse of another, a day after the fight, is all fake, as there is no known Indian that was killed near Fort Misery. McConville also says that the Indians kept on firing at them all day. This is also fake. They had been ordered not to waste ammunition; as the soldiers [volunteers] were in their dugouts, and only occasionally their heads sticking out. Those soldiers fired at innocent Indians that were looking on from a distance. My uncle, who was married to a niece of Chief Joseph, did not follow the warring party over the Lolo Trail.

"My uncle told me also that the warriors were led in the Fort Misery fight by Pahkatos, Wahchumyus, and Ollokot."

YELLOW WOLF:
His Own Story

✪

Battle of the Clearwater

The Clearwater River, flowing almost due north, lies some fifteen miles east of where we saw the Nez Perces on July 5, in the preceding chapter. Here the Indians had gathered to await developments. General Howard had meanwhile lost track of his extremely mobile opponents. As we see in this chapter, it was only more or less by accident that he stumbled upon their camp.

Our party, in revisiting the sites of the war, climbed to the summit of the formidable high tableland known as Battle Ridge, where on July 11 and 12, 1877, the battle of the Clearwater was fought. Yellow Wolf led the way directly to the most narrow point of the ridge. Here, from the brow of the canyon skirting the north side of the battlefield proper, we had an unobstructed view of the country for miles to the north, where General Howard's army first came in sight. With another unhurried look around, the old warrior resumed his story.

IT WAS about ten o'clock in the morning, a sun or so after we took horses from soldiers on Possossona. Some boys and men were racing horses on the narrow strip of level land along the Clearwater below our camp. I was sitting on my horse watching them, when Wemastahtus called to me, "Yesterday a soldier was killed below here. I saw him."

I rode down to see the dead soldier. I found him lying by the trail. He had a mustache, but nothing else appeared about him to note. It was afterwards thought he had run away from the army. Alone, he could not defend himself.

Just then I heard a noise at the races. I moved away a

short distance, dismounted and sat down on a boulder. I could still hear an excitement at the races. I sat there some time, thinking. Then I heard the boom of a gun report. Sounded like the shot of a big gun—a distance away. I listened hard! It was a strange sound passing through the air that I now heard.

Then came a loud explosion near the racers. That shell-shot was from the high mountain bluff beyond the river—north side of this canyon. Immediately a scout came riding hard down the slope from that direction. Waving his blanket, he called across the river, "Soldiers surrounding us! Soldiers surrounding us!"

It was sure enough! I saw soldiers strung out a long way off; far up along the mountain's brow.[1]

I jumped on my horse and galloped to camp. I stripped for the battle. I got my rifle and cartridge belts, two of them. One I wore around my waist; the other, across my left shoulder and under the right arm. I always carried them that way.

The chiefs called an order, "Split up! Make three bodies!"

About twenty of us young warriors joined together. Chief Toohoolhoolzote was our leader. The other two companies must stay at camp. We hastened upriver a short ways. We crossed and rode into the timber. We

---

[1] Harry Lee Bailey was in the battle of the Clearwater as second lieutenant, Company B, Twenty-first Infantry, and was breveted for bravery. In regard to the opening of the fight, Bailey wrote me under date of Jan. 29, 1934:

"The Indian camp was passed by General Howard with only a vague idea of the Indians' location, and we were one or two miles beyond the camp location before—we might say—the Indians discovered us. Possibly someone at the end of our long column might have seen the Indian camp, or some Indian coming from it, and passed up the alarm. I do not know which. The gatling guns and howitzer were rushed to the rim of the high cliff to our left and we fired some volleys which may have been the real awakening of the enemy. . . . Apparently they were without any good outposts and were really ignorant of our so near approach."

General Howard in his official report states that the Indians were discovered by his aide-de-camp, Lieutenant Fletcher, about twelve o'clock, and it was judged from their motions that they "had just discovered our approach." It was one o'clock when a "howitzer and two gatling guns were firing towards the masses of Indians below." ("Report of the General of the Army," 1877, p. 122.)

YELLOW WOLF'S RIFLE
Not until shortly before the Clearwater battle did Yellow Wolf secure his own rifle, at which time his mother brought it to him secreted in her pack.

LOOKING DOWN THE CLEARWATER
Along the base of "Battle Ridge" on the right. It was on the summit of this ridge or plateau where the main battle was fought.

PHOTO BY BENNETT

NORTHWEST SLOPE OF CLEARWATER BATTLEFIELD

The Clearwater River flows along base of gentle slope at extreme left of picture. Toward left skyline may be seen the white house and the thorn-bush clump where Yellow Wolf helped build a rifle pit.

WOTTOLEN (RIGHT) AND HIS SON

Seated: Wottolen, the famous warrior, in his old age. Standing: Many Wounds, his son, who served as interpreter for much of Yellow Wolf's narrative.

THE SMOKING LODGE

Behind this rampart of rocks the aged men and other noncombatant Nez Perces
were safe from flying bullets.

DOWN THE CLEARWATER FROM THE BATTLEFIELD

Showing mouth of canyon up which the Nez Perces withdrew and proceeded to
Kamiah, Idaho.

hurried up the wooded slope of a canyon, leading to south side of this battlefield.

I was ahead as scout, and reached the ridge-brow first. Looking north, I saw many soldiers. They were getting ready for the war. I saw a big bunch of them heading down toward our camp across the river. Pointing, I called to the others, "Can you not see the soldiers? What they are doing? Let us go closer and do shooting!"

We ran our horses across the flat, down into this canyon and up the other side a ways. We tied them in some small, scattered timber, and hurried afoot up to the flats.

We had to stop those soldiers going to our camp!

A few other warriors joined us, making about twenty-four to fight General Howard's army.

You see a white house far away to the left yonder? It is in foreground of trees. That black spot to its right is a thornbush clump. We were left of that thicket only a few steps.

I heard our chief call, "Come, boys! We will make a rifle pit."

At that place we worked fast. Piling up stones, we soon had a good shelter.

Chief Toohoolhoolzote then said, "Stay here. I am going up a short way."

Holding close to earth, the chief crawled up the hill. He did not pass from our sight. Soon we heard a rifleshot. Our chief had killed a soldier.

His rifle a muzzle-loader, it was a little time before we heard a second shot. Another soldier had been killed.

Smoke of that last shot drew a storm of bullets. But they did no harm. Chief Toohoolhoolzote's *Wyakin*[2] was strong.

---

[2] *Wyakin* is discussed in Appendix A, end of volume.

We were firing whenever soldiers could be seen. Bullets were striking our stone fort. Chief Toohoolhoolzote crawled back to us. The firing was making our horses uneasy. They might break loose. Toohoolhoolzote gave command that four go hold them, the rest to stay and beat back the soldiers. None of us were hit, but we saw some of our bullets found marks.

Soldiers were strung out a long ways and advancing. Some were close to us. Indians and soldiers fighting—almost together. We could not count the soldiers. There must have been hundreds. Bullets came thicker and thicker.

Our chief looked around. It was early afternoon. A long while before dark would come. He saw we were hemmed in on three sides and gave orders that we go. He was last to leave. We crawled a ways, then ran. We hurried, for bullets were singing like bees. My heart beat fast. Thinking only for escape, I ran away from my waiting horse. Nobody stopped for horses. All were running to cross the ridge about where we are now standing. I, too, kept on for a little ways.

Then I came to myself. I missed my horse, and I grew hot with mad! I made myself brave! I turned and ran for my horse—many soldiers shooting at me.[3] Why, I did not care what I ran into! I got my horse and led him away. The boys caring for the horses had escaped on their own. The enemies got all the others.

With soldiers still shooting, I jumped on my horse and galloped down the hill. Crossing the canyon, I came to left of here. As I drew up to higher ground, bullets fell about me. I could see dust spurt up where they struck

[3] The panic of the young warrior was dispelled by his sudden realization of the disgrace that would be his were he to lose his horse under such circumstances. The record he had established on the White Bird field had to be maintained. Death would be preferable to the loss of those laurels.

the earth. I whipped my horse for all in him. A swift horse, light black [brown] in color. He began slowing down, breathing hard. I whipped the more, and finally we passed over the saddle ridge just west of here. Out of sight of the soldiers, my horse could take a good rest.

While making that ride, I thought it my last day. My feelings were that I was not much excited. Before that time, my uncle, Old Yellow Wolf, had said to me, "If you go to war and get shot, do not cry!"

I remembered that instruction. It helped me to be brave. If we die in battle, it is good. It is good, dying for your rights, for your country.

When I reached timber south of this saddle ridge, I dismounted and tied my horse. I came where some older men had built the big "Smoking Pit." Sheltered from all danger, I saw lots of people there smoking. Most of them old, they were not fighting. I passed them. I did not like tobacco or any kind of smoking. I was afraid to smell it. I ran eastward to where I heard shooting.

I came where four men were fighting. They were my uncle, Old Yellow Wolf, Otstotpoo, Howwallits [Mean Man], and Tomyunmene. The three older men's faces were bleeding. Rock chips from flying bullets were doing the work.

These warriors had rifle pits among some boulders. Not too big, the rocks, but about right size for conceal- ment. I dropped down behind one of them.[4] We were

---

[4] A few rods north of a boulder barricade in the head of a small "draw" at the uttermost southeastern angle of the Nez Perce defense—where fought the Three Red Coats and others comprising the flower of White Bird's and Toohoolhoolzote's bands—was located the rifle pit of Yellow Wolf and his fighting mates named in his narrative. These two pits, according to Colonel Bailey, were in the most exposed section of patriot defense. Yellow Wolf pointed out the site of his barricade, but not a boulder of its construction remained. All had been removed to make place for the plow. The pit had been formed of a single row of boulders placed in elliptical fashion, with no excavation whatever. The stones were of a size that one man could readily carry from the lower ground some rods to the south. The occupants fought lying prone.

now five, all fighting in thick smoke. Like smoke rolling up from burning woods. My uncle was shot in the head and lay dead for a while. But returning to life,[5] he helped on with the fight.

This fighting was with the cavalry only. Later, foot soldiers came. I did not know which officer was in charge, unless General Howard. I watched for him, but did not see him.[6]

Most shooting was now from the whites. I heard the cannon guns and was scared. I lay close to the ground. I did not know to shoot or not. I heard my uncle say, "I am thirsty! I will crawl to the *koos* [water] and drink."

He did so, and came only part way back. I saw him crawling slowly, rolling a boulder ahead. Hidden behind that not large boulder, he advanced for closer shooting at the soldiers. He passed from my sight. I heard him shoot a few times.

Wishing to check statements from other warriors, I interrupted here and asked if it were true that the soldiers were unable to determine from what point the Indian bullets came, even in open ground. Yellow Wolf replied, "The little boulder is good for hiding behind. Our rifle pit was already made." I could see he meant that the outcropping rocks served the same purpose as a dugout rifle pit.

I lay flat, seeing nothing, hearing only the battle. I did not know all had left when the soldiers' firing was the hottest. Other warriors all gone, and still I lay there.

One of the brave men, looking back, saw me and thought, "Why is he lying there? Must be wounded!"

Sounds came to my left ear. A voice speaking, "Who are you, lying flat? Soldiers are close coming!"

[5]An unconscious state is always spoken of by the Indians as "death," "being dead." The recovery from such a state they commonly describe as "returning to life," "getting life again."

[6] Yellow Wolf's watching was in vain. General Howard and his staff were in a barricade composed of pack saddles, baggage packs, provision cases, and general camp dunnage. It was situated on the east side of the battlefield, where all were well beyond the reach of Nez Perce bullets.

I looked to my left. I saw nobody. I did not get up. I heard the same voice again, and a whip struck me. What I heard was, "Heinmot Hihhih! Are you wounded? Why you not shooting? Kill some soldiers. They will kill you if you do not defend yourself!"

When I heard that voice, I was convinced what to do. I raised up. It was Wottolen [Hair Combed Over Eyes] who had called me, who had struck me. He was one of the commanders. Soldiers, armed, were about thirty steps from me. I grew mad to see them so close. Struck with the whip, I showed myself brave. I now was not afraid of death. From between the boulder rocks, I pushed my rifle. I fought like a man, firing five or six shots. Just then I heard heavy breathing. Otstotpoo had come back to me. Hearing the firing, he knew I had been left alone.

He said to me, "Dear son, we are going to die right here! Do not shoot the common soldier. Shoot the commander!"

I understood. I looked for an officer. He was just back of his men. All were crouching. I fired, and that officer went down. Another one seemed taking his place, I dropped him. Those officers did not get up.[7] No one now to drive the common soldiers, they fell back in retreat. Those two officers killed, common soldiers retreating, the warriors returned to their rifle pits.

The soldiers were being whipped in another part of the field.[8] A supply train coming from the south was nearly

---

[7] General Howard's official report shows no wounds nor fatalities among his commissioned officers, but Sergeant James A. Workman and Corporal Charles Marquard, both of Company A, Fourth Artillery, are listed as killed; and Corporal Charles Carlin and Musician John G. Hineman, of Company I, Twenty-first Infantry, are listed as "died enroute from the field to the hospital." ("Report of the General of the Army," 1877, pp. 132-33.) It was not unusual for artillerymen to take the place of infantrymen where battery guns were not practical.

[8] Toohoolhoolzote's valorous twenty-four alone stood the brunt of the first hour and a half's battle. Their only loss was the twenty head of horses which

captured by warriors of the other two bodies who came up from the camp. They almost took that train.[9] Of course I was not in the fighting there. Not all three companies of warriors could leave camp until they saw the soldiers being held on the mountain.

Came complete sundown. The firing almost quit. With darkness was heard only occasional shots. The five chiefs gave order, "Warriors, do no more fighting tonight!"

Half the warriors went down to camp. Women, children, and old people to be guarded. Horses must not be lost. The others of us, we did not run from the soldiers. Only did what the chiefs commanded.

I had only moccasins and breechcloth. But with the darkness, I did not leave. About midnight came stronger cold. It was then I left my pit. The big Smoking Lodge where no-fighters stayed, smoking and counseling, safe from bullets, was many rods southwest. I found several men lying there. I did not stop. I saw one man lying where horses were tied. I asked to sleep with him on account of the cold. He answered "Yes." Then I knew my own brother [cousin], my aunt's son, Teminisiki [No Heart]. As I lay down with him, I heard a woman speaking, "May I stay with you? I have no blanket. I get cold!"

My brother replied, "Come on! Get here between us! You will keep warm."

The woman did as invited. I remembered instructions from old people. In wartime man cannot sleep with woman. Might get killed if he does. Because of this, I

they had been obliged to leave behind. After it seemed demonstrated that General Howard could be held to the region where he was first discovered, the other two bodies of warriors, no longer needed to guard the families, went out upon the field and engaged in the battle as here described by Yellow Wolf.

[9] See Appendix I, this chapter.

got up and went back to my rifle pit. No shirt. No leggings. Only breechcloth and moccasins. Just as stripped for war. I stayed there until daylight. Stayed until the fighting began again.

My brother Teminisiki was killed in our next hard battle, the Big Hole![10]

* * *

APPENDIX I

Of this attack on his supply train, General Howard says:

" . . . four hundred men held a line of two miles and a half in extent. My main pack train had passed by this position. A small train with a few supplies was on the road nearer us.

"The Indian flankers, by their rapid movement struck the rear of the small train, killed two of the packers and disabled a couple of mules loaded with howitzer ammunition. The prompt fire from Perry's and Whipple's cavalry saved the ammunition from capture. I had previously sent an orderly to conduct the train within my lines; the fierce onset of the Indians requiring greater haste, Lieutenant Wilkinson, aide-de-camp, being sent, brought in the trains under cover of Rodney's [artillery] and Trimble's [cavalry] companies." ("Report of the General of the Army," 1877, p. 122. See also Howard, *Nez Perce Joseph*, p. 159.)

That General Howard's supply train was more nearly captured than is revealed by his official report, is disclosed by the following from interpreter Williams.

"Some years ago I was told by one of General Howard's Nez Perce scouts named Mathews, that the soldiers were driven back onto the General's lines or headquarters in a swarm, and that he heard an Indian calling at the top of his voice that he had the cannon in his possession, but was alone. Of course he lost it when General Howard charged his men back again.

"This Indian was supposed to have been one of the four that were killed in that battle; for no warrior was ever heard to speak

---

[10] One other fatality during the course of the Nez Perces' flight was attributed to the violation of the taboo referred to by Yellow Wolf. See Appendix A, "*Wyakin* Powers," end of volume, for further discussion of this subject.

about taking the big gun. Red Thunder was the only Indian killed near that part of the field.

"A man who said that his name was Adkinson, and that he had served in General Howard's army, told me it was a single Indian who killed the head packer and captured two mules loaded with ammunition, but could not hold them lone-handed. The Indians were scattered—not many at any one place at that time."

YELLOW WOLF:
His Own Story

❂

CHAPTER 7

Indian Withdrawal from the Clearwater

In the battle of the Clearwater, General Howard, for the only time, came within striking distance of the Nez Perce force. With the General, it was a great achievement, and he prefaces his description of that event with a grandiose elaboration, where he says:

"Joseph, in consequence of his success at White Bird, his eluding me at the Salmon, his massacre of Rains, and his escape from Whipple, and his skirmishes with the volunteers, as well as his aiding Looking Glass in avoiding arrest, had come to boast of his prowess, so that he was rather inclined to try his hand with me." *(Nez Perce Joseph*, p. 155.)

Again, General Howard in his summary of this battle, states:

"We had, on our side, put into the engagement, for these two days, four hundred fighting men. The Indians, under Chief Joseph, over three hundred warriors; also a great number of women, who assisted in providing spare horses and ammunition—as did our 'packers' and horse holders,—thus forming for them a substantial reserve." *(Nez Perce Joseph*, p. 166.)

These Army accounts seem pretentious when compared with the Indian version of this battle, which some of them denominated as a "skirmish."

NEXT morning began the fighting again. In first skirmishing it seemed soldiers had drawn a little nearer. Had made barricades during the night. Four of us were fighting from behind our boulder shelter. The same warriors, same barricade as the night before. Shots from the soldiers were not scattering. Their volleys became one continued roar. I paid attention to myself only, what I was doing. I thought nothing about the warriors with me.

I got a bullet here in my left arm, near the wrist.[1] When it struck me, I rolled on the ground, it hurt so. But I said nothing! Then I was hit just under my left eye. It was a piece of bullet or a chip from the boulder. Blood ran down my face. That eye was dimmed for the rest of my life.

The battle continued some hours. It must have been about ten o'clock, and soldier bullets still rained. Of course there was some cannon shooting. The soldiers began leaving their shelters, coming towards us.

Suddenly I heard my partner, Wottolen, call to me: "Nobody here! We will quit!"

I raised partly up. No Indians could be seen fighting. All had left the battle![2] Wottolen and myself were holding back the troops.

I now understood why soldiers crowded so. *No warriors opposing them!*

All yesterday fighting; all this morning they did not crowd us. But now, meeting no Indian bullets, they came charging bravely.

Then I ran, again forgetting my horse. I ran back where he was tied in the timber edge. Mounting, I started down the mountainside. It was through woods, open places, over rocks and steep bluffs. But my horse never missed footing. Crossing the river and reaching where the now empty camp stood, I heard a woman's voice. That voice was one of crying. I saw her on a

---

[1] A bullet could easily be felt under the skin inside the left forearm, where it had entered without bone injury.

[2] The withdrawal of the Indians was not occasioned by fear of the soldiers, but rather by dissension among themselves, as Yellow Wolf later in the chapter intimates. In 1926, Wottolen thus described to me the situation: "The fight was for two half days, and then the warriors quit. They quit for a reason. There was a quarrel among the Nez Perces. Some kept riding back and forth from the fighting to the camp. That was not good. The leaders then decided to leave the fighting, the cowards following after. I did not know this and was left behind. I could hear shots from but one gun, and I hurried to see what was wrong. I found only Yellow Wolf. All others gone. It was his rifle I heard. I called him, then thought to save myself."

horse she could not well manage. The animal was leaping, pawing, wanting to go. Everybody else had gone.

I hurried toward her, and she called, "Heinmot! I am troubled about my baby!"

I saw the baby wrapped in its *tekash* [cradleboard] lying on the ground. I reached down, picked up the *tekash*, and handed it to the woman. That mother laughed as she took her baby. It was the cannon shots bursting near that scared her horse. She could not mount with the little one. She could not leave it there. Riding fast, we soon overtook some rear Indians entering the canyon. We were then out of reach of cannon shots fired from the high mountain bluff.

This woman with the little baby was Toma Alwawin-mi [possibly meaning Spring of Year, or Springtime], wife of Chief Joseph. Her baby girl was born at Tepahle-wam camp a few days before the White Bird Canyon battle, but it died in the hot country [Indian Territory] after the war.

I did not ask why she was as I found her. Chief Joseph left the battlefield ahead of the retreat. Seeing it coming, he hurried to warn the families. He could not leave his wife had he known. The women were all supposed to be ahead. A bad time—everybody busy getting away.

Here, taking advantage of a pause in the narrative, I informed Yellow Wolf of General Howard's claim that in their abandoned camp many dead and wounded horses were found as a result of the cannon fire,[3] to which he replied:

---

[3] In his official report General Howard states: "The wounded and dead horses showed that our artillery had reached their camp. . . ." ("Report of the General of the Army," 1877, p. 124; also Howard, *Nez Perce Joseph*, p. 166.) But Major J. C. Trimble says of the appearance of the abandoned camp: ". . . the only living objects that were abandoned by them were about half a dozen crippled horses and one poor, aged squaw." (Brady, *Northwestern Fights and Fighters*, p. 147.)

I am telling you all I know about the cannon fighting. During the battle one shell exploded west of the barricaded Smoking Lodge. When I came down from the mountain, only two Indian men were in sight. They were a good distance away, riding hard to escape. Joseph's wife and baby only were left in camp. No dead horses killed by cannon shots were there. Usually at all camps a few lame or sick horses were left.

This fact being amply verified by different warriors questioned, I continued, "General Howard states that fifteen Indians were killed in this battle, and eight others were found dead on your trail as a result of wounds received in fighting, making twenty-three in all, and that about forty were wounded and forty taken prisoners."[4] There came the quick retort:

Not true! Only four warriors killed. First was Wayakat [Going Across], killed instantly. Second man, his partner in the fight, was Yoomtis Kunnin [Grizzly Bear Blanket], who lived a few hours after shot. Howwallits, also fighting there, was slightly wounded. He died years later on lower Snake River. The three were fighting near where we are now sitting. A few trees, three, maybe five, stood there.[5]

---

[4] Again quoting from General Howard's official report: "I reported at the time 15 Indians killed and a large number wounded.
"After that 8 dead were found on their trail, of those who died from mortal wounds, making for this battle 23 warriors killed; and there were at least twice as many wounded. Twenty-three prisoners, warriors, and 17 women and children were subsequently secured in the pursuit. Our loss was 2 officers and 22 enlisted men wounded and 13 killed." ("Report of the General of the Army," 1877, p. 124.)
So much for an "official report." Surviving warriors and women all declared that no Indian died on the retreat from the Clearwater field, and even though they had, their bodies would not have been left "on their trail." Chief Peopeo Tholekt, a warrior of the Chief Looking Glass band vehemently protested: "If General Howard claims dead Indian warriors were found along our trail from Clearwater, he tells big mistake. No one died between Clearwater battle and Big Hole in Montana. General Howard himself seemed not wanting close up with live Indians having guns."
On this score the late Colonel J. W. Redington wrote, alluding to the last battle: "Such adroit concealers of their dead were the Nez Perces, that despite the fact that the Indians were compelled to bury their dead within the confines of their besieged camp, not one grave could be found."
See Appendix I, Chapter 8, for more about General Howard's "catch" of prisoners in his Clearwater campaign.
[5] These trees, pine or fir, one of them rather large, formed a scattering group on the north slope of the canyon several rods to the east of where Yellow Wolf

Third man killed was Heinmot Ilppilp [Red Thunder]. Killed in timber edge at break of canyon, south side of battlefield. Many small bushes there were nearly cut down by soldier bullets. These three men killed and one wounded in earliest fighting.

Lelooskin [Whittling] was fourth man killed. Killed in his rifle pit after dark.[6] His partners, Kosooyeen and one other [name unknown], escaped to safer rifle pits. Wayakat and Lelooskin were so close to the enemy lines when they were killed that both bodies were left.

No Indians died on the trail from wounds. Just one man was bad wounded, Kipkip Owyeen [Shot in Breast]. Bullet went in back of shoulder and came out through his breast.[7] That is how he got his name. Had no good name before that time. Pahkatos was wounded in right hand. Three others were lightly wounded, two of them warriors. One was my uncle, Old Yellow Wolf, in the

---

crossed the saddle ridge in his flight from their abandoned rifle pit. The trees have been felled, the stumps alone remaining. The ground here, so Yellow Wolf stated, was bare at the time of the battle. It is now overgrown with a tangle of useless brush, which necessitated quite a search before the stumps could be located. We added a few additional boulders to the grave of Wayakat, who was buried by his mother two or three days after the battle, at the foot of the tree where he was killed.

[6] Lelooskin was the dead warrior that Lieutenant Harry L. Bailey speaks of noticing when the final charge by the troops was made:

"Warrior White Thunder or Yellow Wolf, certainly is right about the positions of some of the Indians' boulder rifle pits being close to our skirmish line, for the one which I had bombed by our Mountain Howitzer (in the night) was not more than thirty or forty yards from my own position during most of my fighting, and in it, as we made our final charge, I saw the Indian with the triangular hole in the forehead of whom I have written you before.

"And it was from that pit that a shot was fired at me as I was starting back to join the line, after asking my Captain by calling out in the darkness, and finding myself alone far in the front. That was a 'close call' as the soldiers would say."

[7] Kipkip Owyeen was wounded while "making himself a brave man." He rode from the south towards the soldiers' battle line. Coming within easy rifle range, he circled widely and was returning in a slow gallop to his own lines when a bullet entered his back and came out through his breast. As the shot did not cause him to accelerate his speed, this display of fearlessness made him a "great warrior."

Kipkip Owyeen had been given the "power" of the buffalo bull, and immediately upon receiving the bullet he resorted to the Indians' greatest of wound remedies, cold water. Descending the mountain with a companion, he submerged himself in the Clearwater for a time, bathing his wound. Then, leaving the stream on all fours with hands closed in imitation of hoofs, he walked about emitting the low, deep rumbling bellow of a challenging buffalo bull. Soon clotted blood gushed from the gunshot, and after his companion applied bandages, he remounted his horse and returned to the fight. He went through the entire retreat, recovered completely, and died about 1906.

rifle pit as I have told; the other one was Elaskolatat, known to whites as Joe Albert.

The oldlike man, Howwallits [Mean Man], was hurt by cannon firing on camp. No other person was wounded at camp that I ever heard.

Not one prisoner taken by soldiers in Clearwater battle.

One other phase of General Howard's summary of the Clearwater fight was in my mind, and I said, "General Howard claims that you were badly whipped at the Clearwater, and that to get away from him, you hurried across the Lolo Trail into Montana."

The old warrior's rebuttal was fraught with fire:

We were not whipped! We do not acknowledge being whipped! When counted, we had many young fellows who should have been in that fight. They held lots of counsels, while some—not many—were in rifle pits. There were big smokes in the Smoking Lodge. That is good, if old people alone!

Our commanders were not scared of bullets, not afraid of death. The Three Red Coats[8] wanted all the young men to go on horses to fight the left wing [cavalry] of General Howard's soldiers. Make it the last fight. Whichever side whipped, to be the last fight. But it was not to be. Many fewer than one hundred warriors met the hard fighting here, as throughout the war. The families were camped across the river from the soldiers. Many of the Indians talked, "Why all this war up here? Our camp is not attacked! All can escape without fighting. Why die without cause?"

We were not whipped! We held all soldiers off the first day and, having better rifle pits, we could still have held them back. Not until the last of us leaped away

---

[8] The Three Red Coats are described in Note 4, Chapter 3.

did soldiers make their charge. Some tepees, robes, clothing, and food were left. The women, not knowing the warriors were disagreeing, quitting the fight, had no time to pack the camp. Chief Joseph did not reach them soon enough.

But we were not whipped! Had we been whipped, we could not have escaped from there with our lives.

We could not have stopped General Howard at Kamiah crossing. We were not scared at that crossing. We did not cross the Clearwater until next morning. We then waited into the third sun for General Howard to cross and give us war.

He would not cross. It was then we started over the Lolo Trail.

Had we been whipped we could not have passed the Lolo barricade.

We could not have beaten General [Colonel] Gibbon at Big Hole.

We could not have captured 250 good horses at Horse Prairie.

We could not have captured General Howard's pack mules at Camas Meadows.

We could not have held off the new army [Colonel Sturgis] at Canyon Creek.

We could not have captured the big supplies at Missouri River Crossing.

We could not have stood against General [Colonel] Miles during four days.

No, it would not have been best to fight to the death at Clearwater. Standing before General Howard's soldiers was not too dangerous. Nothing hard! Wottolen and myself alone held them back after all Indians had quit the fight, left the ridge!

Across the Lolo Trail and into Montana

Following their retreat from the Clearwater battle, the Nez Perces on July 13 crossed over to the east bank of the Clearwater River at Kamiah, Idaho. For a people so badly "whipped," they showed but slight concern because of the close proximity of their numerically stronger enemy. By General Howard the opposite is conveyed:

"They [the Nez Perces] are then immediately pursued, and faintly attempt to make a stand at Kamiah, on our side of the river, but again are driven, with loss of provisions and morale. ... They are then pressed beyond the river along the Lo Lo trail, their fighting force having been reduced at least one third." ("Report of the General of the Army," 1877, p. 125. See also Howard, *Nez Perce Joseph*, p. 168.)

The stay of the Nez Perces at the crossing for the greater part of two days is history. That they loitered for the purpose of giving battle, should Howard attempt to cross to their side of the Clearwater, is obviously true. And it appears equally true that General Howard courted no such honor, even after the Nez Perce fighting force, as he claimed, had "been reduced at least one third."

In this chapter Yellow Wolf covers the period of eleven days (July 17-28) which were spent in following the Lolo Trail to the pass into Montana. He then relates how, after making the Lolo treaty—an act unprecedented in Indian warfare—with Montana settlers, the band passed peacefully up the Bitterroot Valley and finally camped at the Big Hole River.

HURRYING from the Clearwater battle, we left many things in camp. We traveled to Kamiah, named for some useful plant growing there.[1] We did not cross the river, but camped on its bank.

---

[1] The spelling of this name and its definition vary. Interpreter Many Wounds writes it "Kamlahpee," with the comment, "That is my spelling. It sounds like to mean 'Plenty Camas Roots.'"

With coming light next morning, skin boats were made for the crossing. While this was doing, scouts back on the trail from a distant butte waved the blanket signal: *"Danger!"*

Soon a scout came running his horse and called from the bluff:

"Soldiers following us! Soldiers coming fast!"

Crossing the families to north side of the river was easy. While this was doing, we saw soldiers riding down the distant hill toward us. We found hiding and waited for soldiers. When they reached the riverbank, we fired across at them. Many soldiers jumped from their horses and ran to any shelter they saw. Others galloped fast back toward the hills. We laughed at those soldiers. We thought we killed one.[2]

No more fighting, a few stayed to watch. The others went home to camp. We remained there all day and all night. But the soldiers were afraid to cross and have a battle. Next morning we saw General Howard dividing his soldiers. Some left, riding down the river.

There was another trail.[3]

The chiefs called the command, "We will move camp!

---

[2] On this episode at the Kamiah crossing of the Clearwater, General Howard enlarges: "As Perry's and Whipple's cavalry neared the enemies' crossing and were passing the flank of a high bluff, which was situated just beyond the river, a brisk fire from Indian rifles was suddenly opened upon them. It created a great panic and disorder; our men jumped from their horses and ran to the fences. Little damage resulted, except the shame to us and a fierce delight to the foe." (Howard, *Nez Perce Joseph*, p. 167.)

Colonel Harry L. Bailey writes (January 30, 1934): "The soldier wounded as we sat about on the river bank was of the Artillery, and I was at his side almost at once. The wound proved a red ridge where the hair parts on top, only superficial, but it shocked the man considerably and caused him a lot of vomiting for a few minutes, and I believe he soon recovered. I had been remarking that we should seek some cover, when the shot made us realize that without further lessons."

[3] Of this incident, General Howard says: "There was a junction of trails beyond him [Joseph], fifteen or twenty miles off. Could I but get there! Perhaps I could by going back a little, then down the river and across; quick, indeed if at all, and secret! ... But their eyes were too sharp for the success of this maneuver, for I had not proceeded more than six miles before the Indians began to break camp, and to retreat, in good earnest, along the Lo Lo trail, toward Montana and the east." Howard, *op. cit.*, pp. 168-69; also "Report of the General of the Army," 1877, p. 124.)

No use staying here. They do not want to cross and fight us!"

Then we packed up and went. We left the soldiers on their side of the river and fixed camp at place called Weippe.[4] Here we found Indians who had not been in the war. They were Chief Temme Ilppilp's [Red Heart] band. Friendly to both sides. Next morning, coming daylight, one of General Howard's Nez Perce scouts came riding in. Before he came, some of our friends advised him, "You better not go over where those warriors are."

But he came and said to these Indians, "It will be best to come on your own reservation. There you will be safe."

"We will go," answered most of those Indians. There were about twenty of them, men, women, and a few children. They had not joined us. Never had been in any of the war. Coming from Montana, they had only met us there.[5] Those Indians not joining with us in the war now bade us all good-by—a farewell, that we would never return to our homes again!

An old medicine man, Hatya Takonnin[6] had come to see his son, Heinmot Tootsikon [Speaking Thunder], who had joined our band to go fight the soldiers. He was a strong young man, and his father said to him, "I want you home with me. Death awaits you on the trail you

---

[4] Pronounced by some, "Oyipee." An ancient appellation for which no definition could be determined. One aged tribeswoman defined it as "Unstrung Beads," the cord broken through accident. An ancient Nez Perce stamping ground, because of the plentiful camas, it was described by interpreter Hart as a "swampland with fir and pine growing in diamond shape where the creek comes in, must be six or seven miles, the diamond." It was about ten miles northeast of Kamiah, where the Clearwater was crossed.

[5] Chief Red Heart and his band had been absent in the buffalo country during the acute brewing of the war. When they learned of it upon their homeward way, they stopped at Weippe for the very purpose of avoiding any connection with the conflict. This claim has been amply verified by every warrior interviewed.

[6] The English translation of this name may be termed dual in its essence: *i.e.,* either "Accompanying Cyclone (or Wind)," or "Accompanied by Cyclone." It is a compound of Hatya, "Cyclone" or "Wind," and Takonnin, which means either "Accompanying" or "Accompanied."

are taking. I see the future. It is dark with blood! I do not want to know you are killed. All going will die or see bondage."

Heinmot Tootsikon answered, "No! I do not care to return home! I want to go with my brothers and sisters. If I am killed, it will be all right."

Tears visited the old man's eyes. Then, clearing his eyes, he spoke again to his son, "I am willing that you go. It is all right for you to go help fight. But soldiers are too many."

Heinmot Tootsikon went with us, and his father returned home. A good warrior, Heinmot went through all fights holding to his life. Captured at the last battle, he was sent to the Indian Territory with others. He died in that Eeikish Pah [Hot Place].

We did not hurt the scout from the soldiers. He came friendly, as a friend to the Indians. It was all right for Chief Red Heart not to join with us. It was all wrong for General Howard to send them as prisoners to Vancouver.[7] They were peaceable Indians. They wanted no war.

After Chief Red Heart's people were gone, we packed up and moved. We traveled to Siwishnimi [Mussel Creek], high in the mountains. We found some mussels there. When we were unpacked, one scout, Wetyettamaweyun [I Give No Orders] came and gave announcement, "Soldiers coming! I am wounded!"

He was shot through the upper arm. They had nearly killed him! Only short miss from fatal shooting.

One of the chiefs then rode about calling orders,

[7] Unmistakably noncombatants, these peaceful campers as "prisoners" served to augment the glories of General Howard's Clearwater victory, for they were the "prisoners" previously cited (Note 4, Chapter 7) in the General's official report: "Twenty-three prisoners, warriors, and 17 women and children were subsequently secured in the pursuit." ("Report of the General of the Army," 1877, p. 124.) For their later experiences, see Appendix E, end of volume.

"Soldiers coming! We must move from this place! We will give them this road!"

We moved camp about half mile from the road. When unpacked, the warriors went back to our first stop. Watched for soldiers all night. One of them said, "Half of you go back to camp." This was done. The rest of us stayed there.

The seventeen scouts went back on the trail. I was one of them. It was a small creek we came to where we stopped. We heard a voice, and we heard a second voice. It was our language, talking about horse tracks. We heard, "There are fresh tracks! Tracks made this morning!"

We watched through the brush. Just a few of them, and we got ready to shoot. We fired and killed one. They were General Howard's scouts, some of his "good men." They ran from us. One of the warriors lifted up the one we shot and saw he was not quite dead. Nobody spoke to him, and the warrior shot him through the heart.[8] We recognized those Christian scouts, their white man's names. The one killed was John Levi. Abraham Brooks and Jim Reuben were wounded, but they escaped with others.

For about six days, coming through the mountains we saw no more fighting. Scouting on our back trail, I, with others, saw no enemies. Seventh day one man from scouts ahead came riding hard to our evening camp and reported, "Soldiers in front of us! Building fort! They

---

[8] General Howard had sent Major Mason with the cavalry, some Nez Perce scouts, and McConville's volunteers "to pursue the hostiles for two marches," and when "within three miles of Oro Fino Creek, his scouts ran into the enemy's rear guard. Three of them were disarmed, and one wounded, and one killed. One of the enemy was killed and two pack-animals captured." ("Report of the General of the Army," 1877, p. 124.)

None of the Nez Perces was either killed or wounded; nor did they lose any pack animals. Had they withheld their fire, this ambuscade of seventeen could have sadly worsted Major Mason's entire command, but as it was, neither his cavalry nor his volunteers ventured a forward movement after the first gunfire.

are heading us off. In a little while we will see the soldiers. They know our camp!"

There are high mountains and a narrow pass where the soldiers were camped. They had built a long log barricade across the trail.[9] That was the trail we had thought to travel. I saw Salish Indians at the soldiers' fort. They seemed quite a bunch. All had white cloths tied on arm and head. This, so as not to shoot each other. So the soldiers would know they were not Nez Perces. They were helping the soldiers. Always friends before, we now got no help from them, the Flatheads. No help any time.

We camped a ways above the soldiers, at Nasook Nema [Salmon Creek]. There was no fight. The chiefs met the soldiers. It was a council, a peace talk. Whatever was said, whatever was done, each party returned to its own camp. The chiefs returned, declaring, "We must move our camp!"[10]

Early next morning the families packed to move. We found a different way to go by those soldiers. While a few warriors climbed among rocks and fired down on the soldier fort, the rest of the Indians with our horse herds struck to the left of main trail. I could see the soldiers from the mountainside where we traveled. It was no trouble, not dangerous, to pass those soldiers.

Later two or more Indians, while moving, took the

---

[9] This barricade was at "Fort Fizzle," renowned in the history of the Nez Perce campaign. The site is now marked with a timber monument. It was here that Captain Charles C. Rawn, of the Seventh Infantry, commanding Post Missoula, with a force of five commissioned officers and thirty enlisted men ("Report of the General of the Army," 1877, p. 500), and from one to five hundred volunteers, took up his place like Horatius at the bridge, heroically sworn to an oath of "They shall not pass."

[10] The peace talk referred to by Yellow Wolf was a truce or armistice proposed by Looking Glass. Captain Rawn felt that his official duty compelled him to reject any peace proposal; but the Montana settlers, who had ever been on the best of terms with the Nez Perces, saw no reason why they should not accept the Indians' guarantee of a peaceful passage through Montana. The settlers, therefore, without the knowledge—or at least without the consent of Captain Rawn—ratified the armistice. By the Nez Perces, this "treaty" was regarded as an actual cessation of war. They expected no further trouble or hostilities.

wrong trail, the main trail. Reaching the soldiers' camp, they were captured.[11]

Of course, during that day we rode around the soldiers, some of us young fellows stayed back as scouts. One white man, maybe a scout, bothered us. Two of us chased him. He got away, and we did not see him any more.

We traveled through the Bitterroot Valley slowly.[12] The white people were friendly. We did much buying and trading with them.

No more fighting! We had left General Howard and his war in Idaho.

But there was something—a feeling some of us could not understand. One morning a young man who had medicine power rode about camp, calling loudly to the people, "My brothers, my sisters, I am telling you! In a dream last night I saw myself killed. I will be killed soon! I do not care. I am willing to die. But first, I will kill some soldiers. I shall not turn back from the death. We are all going to die!"

This young man was Wahlitits, one of the Red Coat warriors. He was killed only a few days later in our next battle, the Big Hole. He killed one soldier, maybe more, before he died.

---

[11] The four captured Nez Perces were the following unarmed noncombatants: John Hill, half-blood Delaware-Nez Perce, on his way to join his family in the Bitterroot Valley; Thunder Eyes, known to the whites as George Amos; Hopan, an old man; and last, a "squawman" (in the Indian sense of a person half man and half woman.) None of these were warriors; but whether or not they were peace emissaries from the Nez Perce camp is a matter of speculation.

[12] Following the Lolo treaty, the Indian procession had a clear front through the Bitterroot Valley, conceded openly by the volunteers—and perhaps tacitly by Captain Rawn, of the Army. But it is said that Lieutenant Andrews, of the citizen contingent, with a few comrades—their courage braced by liberal libations from a goodly-sized demijohn brought in by a Missoula saloonkeeper—swore to stop the Indians. Hurrying ahead, they formed their line of battle directly across the enemy's line of march. When the Nez Perce vanguard came in sight, and their challenging war whoop woke the morning echoes, the guardians of the Bitterroot Valley fled without firing a shot. Sam Scott, one of the contingent, said when later narrating the incident, "I don't know what I did with my gun. Somehow I lost it. I remember using my hat to whip my horse to a swifter pace. Although he was a fast runner, I thought that I never was on a slower mount. The Indians did not fire on us, nor did they appear to hasten their gait. Perhaps they thought we were staging a free riding exhibition for their amusement."

Lone Bird, a brave fighter, also rode about one camp wanting more hurry. His voice reached all the people as he warned, "My shaking heart tells me trouble and death will overtake us if we make no hurry through this land! I can not smother, I can not hide that which I see. I must speak what is revealed to me. Let us begone to the buffalo country!"[13]

We reached the Big Hole, our old camp when going to and from buffalo hunting. Good feed for horses. We would stay several days. The women would cut tepee poles to take with us. Those poles must be peeled and dried for the dragging.

It was next morning, after our first night at Big Hole, that it happened. Two young warriors said to an old man, "Loan us your horses."

"No," said old man Burning Coals.[14] "I will not loan you my horses."

Not getting the horses, nothing could be done. It proved bad.

Puzzled by this attempt at horse-borrowing, I asked, "What was bad in the old man's refusing to loan his horses?" Yellow Wolf answered:

One man, Wottolen, had strong powers. That first night he dreamed of soldiers. Ten, maybe twelve, of us wanted to scout back over the trail. If no enemies were found crossing the mountain, we would go on to the Bitterroot Valley. Had the scout been made, many

---

[13] See Appendix I, this chapter.

[14] Burning Coals was better known as Waptastamana (Blacktail Eagle—explained as "two or three black eagles coming down from the sky slowly and together"). With horses and cattle running into four figures, he was reputed the wealthiest member of the Nez Perce tribe. His fortune in gold, said to be cached in a bluff of the Salmon River, has never been unearthed. Old and broken, he was one of those whose names swell Colonel Miles's list of "100 warriors" surrendered to him at the last battle. ("Report of the General of the Army," 1877, p. 631.) He died in exile in the Indian Territory.

Indian lives would have been saved. The soldiers, trapped before reaching our camp, none of them could have escaped. All would have been killed. Sarpsis Ilppilp and Seeyakoon Ilppilp had no good horses. Best race horses must be for the scouting. Old man Burning Coals had such horses. But he liked his horses and refused to let them go.

Chiefs Looking Glass and White Bull also opposed our going. Looking Glass was against everything not first thought of by himself. White Bull always sided with him. They said, "No more fighting! War is quit."

They would not mind Wottolen. The scout was not made!

That night the warriors paraded about camp, singing, all making a good time. It was first since war started. Everybody with good feeling. Going to the buffalo country! No more fighting after Lolo Pass. War was quit. All Montana citizens our friends. This land had belonged to the Flatheads, our old-time friends. They called it Iskumtselalik Pah; meaning "Place of Ground Squirrels,"—the kind you call "picket pins." Lots of them hatched here.

It was past midnight when we went to bed.

❊   ❊   ❊

APPENDIX I

Various writers have set forth the picturesque theory that impending disaster for the Nez Perce camp in its loitering passage through the Bitterroot Valley was foretold by their Dreamer medicine men. For example, Lieutenant C. A. Woodruff, Colonel Gibbon's adjutant in his Nez Perce campaign, reports:

"The Indians seemed in no great haste. White Bird is said to have scented danger and urged a more rapid movement. One of their medicine men had cautioned the chiefs that death was on their trail.

" 'What are we doing here?' he asked. 'While I slept my medicine told me to move on—that death was approaching. If you take my advice, you can avoid death, and that advice is to speed on through this country. If we do not, there will be tears in your eyes.'

"But Looking Glass replied, 'We are in no hurry, the little bunch of "walking soldiers" at Missoula are not fools enough to attack us.' " (*Contributions to the Historical Society of Montana,* Vol. VII, p. 104.)

Undoubtedly Lieutenant Woodruff got the foregoing from Duncan McDonald's "Nez Perce War of 1877; Indian History from Indian Sources," published in the *New Northwest,* Deer Lodge, Montana, 1878-79. McDonald, an intelligent half-blood Nez Perce, visited Chief White Bird in his camp with Sitting Bull in Canada. He relates that White bird told him of urging more haste on the part of Chief Looking Glass, who seems to have dominated the movements of the camp; but to no purpose.

"Why do you allow the camp to drag lodgepoles?" White Bird is quoted as chiding, insisting that the poles be discarded.

McDonald quotes another medicine man as exhorting the leader, only one day before the Big Hole battle—the Nez Perces were camped there two nights before the attack—"What are we doing here?" After singing his song, he continued, "While I slept, my medicine told me to move on; that death is approaching us. Chief, I only tell this because it may be some good to this camp. If you take my advice, we can avoid death, and that advice is to speed through this country. If not, there will be tears in our eyes in a short time."

When Yellow Wolf was informed of the foregoing versions, he commented briefly, "I think those reports came from what I just told you. They could not come any other way. Had there been such prophecies as you speak of, I would have known them."

It is history that all lodgepoles were abandoned at the Clearwater camp, and that none were brought over the Lolo Trail, nor through the Bitterroot Valley. In his official report, Colonel Gibbon says in part of his pursuit of the Nez Perces through the region in question:

"No accurate estimate of their strength could be made, as many of them occupied simple brush shelters. It was observed, also, that . . . no signs of tepee poles nor travois for wounded were seen on the trail." ("Report of the General of the Army," 1877, p. 69.)

The first night on the Big Hole prairie was spent without tepees. The next day the women cut and peeled the poles and set up their lodges in regular order. They expected to remain there until the poles were seasoned and dry for dragging to the land of the Crows and of the buffalo. This fact has been sustained by every member of the band questioned, both men and women.

At the Big Hole: Surprise Attack

Having ascertained that the Nez Perces were on their way to Montana, General Howard telegraphed the Adjutant General, Division of Pacific, San Francisco, on July 27 as follows:

"Can not troops at Missoula or vicinity detain Joseph till I can strike his rear? . . . My troops will push through rapidly."

Thus, while the Nez Perces were camped unsuspectingly on the Big Hole prairie, Colonel Gibbon had approached with a considerable force. The Colonel gives this account of the surprise attack on the Indian encampment:

"The command was now halted, and all lay down to wait for daylight. Here we waited two hours in plain hearing of the barking dogs, crying babies, and other noises of the camp. . . . All pushed forward in perfect silence, while now scarcely a sound issued from the camp. Suddenly a single shot on the extreme left rang out on the clear morning air, followed quickly by several others, and the whole line pushed rapidly forward through the brush." ("Report of the General of the Army," 1877, pp. 69-70.)

In revisiting the site of this battle, Yellow Wolf stood some moments silently surveying his surroundings; then he commented: "It all comes back like a picture, what I saw, what I did, so many snows ago."

BEFORE leaving Idaho one of the chiefs—I do not remember which one—had ridden all about our camp announcing, "We may first go to the buffalo country, and then afterwards join Sitting Bull in Canada. Crossing this mountain, leaving Idaho, we will travel peaceably. No white man must be bothered! Only enemies here we fight. Trouble no white people after

112

passing the Lolo into Montana. Montana people are not our enemies. Enemies only here in Idaho.[1]

"When we reach Sitting Bull, we will hold council. Whatever is there decided will be done. Delegates will be sent to talk with officers of the Government. If agreed we return to our homes, all right. We will return. If agreed to take land in Montana near the Sioux, that will be done for us by the Government.

"Across the mountains kill no cattle-beeves, while the food we take with us lasts. At Clearwater fight, we lost plenty food for reaching the buffalo country. Only if our women and children grow hungry will we take cattle or whatever food we find—as taken from us.

"On that side of the mountain, we will shoot no citizens, no uniformed soldiers who do not shoot against us. The war we leave here in Idaho."

These were instructions from the chiefs. Strong laws, nor were they broken. The chiefs thought the war ended. To be no fighting in Montana. But not so, the Montana people.

They did not regard the peace made with us there at Lolo Pass.

Because of that lie-treaty we were trapped.

Trapped sleeping, unarmed.

Through the Bitterroot Valley they spied on us while selling us vegetables, groceries, anything we wanted.

Sold whisky to some, almost making trouble.

---

[1] In Indian warfare leadership devolved upon seniority and experience. Chiefs White Bird and Toohoolhoolzote, being both incapacitated by age, Chief Looking Glass was next in line. As he not only was of chieftainly descent, but also knew the buffalo country and had met enemy tribes in battle, he was accorded the leadership. His self-centered arrogance, however, unfitted him for such a trust. Ignoring prophecies of impending danger (as related in the preceding chapter), Looking Glass permitted time-killing loitering during the passage of the Bitterroot Valley. His worst lack of judgment was shown when he decried the proposed precautionary back-scouting of their own trail. Had he not been bloated with self-exaltation, he would not thus have opposed the wishes of a dozen tried warriors, some of whom were renowned for wisdom and achievements in tribal warfare. Upon Looking Glass must fall much of the blame for the disaster at the Big Hole.

They spied on us crossing the mountains when we thought not of foes.[2]

The next morning on our way to the lower river bottom where the Nez Perce village had stood, interpreter Many Wounds stopped at a bank of drifted sand and, under Yellow Wolf's direction, drew a diagram of the ill-fated camp. (Yellow Wolf had no ability as a draftsman, although he was fairly good at word-picturing.) The tepees were shown in rather irregular, compact form with a partly open court in the center, corresponding in general with a pen drawing by Chief Peopeo Tholekt, made at a later day. Both delineations negated the methodic, straight-line V-shaped village so generally described.

The sand-picturing completed, we crossed the stream on the old pole-floored bridge to which Yellow Wolf refers in his narrative, and found ourselves upon the Nez Perce camp site and the battlefield proper. Under Yellow Wolf's guidance we walked north to within a few paces of the apex or tip of the old camp or village.

He designated a spot near the riverbank where the tepee in which he was sleeping had stood when the first gunfire of the attack broke upon them. For a full five minutes he stood, his keen eyes sweeping all points of the field. Then facing west, whence the enemy descent had come, he began in his usual evenly modulated tone:

Before the soldiers charged from the hillside, I heard a horse cross the river slowly. Heard it pass down the camp, out of hearing. Minthon was with me, and we afterwards agreed that it must have been a spy.[3]

---

[2] There can be little doubt that the Nez Perce camp at the Big Hole was spied on. Chief Joseph, in his *Chief Joseph's Own Story*, laments that the realization dawned on them too late that three passing horsemen—supposedly stockmen or miners—were, in reality, spies.

Yellow Wolf, early in the evening of our arrival on the battlefield, had pointed out where, the morning following the pitching of their camp, two white men had been seen riding out from the open timber to the north. They had passed eastward along the barren hillside. Mounted Indians hurried across the river bottom where they expected to intercept the strangers and learn their business. But the horsemen had disappeared. Not suspecting major danger, the Indians made no effort to apprehend them. They could have overtaken them easily and killed them had they been so inclined. After the battle it was decided that the white riders had been spies. Yellow Wolf recalled how the small Indian boys afterward reported seeing two men wrapped to their eyes in grayish blankets (unlike those the Indians wore), with pulled-down hats, loitering near where the lads were at their games on the eve of the battle. The boys said one of the faces showed white in the firelight. (See statements of Red Elk and White Bird the younger, Appendix I, Chapter 10.) The warriors at the time were parading and singing about the camp and indulging in a round of general rejoicing—the first since the opening of hostilities. They firmly believed that the war had been ended by the Lolo treaty.

[3] About the espionage of the Nez Perce camp, Mr. Andrew Garcia, venerable Montana pioneer, writes me:

114

But we did not think of enemies at the time. This tepee here was not my home, and I was without my rifle. Chief Joseph's tepee, my home, was near upper end of camp. My gun was there. Only very few warriors had guns ready when the attack came.

It must have been about three o'clock in morning, just before daylight, when I heard it—a gun—two guns! I knew not what was the trouble! The sound was like a small gun, not close. I was half sleeping. I lay with eyes closed. Maybe I was dreaming? I did not think what to do! Then I was awake. I heard rapidly about four gunshots across there to the west. We did not know then, but it was those first shots that killed Natalekin, who was going to look for his horses.[4] This gunfire made me wide awake. Then came three volleys from many rifles, followed by shouting of soldiers.

I grabbed my moccasins and with others ran out of the tepee. I had only my war club.[5] We stopped where we are now standing. Men and women were lying flat on the ground, listening. I saw one woman so—over there only a few feet away. I heard her call out, "Why not all men get ready and fight? Not run away!"

I did not know her. When I heard this, it convinced me she was right. Minthon, a younger boy than I, was also convinced. He gave me his gun. It had but one shell. I walked to here [four paces]. I saw a man running this

---

"I well knew H. L. Bostwick, scout and post guide at Fort Shaw, where Colonel Gibbon held command. A half-blood Scotchman of determined mind, he ill-brooked military restraint. He is reputed as having rebelled against going afoot in a night reconnoitering of the Nez Perce camp, but rode his iron-grey saddler through the willow thickets with no particular attempt at concealment of movement. Doubtless he reasoned that the tramp of a horse would be less likely to attract the unfavorable attention of the enemy than would the sly movements of a footman. The animal could well be a rambler from their own herds, while the idea of a mounted spy passing noisily through the brush would be too rash to be entertained."

It was doubtless this daring Fort Shaw scout that Yellow Wolf heard crossing the river. Bostwick fell in the ensuing battle.

[4] See Appendix I, this chapter.

[5] A description of this weapon, which until recently retained the ghastly stains of conflict, is given in Appendix B, end of this volume.

way. It was now nearly daylight. He came close and said, "Wahchumyus [Rainbow] is killed!"

I thought that must be a mistake. But he was killed early, before the sunrise.

A man was standing here near the water. He was wearing a black blanket. It was Pahkatos Owyeen [Five Wounds]. He seemed thinking to himself. Stepping one way, then another. Restless and not easy in mind. I knew his feelings. Thinking, but not talking. After a moment, he said, "Any you brothers have two guns? Let me have one."

Pahkatos had been wounded at the Clearwater. Fingers of right hand, but no bones broken. Had his fingers wrapped together. I was standing back there. One man, a little ways off, came stepping. Holding out a rifle, he spoke in quick words, "Take this gun. It has five shells in magazine and one in barrel."

Pahkatos took the rifle with the remark, "They are enough." He dropped his blanket. I do not know if he crossed the creek here or up there near the willows [forty feet]. He entered the willows on the opposite side of the stream. The last I ever saw of him. He was killed later in the fight. A powerful warrior, he had fought in the buffalo country to the east. Was known to all the tribes.

Watyo Chekoon [Passing Over (head)], also strong in war, crossed the creek from the main body of Indians. Later, going where bullets flew like hail, he escaped a great danger. Came through it all.

The soldiers had not reached our part of camp. Never did cross the river at this point. The hard fighting was at upper half of the village.

I ran up that way towards the fighting. I saw a

warrior hurrying along the line of tepees, and I went with him. Going only a short ways, another man joined us. We ran, maybe half a quarter mile, when we saw soldiers along the creek, upper part of the village, we were about midway the camp when I saw a man coming toward us. I stopped, the other two men going on. He was walking stooped, blood running from his head. His name was Jeekunkun [Dog], mostly called John Dog.[6] I said to him, "Trade me your gun! You have plenty of cartridges and I have none. Trade, and then get away from danger!"

The wounded man answered me, "No! I must have the gun. I do not want to die without resisting!"

I met another young man wounded in the right arm. He was carrying his gun in his left hand. He, too, refused to trade guns. His name was Temme Ilppilp [Red Heart], and he was wounded worse than I saw [stomach wound]. He died at the second camp from the battle.

I hurried on to about here [past midcamp] and saw a soldier crawling like a drunken man. He had a gun and belt full of cartridges. I struck him with my war club and took his Government rifle and ammunition belt.

I saw teeth loose in his mouth, and easily took them out. I had never seen such teeth.[7] They must be around here somewhere yet.

I now had a gun and plenty of shells. As I have shown

---

[6] Chellooyeen (Phillip Evans) said that as he was leaving the battlefield, he met Jeekunkun with a dark streak of blood between his eyes. He appeared to have a skin wound on the forehead, which dazed him and made him unable to answer questions. It later developed that he was momentarily rendered unconscious by the shot. Jeekunkun was of the Asotain or Looking Glass band. Maintaining his reputation as a warrior, he escaped from the last battle to Sitting Bull's village in Canada, thus avoiding the ignominy of surrender. After several years he returned to Idaho and settled on the Lapwai reservation.

[7] In response to an inquiry, Sergeant C. N. Loynes writes (January 18, 1928):
"It is possible that the soldier who had false teeth might have been Captain Logan, for he was in the service prior to the Civil War and rose from the ranks for valor during that war. I never knew of any soldier having false teeth. They of course, would not be accepted at enlistment with them. Among the enlisted men, a man with false teeth would have been known."

you, I was in lower part of camp when the attack came. I hurried to join in the battle, which had grown hot. At first the warriors had no guns, but now a few—a very few—had found rifles. I came near a small willow thicket. I heard yelling, screaming. I recognized Iskatpoo Tismooktismook [Black Trail]. He came stooping and said to me, "My nephew, I got shot. I am wounded! Shot through the shoulder."

Iskatpoo was a good warrior, a brave warrior. But he was overcome by the too-numerous enemies.[8]

From here where we stand I saw soldiers come stepping forward. Nothing could stop them! As I said, but few warriors had rifles in their hands. Sleeping when soldiers fired on our camp—there must have been two hundred of them—we knew not at once what to do. Of course, not well awake, it was hard to get arms quickly.

These soldiers came on rapidly. They mixed up part of our village. I now saw tepees on fire. I grew hot with anger. Women, children, and old men who could not fight were in those tepees. Up there above that old pole bridge crossing the creek—about one hundred steps from the blazing tepees—I heard an Indian voice loudly announcing:

"My brothers! Our tepees are on fire! Get ready your arms! Make resistance! You are here for that purpose!"

It was Kowtoliks[9] talking, a brave warrior. He was answered with war whoops by those who had guns. There must have been one hundred soldiers in that part of the camp.

---

[8] Black Trail was a man of middle age, respected and well liked. He was among the surrendered at the last battle and was exiled to Indian Territory. His wound—a broken left collarbone—never properly healed, and when he was working in a sawmill, it was reopened from too heavy lifting. Black Trail died as a result.

[9] Kowtoliks, as explained by the interpreter, is descriptive of the hair and bones of human dead scattered about by wild animals.

An Indian with a white King George blanket about him was standing farthest up the river, alone. Of the Paloos Waiwaiwai band, his name was Pahka Pahtahank [Five Fogs].[10] Aged about thirty snows, he was of an old-time mind. He did not understand the gun. He was good with the bow, but had only a hunting bow. I thought, "If he had good rifle, he could bring death to the soldiers."

He was just in front of his own tepee.[11] Soldiers were this side, not far from him. He stood there shooting arrows at the enemies. The soldiers saw, and fired at him. That Indian stepped about a little, but continued sending his arrows. Three times those soldiers fired and missed him. The fourth round killed him.[12]

Looks wonderful to me, three volleys—not exactly volleys together—should miss him not more than ten steps away. I do not know if he hit any soldiers.

At Kowtoliks' voice, about ten warriors—not more—

---

[10] Pahka Pahtahank signifies "Five Fogs," or "Dark Cloudy Days Five Times Repeated." Popular and well liked, Five Fogs was the son of the Paloos chief, Hahtalekin.

The bow used by Pahka Pahtahank with its quiver and ten remaining arrows was picked up on the battlefield and came into the possession of S. G. Fisher, leader of a band of Bannack scouts who later joined General Howard at Camp Benson. Chief Fisher in after years turned this relic of a pathetically lost cause over to Colonel Frank Parker, an associate scout, at whose death it was passed on to the author by Mrs. Parker.

The sinew-backed bow with its original sinew cord measures thirty-two inches. The quiver, of light half-tanned deerskin and red flannel with a short fringe along the under edge, is twenty-six inches in length. The arrows vary from twenty-four to thirty-three and one-half inches, the five shortest being tipped with points fashioned from hoop iron of Indian workmanship. Three of the shafts are lightly grooved, supposedly to permit a freer flow of blood. Perhaps, too, these grooves may hold some occult significance, such as the lightning's streak in its speed from the bow. The remaining five are worked to long, tapering points flattened on one side, evidently for splicing thereon a piercing point fashioned from the semipoisonous greasewood, or a kindred shrub known as mahogany. These latter shafts are in some respects lacking in finish and were apparently fashioned while on the retreat. All are winged with hawk and eagle feathers, one of them sharply spiral or rotary, and all are badly frayed and worn. They bear traces of war paint.

[11] In September, 1937, under the auspices of the "Big Hole Good Roads Association," the writer staked Big Hole battlefield historically from the Nez Perce depiction. Stakes consecutively numbered were driven at various tragedy and tepee sites, and each recorded. The stakes were then surveyed and this additional boundary included in the "Gibbon Battlefield National Park." With this explanation, subsequent notes of this nature will be understood. Stake No. 50 marks the site of Five Fogs's tepee.

[12] Stake No. 49 is where he fell.

started for those soldiers. I hurried to get a closer position, closer and hidden.

Proceeding another sixty paces, Yellow Wolf halted where had been the southern extremity or base of the village, and about twenty steps from the riverbank. He stood silent, though keenly alert, for several minutes before resuming his narrative:

What I show you from here was just a few men who drove the soldiers back at this point. Only about ten brave warriors made here a desperate stand after Kowtoliks called that the tepees were afire. Some had already mounted horses and were fighting, scattered. Others were in the willows fighting. I joined to save the tepees.

I came against the soldiers on side opposite the other warriors. Those warriors—not more than ten—were scattered, shooting from sheltered places.

From all sides we mixed them up. I made an advance against some soldiers. Got close enough to take good aimed shots. Three of those same enemies went down. I only know I shot fast and saw each time a soldier fall. I rushed in. Took guns and cartridge belts from those three soldiers. That is the custom of war. Those guns afterwards were used by other Indians.

We now mixed those soldiers badly. We could hit each other with our guns. It was for the lives of women and children we were fighting. If whipped, better to die than go in bondage with freedom gone.

Those soldiers did not last long. Only about thirty at that place were left standing. Scared, they ran back across the river. We could not well count how many dead soldiers, but we killed a good few. They acted as if drinking. We thought some got killed by being drunk. I saw four killed before getting this far up. I had not time to see what others were doing at this place.

I am telling you true! Those soldiers hurried back across the river. Too many of them falling, and they ran.

We followed the soldiers across the stream. I waded it just below that old pole bridge. Of course there was no bridge then. Reaching that open space among the willows, I saw a soldier only a few steps ahead of me. Stepping cautiously, stooping, looking among the willows with gun ready [Yellow Wolf was pantomiming his story], he did not see me approach. I got within four steps of him. I would touch him while he lived. He must have felt me back of him. Whirling, he brought his gun around. But I was too quick. My bullet went through his breast. He fell and did not move.

A young man, this soldier wore a uniform. I took his gun, cartridge belt, and trench-digging knife. I quickly gave the gun and ammunition to a warrior who had none.

The soldiers were now running to the hill. Desperate fighting in the brush, among the willows, and in open places. Close pressed, the soldiers hurried up the bluff. On the flat they stopped to barricade themselves. Had all the warriors had guns, not many soldiers would have reached the bluff.

Up to this time not twenty Indians had rifles. Every gun taken was quickly used. When they could, soldiers spoiled those of partners who were killed. They broke a few Indian guns as well.

Casually passing along the river where it turns suddenly in a great sweep towards the western mountain, Yellow Wolf paused. Studying its eroded bank, he spoke half musingly: "Looks some change in this bank." And then:

It is a wonderful story I am telling you. When I reached here, desperate fighting was being done. I saw a soldier standing like this:

121

Yellow Wolf, stepping down the bank, stood motionless at the water's edge, facing east, with his head turned north toward where Wahlitits and his wife were killed—more of which later—.

Like this that soldier stood, the lower part of his body hidden by the bank. Some kind of marks or stripes were on his upper arms or shoulders, as if an officer. I thought he was alive, and brought my gun to shoot. He could see me, but did not move. Then I understood.

That soldier was dead![13]

When I saw him so facing where Wahlitits and his wife lay, I was convinced one of them had shot him. There seemed no other way he was killed. He was the only dead man I ever saw standing.

The narrator paused meditatively. As if comprehending that his story would be discredited, he added earnestly:

While I am talking, I am convinced of this. My chiefs were here then. Now I am alone, succeeding them. No witnesses, this is why I feel to tell only truth of what I saw in battle, of what I myself did. You must know I am speaking true. What I, Yellow Wolf, saw and did, only.

A tepee stood above that of Wahlitits. It belonged to Wetyetmas Likleinen [Circling Swan], a large man. He died here, fighting at his tepee home.[14] Never went anywhere. He did not run. His wife was killed here. Their tepee stood close to White Bird's, to Toohoolhoolzote's, and to that of Chuslum Moxmox [Yellow Bull].[15]

Now I speak of another of the best warriors. He was killed there at the next tepee downstream.[16] Only a few

[13] Stake No. 13, Big Hole battlefield. Such cases of rigidity in death are not wholly unusual.

[14] Stake No. 22, Big Hole battlefield.

[15] The warrior Chuslum Moxmox (Yellow Bull) also had another name, probably a prewar cognomen: Weyatanatoo Wahyakt (Sun Necklace).

[16] Stake No. 23, Big Hole battlefield.

DIAGRAMING THE BIG HOLE BATTLEFIELD

Yellow Wolf (in light-colored hat) studying a sand diagram of the battlefield as traced by Many Wounds.

HUNTING BOW AND ARROWS

This weapon was used by Pahka Pahtahank in the battle of the Big Hole.

SLOPE ABOVE THE BIG HOLE RIVER   PHOTO BY McWHORTER

The first shots of the surprise attack claimed the life of Natalekin just in front of the prominent clump of bushes on the hillside.

TIMBERED SLOPE OPPOSITE THE NEZ PERCE VILLAGE SITE

The pole bridge, in foreground is comparatively recent and marks the site of the Indian trail crossing the Big Hole River. Gibbons men retreated to & entrenched themselves in a position about one half mile south west of the slope shown in the background of this picture.

YELLOW WOLF RE-ENACTING A BATTLE SCENE

"I got within four steps of the soldier. . . . He must have felt me back of him. Whirling, he brought his gun around. But I was too quick. My bullet went through his breast." This action occurred in the old trail near where it crossed the Big Hole River as shown in picture above.

A STRANGE DEATH

Above: Brush along the river outlines the sweeping curve of the Big Hole.
Among the willows in the distance Yellow Wolf saw a soldier *standing* rigid in death.

Below: Yellow Wolf demonstrates the position in which he saw the soldier.

steps from Wetyetmas Likleinen. His name was Tewit Toitoi.

Here by his tepee[17] sat smoking, Wahnistas Aswetesk, a very old man. He was shot many times! As he sat on his buffalo robe, one soldier shot him. He did not get up. Others shot him. Still he sat there. Others shot him. He did not move. Just sat there smoking as if only rain-drops struck him! Must have been twenty bullets en-tered his body. He did not feel the shots! After the battle, he rode horseback out from there. He grew well, but died of sickness in the Eeikish Pah where he was sent after the surrender. The wounds did not seem to grow. It was just as you see mist, see fog coming out from rain. We saw it like smoke from boiling water [steam], com-ing out of his wounded body. He was not shot in the head.

Several dead soldiers lay scattered around here. More were killed farther up the village.

Proceeding thirty-two steps upstream, Yellow Wolf continued:

I saw here a dead Indian lying under the riverbank, his leg in the water. His name was Lazzykoon, as pronounced by the whites, but we called him Allezyahkon—an old-time name with meaning known only to the oldest Indians. His age about sixty snows, he was not classed as a fighter. His son was Lahpeealoot [Two Flocks on Water; later known as Phillip Williams]. Lazzykoon had often said to his son: "If the Nez Perces go to war with the whites, we will not go. Our family will not join them."

Fifty steps farther upstream, he went on:

---

[17] Stake No. 24, Big Hole battlefield.

123

I saw another Indian lying here dead under the bank. He was about thirty years old and died fighting. His name was Wookawkaw [Woodpecker].

Besides the three soldiers I saw fall as I shot, I saw four others killed a little below here. I do not know how many were killed all counted, but more were killed above here.

In meantime there was hard fighting among the brush. I will show you where some bad struggles took place.

Yellow Wolf now piloted us to the west side of the stream and, passing directly by the place where he had been victor in the rifle duel with the young soldier, he headed across the open bottom land over which Colonel Gibbon's most unobstructed charge had been launched. Yellow Wolf pointed out, near the west bank of the river, where it bends towards the mountain in a great sweeping curve, a well-preserved buffalo wallow which the troops passed in their morning onslaught against the sleeping village. Without a hesitating step, our guide proceeded some hundreds of yards and stopped near a large circular clump of willows flanked by a much smaller clump. After his usual moments of reverie before speech, he told the following:

I have told you that Wahchumyus [Rainbow] was killed early in the fight, before sunrise. What happened here I did not see. But it is true as told me by witnesses. They have also told it to you. I was here after the fight. I saw the dead in the same positions as when they fell.

At this place a tall soldier—must have been near seven feet—and a short Indian met. The Indian, Wahchumyus, stepped from behind that small bunch of willows. The soldier came from back of this big cluster. About four steps apart, both raised guns at same time. The Indian was the quickest, but his gun snapped. The tall soldier shot him through the heart. He fell backwards, dead.

Wahchumyus was a great warrior, brave in all fighting. He had whipped in many battles in the buffalo country. All the tribes knew and feared him. His name was strong over all the land. That big soldier had killed one of our best warriors.

When Wahchumyus fell, the tall soldier turned and ran south. He passed Wahchumyus on his left. He sprang behind those bushes [about fifty feet to the south]. Other soldiers were passing close, hurrying to the hill. Hohots Elotoht [Bad Boy Grizzly Bear] was back of those willows. Both their guns were empty. They clubbed with their guns, then grabbed each other. They wrestled. The big soldier was too much for the short Indian and threw him. Both struggled for their lives. The big soldier was on top. The Indian called twice to his *Wyakin* for help. He was heard and was given strength to break from his enemy.

The two stood up. Not equally matched, again Elotoht was thrown. His arm doubled under the tall soldier who was now choking him. Elotoht could no longer free himself.

A brave warrior, Lakochets Kunnin, came running. He shot the tall soldier and killed him. The bullet broke one bone in Elotoht's arm above his wrist.

A few Indians hiding from the fighting witnessed the killing of Wahchumyus. Saw the fight between Elotoht and the big soldier. But none offered help. Towassis [Bowstring] was there. He did nothing—was not a fighting man. Owhi, standing away back like a looker-on, saw it all.[18] From the Yakimas, he was not a Nez

---

[18] Owhi, the only alien among the Nez Perces (except for the footless ex-slave Seeskoomkee), was a Yakima who fell in with the band as they were passing through the Bitterroot Valley, shortly before the Big Hole battle. At the Colville Indian Agency, Owhi dictated a manuscript concerning these events, particularly the death of Wahchumyus. His account is so remote, however, from all other narratives obtained that its authenticity must, unfortunately, remain clouded in doubt.

Perce. He did no real fighting, always keeping out of it.

Pahkatos, killed a few hours later than Wahchumyus, approached the closest of any of the warriors to the soldier trenches. He got killed purposely. Wahchumyus and Pahkatos had been partners fighting the Sioux [Assiniboins] in the buffalo country. These two war mates had agreed that both should die the same day. In the same battle, as had their fathers. The death of these two mighty warriors was a great loss to our fighting strength. They were strong in planning battle.

Lakochets Kunnin was a fine young man, a brave warrior. He knew not fear. Scared at nothing! While driving the soldiers to the timbered flat, it was at foot of bluff, right by the trail, it happened.[19] Lakochets there, where I showed you, mixed a soldier in a hand to hand fight. The soldier had a gun and was getting the best of Lakochets. Peopeo Tholekt rushed in and wrenched the gun from the soldier, and Lakochets then killed him. It was hard struggling and the soldier would have come out best had Peo not been quick.

Under Yellow Wolf's leadership we now turned back to the old village site.

❈ ❈ ❈

APPENDIX I

J. B. Catlin, commanding thirty-four volunteers, says of this episode, in part:

"Our skirmishe[r]s were advanced a short distance where we remained for signs of coming daylight when a solitary Indian came out from the lodges riding directly toward us, evidently going to their herd of horses. . . . My men had been instructed and the poor devil paid the penalty. Some four or five of the boys helped him on his way." ("The Battle of the Big Hole," *Historian's Annual Report, Society of Montana Pioneers*, 1927, p. 11.)

---

[19] Stake No. 107.

AT THE BIG HOLE: SURPRISE ATTACK

T. C. Sherrill, a volunteer in Colonel Catlin's company, seems to have this Indian afoot:

"While we were lying in wait, hardly breathing, one Indian herder, who could not see a group of us crouched down in a hollow, came straight toward us, not knowing of our location, and walked up within six yards of us. We knew he would be right on us in a few seconds and thus give his tribe the signal, so the only thing for us to do was to shoot him down at once, and three of us fired on him at once. This of course was a signal for our men to attack." (E. C. Hathaway, *Battle of the Big Hole,* as told by T. C. Sherrill, pp. 7-8.)

Amos Buck, a merchant of Stevensville, Montana, who had traded with the Nez Perces as they passed through the Bitterroot Valley, and who also fought in this battle as a volunteer in Catlin's company, says of this first Indian killed:

"At three-thirty o'clock, just as morning commenced to show, Dave Morrow asked Captain Catlin, 'Shall we wait for orders to shoot?' Captain Catlin replied, 'Shoot the first Indian you see.' We had not long to wait. The first Indian to make his appearance was a large, well-built fellow who proved to be Cul-Cul-Se-Ne-Na, their great medicine man, who was coming directly toward us, mounted on a large-iron-gray horse. The Indian did not notice our men until he was within a few yards of us; he then put spurs to his horse and attempted to ride through our lines. Four shots were fired almost simultaneously, and the great Nez Perce medicine man was no more. ... Strange to say, when the Nez Perces buried their dead, they would not touch their medicine man. He was left on the battle field unburied. When Howard's scouts were taken to him, they jumped off their horses and each gave a kick, saying, 'No good medicine man.' " *(Contributions to the Historical Society of Montana,* Vol. VII, pp. 124-25, 127.)

When Yellow Wolf was made acquainted with this story, he stated tersely, "Natalekin, killed when going to look after his horses in early morning—first Indian killed—was not a medicine man. Was just a common man, too old to engage in fighting. He could not see very well. He was not buried, because there was no time to bury those killed outside the main battlefield."

That this early-morning victim had defective eyesight, as stated by Yellow Wolf, is suggested also by Lieutenant C. A. Woodruff's remark: "He leans forward on his horse to try and make out, in the dim light, what is before him." *(Contributions to the Historical Society of Montana,* Vol. VII, p. 109.)

At the Big Hole: Savagery of the Whites

As Yellow Wolf has related in the preceding chapter, Colonel Gibbon's surprise attack on the early morning of August 9, 1877, did not turn out as well as expected. The soldiers were repulsed—but not until after they had descended upon the defenseless tepees of the women, children, and Indian men too old to fight. They then retired to barricade themselves on the flat, wooded bluff overlooking the river. Yellow Wolf, standing midway between the wooded flat and the battlefield proper, resumed his narrative.

AFTER the morning battle, after the soldiers ran to the woods, I started back with others to our camp. I wanted to see what had been done. At this place I came to a dead soldier [feigning death]. A knife was in his hand. He lay as he had fixed his position—rifle at right side. When I stooped to get the gun the soldier almost stabbed me. His knife grazed my nose. I jumped five, maybe seven, feet getting away from that knife. Approaching, I struck him with my *kopluts*. He did not raise up.[1] I took his gun and cartridge belt.

Taking those guns made me a chief.[2] I killed a few soldiers. I took some guns and became a chief. It is the custom of the tribe.

We saw another soldier. Wounded, he was afraid or knew not what he was about. One warrior took his gun

---

[1] Stake No. 106, Big Hole battlefield.

[2] Notwithstanding this well-merited promotion which was in accordance with an age-old law of his own and kindred tribes, Yellow Wolf did not aspire to such lofty recognition. Early in our acquaintance he made it known that he preferred not to be addressed as "Chief." His spirit crushed by the ruins of his every hope, he went through life with an empty heart, brooding over the deep wrongs suffered by his people at the hands of a stronger, alien race.

from him, and afterwards, I went back and got his cartridge belt. Something was tied to the belt. I opened it. There was hardtack and a little bacon. Later I ate that lunch. I did not bother the soldier. He could not live.

From then until now, all the tribes know that I have full right to take food from anybody, no difference who. When an act is done at the risk of a warrior's life, it is thereafter known that he is entitled to take food wherever he happens to be.

Here, we recrossed the creek to our camp. It was not good to see women and children lying dead and wounded. A few soldiers and warriors lay as they had fallen—some almost together. Wounded children screaming with pain. Women and men crying, wailing for their scattered dead! The air was heavy with sorrow. I would not want to hear, I would not want to see, again. About ten warriors had been killed when the tepees were fired on before anyone was armed. All this was seen.[3] The chiefs now called to the warriors to renew the fighting where the soldiers had hidden themselves.

In the meantime after the soldiers had been driven back, a citizen soldier was captured. It was over among those biggest willows. He threw his gun away, but someone who helped capture him found it. I heard a voice call out, "Kill him!"

"No! He will tell us some news!"

---

[3] The army commander's concept of this scene is given here:

"Few of us will soon forget the wail of mingled grief, rage, and horror which came from the camp four or five hundred yards from us when the Indians returned to it and recognized their slaughtered warriors, women, and children. Above this wail of horror, we could hear the passionate appeal of the leaders urging their followers to fight, and the warwhoop in answer which boded us no good." ("Battle of the Big Hole," by John Gibbon, in *Harper's Weekly*, December 28, 1895.)

Evidently the piercing war cry of justly enraged fighting men was not heard by the chivalrous colonel with the same complacency with which he had listened to the plaintive intone of "crying babies" at their mothers' breasts, while impatiently awaiting a rosy dawn to pilot his leaden onslaught on the sleeping village.

That was what I heard one man reply. They brought him close to a tepee. Lakochets Kunnin, a young warrior, was leading the prisoner. I did not see from which side of the tepee one man came stepping and joined the group. The man who came from back of the tepee said commandingly, "Do not waste time! Kill him!"

While Lakochets Kunnin stood holding the prisoner, the new man with gun ready without more words shot him. Killed him dead.[4] He then spoke, "No use! The difference is, had he been a woman, we would have saved him. Sent him home unhurt! Are not *warriors* to be fought? Look around! These babies, these children killed! Were *they* warriors? These young girls, these young women you see dead! Were *they* warriors? These young boys, these old men! Were *they* warriors?

"*We* are the warriors! Coming on us while we slept, no arms ready, the soldiers were brave. Then, when we have only a few rifles in our hands, like cowardly coyotes they run away.

"These citizen soldiers! Good friends in Bitterroot

---

[4] As far as can be ascertained, the man referred to was Campbell Mitchell, of Corvallis, Montana:
"When the troops retired to the mouth of the gulch on the morning of the 9th, the warriors were examining the dead. Among them they found a white man, a citizen who was breathing; his eyes were closed and he pretended to be dead, but they saw that he was not though he was severely wounded. They took hold of him and raised him up. Finding that his 'possuming' would not work, he sprang to his feet. Looking Glass was at hand and ordered the Indians not to kill him, reminding them that he was a citizen and that they might obtain valuable information from him. . . . He told them that Howard would be there in a few hours and that volunteers were coming from Virginia City to head the Indians off. While he was talking with them a squaw who had lost a brother and some of her children in the fight, came up and slapped him in the face. He gave her a vigorous kick in return, and one of the warriors, enraged at this, killed him." (Shields, *Battle of the Big Hole*, pp. 79-80.)
The foregoing is unquestionably plagiarized from Duncan McDonald's articles, "Nez Perce War of 1877," published in the *New Northwest*. McDonald, however, states that the volunteer was "not even wounded" at the time of his capture.
Will Cave, enlarging upon Shields, gives the name of the "severely wounded" man caught feigning death, as Campbell Mitchell, and adds: "Unfortunately there is reason for the belief that he died a more fearful death than would have been produced from a gunshot wound." (Cave, *Nez Perce War of 1877*, p. 20.)
A request for information on this implication of torture of a wounded prisoner by the Nez Perces elicited no reply from Mr. Cave. No mention of torture by the Nez Perces is to be found in any of the chronicles or official reports of the battle. Torture would have left its marks on the victim's body, but nothing of the kind seemed in evidence. That a citizen prisoner was taken is conceded, and the reader can judge between Yellow Wolf's depiction and the hearsay version as to his fate.

Valley! Traded with us for our gold! Their Lolo peace treaty was a lie! Our words were good. They had two tongues. Why should we waste time saving his life?"

This warrior, Otskai, was my brother [first cousin]. No reply was made to his talk. All were convinced to his side. He had spoken right. A brave warrior, a good fighter, but at times his head did not act right. Would do things at a wrong time.[5] But nobody could say Otskai was afraid, that he ever hid from the fighting!

The citizen soldier was a young man. We afterwards learned he was prominent in the Bitterroot country. He was wearing poor clothes. At the surrender the Nez Perces were asked, "Who killed the young man prisoner at the Big Hole?"

When asked this by those United States soldiers, nobody answered. Otskai and I were not there. We had escaped, going to the Sioux in Canada. Lakochets Kunnin had also escaped, but he was killed by enemy Indians. Chapman, interpreter in the Indian Territory, asked who killed the citizen soldier, a prominent man. Nobody knew. Nobody would tell. Up to this day, this time, nobody has ever told who killed that citizen soldier.

During the foregoing depiction, we had traversed the entire length of the original camp, and now, guided by Yellow Wolf, we doubled back some distance to learn of other tragic happenings. He designated a spot fifteen paces out from the west line of tepees, and towards the river in the direction from where the charge was made on the camp. After a few moments of silent meditation, the old warrior told the following ghastly story:

Here, alone, stood a small tepee[6], what you call a hos-

---

[5] As evidence that Otskai's head "did not act right," see Chapter 11, for his participation in the capture of General Howard's pack train. Otskai had a powerful, athletic build, and it is said that once, in escaping the civil authorities, who wanted him for some petty offense, he swam the Columbia River, carrying his wife on his back. Otskai was ever averse to talking about his personal exploits. His name, reputedly Salish, has been defined as "Wild Oats" or "Wild Oat Moss." Two Moons, whose father was of that tribe, gave the definition as "Going Out."

[6] Stake No. 5, Big Hole battlefield.

131

pital, erected for a purpose. In this tepee during the night before the attack, the wife of Weyatanatoo Latpat [Sun Tied] gave birth to a baby. Wetahlatpat's sister, Tissaikpee [Granite (Crystal)], an oldlike woman, was with her as nurse. What I am telling you are facts; as I, Yellow Wolf, saw with my own eyes.

As I have already told, we came back from driving the soldiers to the hill to find part of our village in ruins. This tepee here was standing and silent. Inside we found the two women lying in their blankets dead. Both had been shot. The mother had her newborn baby in her arms. Its head was smashed, as by a gun breech or boot heel. The mother had two other children, both killed, in another tepee. Some soldiers acted with crazy minds.

Wetahlatpat was a brave warrior. But we saw him no more in that fight. After helping drive the soldiers to the hill, he came back here. Finding all his family killed, he spent the rest of the day burying them. His sister, a widow woman, he also buried.[7]

I did not see the burying of our dead. The fighting, the scouting, had to be done. In each family, the nearest relations did the burying. If a warrior lost a child or his wife, he quit the fight to bury his dead. If any of his family were bad wounded, he quit fighting to take care of them. Because of this, some of our bravest warriors were not in the fighting after driving the soldiers to the timbered flat. But Ollokot, whose wife was wounded, did not go with the camp. Relations took care of her.

---

[7] Interpreter Many Wounds interposed here and said, "The two older small children of Mrs. Wetahlatpat [Weyatanatoo Latpat] mentioned by Yellow Wolf were in my mother's tepee, where both were killed. My sister, Ipnasa Payutsami, was there also killed. Shot through the head where she lay in her blankets. Sheared Wolf [John Levi], scout for the whites, who was killed in the Lolo ambuscade, was her uncle. Her own two children died at Lapwai after being returned from bondage. During all their captivity, and until their deaths, they were cared for by my mother, Wetsetse. She and the children were returned to Lapwai with other widows and orphans about two years before the main band was permitted to

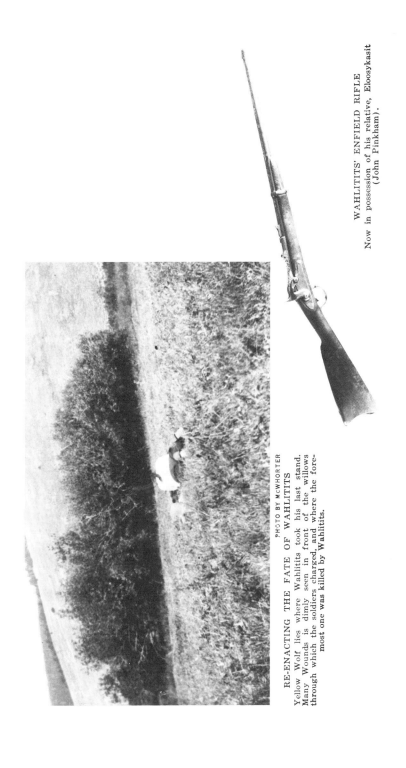

PHOTO BY McWHORTER

RE-ENACTING THE FATE OF WAHLITITS

Yellow Wolf lies where Wahlitits took his last stand. Many Wounds is dimly seen in front of the willows through which the soldiers charged, and where the foremost one was killed by Wahlitits.

WAHLITITS' ENFIELD RIFLE

Now in possession of his relative, Eloosykasit (John Pinkham).

LOCATING A BATTLE SITE

Yellow Wolf (with back to camera) shows where Hohots Elotoht, fighting in a hand-to-hand struggle with a big soldier, was saved by the timely arrival of Lakochets Kunnin.

LOOKING NORTH ON THE BATTLEFIELD

Stake in foreground (No. 106 in historic field tabulation) shows spot where Yellow Wolf narrowly escaped being killed by soldier feigning death.

Yellow Wolf proceeded south to a very slight depression in the ground a few feet in diameter. Designating the scarcely noticeable "sink," he said:

Here[8] Wahlitits was killed early in the fight. It happened immediately after I passed on my way to where the soldiers were mixing the Indians up. His tepee stood just south of here, in the main village line. Like all the warriors, he was bothered to get moccasins and rifle. He sprang out and ran to this place. He dropped flat in the sink behind a log thick as a man's leg. Across this log, his rifle pointed at the willows over there where the soldiers would be first seen. He killed a soldier who stepped from the willows. I do not know how, but Wahlitits was then killed by another soldier. When hit, he must have raised up, for he was found lying on his back.

Wahlitits' wife, a brave woman, was with him. When he fell, she grabbed his gun and fired at a near soldier. I do not know if more shots than one. Some said she killed the soldier who had killed Wahlitits, and then was quickly killed herself.

We found her lying across her husband's body as if protecting him. I heard she had been wounded before Wahlitits was killed. She was the only woman who did fighting in that battle that I knew about.

Wahlitits lay with face to the sky. A brave warrior, he did not turn back from death.[9]

---

return. Many such cases were to be found among the patriot Nez Perces. Wetahlatpat escaped from the last battle and with other refugees had an encounter with the Assiniboins. Never captured, he eventually died at Lapwai."

[8] Stake No. 10, Big Hole battlefield.

[9] For an unreliable account of Wahlitits' death, apparently plagiarized from Duncan McDonald, see Shields, *The Battle of the Big Hole*, p. 52. While Shields did not hesitate to quote McDonald (without credit) when it did not interfere with his partisan, truth-perverting purpose, he adroitly omitted all evidence which tended to show the troopers' horrible brutality in the wanton slaughter of women and children. Indeed, Shields lauds Sergeant Mildon H. Wilson, charged by McDonald with such savagery, as a patriotic hero. (Shields, pp. 76-77.) Because of his supreme arrogancy and niggardly nature, he was dubbed "Nigger Wilson" by the enlisted men in general, so wrote Sergeant Loynes, retired, of Captain Rawn's

APPENDIX I

ADDITIONAL INDIAN ACCOUNTS OF THE BIG HOLE BATTLEFIELD

Not all facts find a place in the annals of history. Wars are waged by two opposing forces, and when the chronicling is left to but one of these—as has ever been the case with our Indian conquests—a clouded and one-sided picture is the inevitable result. Nowhere is this more evident than in the usual treatment by historians of the wanton massacre of August 9, 1877, when Colonel Gibbon's numerically stronger fighting force swept down at early dawn in a veritable avalanche of annihilation upon the sleeping Nez Perce camp beside the Big Hole River.

The following accounts by Indian eyewitnesses throw new light upon that barbarous shambling of women, children, and defenseless old men—an episode hitherto vindicated as "unavoidable" by the laudatory pens of calloused Army officials and other writers. Gathered for the purpose of verifying Yellow Wolf's startling disclosures, these testimonies may be challenged but not refuted.

(1) ELOOSYKASIT

Among the outstanding incidents of the Big Hole Battle is the death of Wahlitits and his wife. This account is told by Eloosykasit (Standing on a Point), known in later years as John Pinkham. Of Chief Timothy's band of Alpowa, he, as a lad of about seventeen years with a younger companion, had gone with horses to participate in the races at Tolo Lake, the great Nez Perce gathering place. Hostilities breaking out, the boys were advised by the chiefs against returning home because of the bad temper of the whites in general. Thus they found themselves unwilling members of the noncombatant contingent of the patriot cause. As a relation of Wahlitits, Pinkham became an attaché of that warrior's family circle, and at the Big Hole camp was domiciled in an adjoining tepee when Colonel Gibbon launched his morning attack. Of the scene which ensued in their part of the camp, Pinkham gives the following depiction:

At the Big Hole camp the Indians had a great time the night before the attack. They paraded and sang all through the camp. Some were gambling at a stick, or bone, game near some brush.

Company I, Seventh Infantry. In contrast to Shields's account, see Eloosykasit's narrative, Appendix I, Chapter 10. Eloosykasit is the present owner of the warrior's needle gun.

When the attack came, just before daylight, Wahlitits and his wife ran to a shallow depression fronting their tepee. Wahlitits placed a very slim and short piece of log on the edge of the depression, facing the river brush. Very poor fort protection. A small bunch of willows was there. This was about fifteen, maybe twenty, steps from the heavy willow thickets through which the soldiers were charging. Wahlitits said to his wife: "Go with people to hiding!"

She started; Wahlitits did not know she immediately returned. He did not see her drop down back of him. Shooting was now going on, and he heard his wife speaking, "I am shot!"

Wahlitits turned and saw her lying there. He called out before the people, before the warriors, "My wife is shot to die! I will not leave her! I will go nowhere! I am staying here until killed!"

Those were the last words spoken by Wahlitits. All near witnessed what he said.

Right away a soldier broke through the willows fronting Wahlitits, who dropped him with a single shot. Then Wahlitits was killed by a soldier, the bullet entering at his chin. I did not see what I now tell, but others told me this about his wife. Though bad wounded, she reached her husband's rifle and killed the soldier who had shot him. She was then quickly killed by other soldiers. One bullet went in here [base of throat] and came out here [lumbar region]. A good-looking woman, she was soon to be a mother.

The great warrior, Rainbow, was only about four steps to left [south] of Wahlitits in this fighting. Lying flat on the ground, he was shooting into the willows. He left when his partner was killed.

The gun I have, Wahlitits had in his hands when killed. He took it from a soldier in the White Bird Canyon fight. Some of his close friends or relations picked it up at the Big Hole, and it was smuggled through to the Indian Territory after the surrender. Of course it went to Swan Necklace, nephew of Wahlitits, then to lesser kinfolks, cousins, and last to me. It was damaged near the muzzle, causing it to be shortened as you now see it.

Sometimes when I think of my relations gone, I take up this gun and look at it. Then they come to me again and I feel better. I can never give up this gun. I knew Wahlitits, a tall, fine-looking man.

After the soldiers were driven to the flat on the bluff, I, with five other young fellows, escaped from there. The oldest of the bunch, I alone had a gun. We were scattered, but came together somehow. Dodging, keeping away from where might be whites, our traveling was slow. Most of the time we had nothing to eat. We suffered terribly from hunger. For days we did not know where we were. We were always afraid for our lives. After long wandering we crossed the Rockies and other wild ranges, and reached the Nez Perce Reservation.

With thirteen others of a returned buffalo hunting party who were not in the war, I was sent to the Territory. After three years John Monteith, Indian Agent, helped me back home again. He knew me when I was younger and was good to me. I then worked for the Agency several years, farming.

(2) PENAHWENONMI (died March 15, 1938, aged 98)

Penahwenonmi (Helping Another), the aged wife of Husis Owyeen (Wounded Head), says of the Big Hole battle:

Only one woman I knew to engage in the fighting—the wife of Wahlitits. Wahlitits did not give back when soldiers charged our camp. His wife was first bad wounded where both lay in a low place fronting their tepee. Their fort was one very small log. Wahlitits shot one soldier who came from the willows, and was then killed by another soldier. He fell back by his wife's side. She grabbed up his gun and shot this soldier, killing him. She changed positions a little and when several soldiers fired at her, she dropped dead. She was soon to become a mother.

There was no fighting in the brush by women as you tell me. [See Shields, *op. cit.,* pp. 60-61, and Brady, *op. cit.,* p. 181.] No women had guns. Only few men got hold of their rifles in the camp fighting. Not until soldiers were driven out did they become armed. The running soldiers reached the woods and flat before guns could be found.

I hid under some willow brush, lying like this [flat on side]. A little girl lay close, my arm over her. Bullets cut twigs down on us like rain. The little girl was killed. Killed under my arm.

At the water's edge lying on river rocks, was a half-grown boy, shot to death. Nice looking, his name was Illatsats. His father, Espowyes [Light in the Mountain], a warrior, was full brother to Yellow Wolf's mother.

Many little children were killed. Out in the open a baby lay on its dead mother's breast, crying. Was swinging one arm shattered by a bullet. The hand, all bloody, hanging by a string of flesh and skin, dropped back and forth with the moving arm.*

---

* Charles N. Loynes, Sergeant, Company I, Seventh Infantry, in a letter to the author tells of witnessing this sight, the most pitiful of all during his army life:

136

ELOOSYKASIT (JOHN PINKHAM)

A relative of the daring warrior, Wahlitits. Escaping from the Big Hole battle, Eloosykasit, then but seventeen years old, returned with five companions to the Nez Perce Reservation, but was sent to the Indian Territory with other prisoners.

WHITE FEATHER

This young Nez Perce girl was severely wounded at the Big Hole battle. She married Andrew Garcia, white pioneer, but was killed by the Blackfect in the summer of 1879. Picture by Government photographer, Fort Benton, Montana, 1878.

WETATONMI, WIFE OF OLLOKOT

Subsequent to Ollokot's death his widow married again, becoming Mrs. Susie Convill. She is shown with a child of her second marriage.

PENAHWENONMI (HELPING ANOTHER)
Wife of Wounded Head. Photo taken at Spalding, Idaho, 1928.

YELLOW WOLF'S MOTHER
This photograph of Yiyik Wasumwah was taken subsequent to her exile in
Indian Territory.

AT THE BIG HOLE: SAVAGERY OF THE WHITES

I saw two women lying in a small tepee, dead. Both had been shot there in their blankets. A newborn baby was in its mother's arms. The baby's head had been crushed.

(3) OWYEEN

Owyeen (Wounded), a woman of venerable age (1926), reluctant to call up harrowing memories, stated briefly:

Everybody was sleeping when the soldiers charged. They set fire to a few tepees. Little children were in some of those tepees. Sleeping in blankets, they were burned to death. We heard them screaming. We found the bodies all burned and naked. Lying where they had slept or fallen before reaching the doorway.

Two small children crossed the creek alone and hid in the brush. Some women and the old medicine man, Kahpots, were there. One woman requested of him, "Why not do something against soldiers' killing? You must have some strong Power?"

Kahpots replied, "I can do nothing. I have tried, but my Power is not effective. I feel helpless. So, my niece, you better look out for yourself, how you can save your life. Go farther down the creek!"

The woman did as directed and was saved. Kahpots, unable to travel farther, had to be left on the trail a few days later, and was killed and scalped by General Howard's Bannacks, and maybe white scouts.

(4) WETATONMI (died May, 1934)

In October, 1926, Wetatonmi, Chief Ollokot's wife, almost blind from tracoma, gave the author the following brief depiction of the Big Hole battle as she saw it:

After the Clearwater fight of part of two days, we moved across the Kamiah River on towards Weippe. There was some fighting at the crossing, but not hard or serious. We kept going, and crossed the Lolo Pass into the Bitterroot Valley. Soldiers tried to stop us in Lolo Pass, but the chiefs paid little attention to them.

At Iskumtselalik Pah [Place of Ground Squirrels] we camped two suns. This was the Big Hole. We saw good tepee poles, and cut them to take to buffalo country. We did not expect more war.

"The Indian woman of whom I told you I saw lying dead with the baby on her breast, crying as it swung its little arm back and forth—the lifeless hand flapping at the wrist broken by a bullet—was outside the tepee. When I think of those terrible scenes, wrongs waged against human beings, I say shame! shame! This great Christian government had power to do differently by those truly patriotic people. It is such rememberances which touch my emotions, and I am led to marvel at the term 'civilization.'"

Ollokot's tepee was on lower [west] side of the camp, down-creek. Chief Joseph's tepee stood a little way above. More people were killed about Joseph's tepee.

Wahlitits was killed. He had helped start the war. His wife was killed immediately after. She shot the soldier who had killed her husband. She was only woman to do fighting. They all ran to hide in the creek or brush. I ran to lower side of the camp.

It was not yet full daylight. I saw a young boy lying dead under the riverbank, near the water. Nearly half-grown, a fine-looking boy. I thought maybe he had been dreaming and, hearing shots, ran out and was killed. I was hardly awake myself when I ran from the tepee. I have never forgotten seeing that boy dead on the rocks by the clear water. Everybody liked that boy.

I ran off far below the fighting. Soldiers saw me in poor hiding and shot at me. I heard many bullets, but they did not hit me. I did not see Ollokot where he was fighting.

Soldiers were driven from camp after they had destroyed many tepees. They ran to the hill. They entrenched, and the fight afterwards continued. The soldiers driven away, people all came back to the camp. They had to see what had been done. The women and children cried loudly. The chiefs and warriors wept to see their bravest dead. Pahkatos, a great warrior, was well known among the Sioux. A man of strong feeling, strong in battle. Never was known to cry and show tears. Rainbow lay dead where the fighting had been hard. He and Pahkatos had grown up together. Always went together when hunting buffaloes or on warpath. Had never been separated for long. He cried over his friend. Cried long. He said, "This sun, this time, I am going to die. My brother is killed, and I shall go with him."

Pahkatos went with his gun towards the soldier trenches. Drawing near them, the first shots missed him. The next shots he fell dead.

We buried the dead, and in the afternoon moved camp. Some warriors stayed to continue the fight, Ollokot with them. Of course, most of the fighting men went with the camp to protect it, if other soldiers were met.

Some wounded died on the trail and were buried. Two women died of wounds. We had travois for worst wounded, but no stretchers. I do not know how many suns we traveled when we had to leave one old man who could go no farther. A medicine man, his name was Kahpots. General Howard's scouts killed him. He has two sons now living.

AT THE BIG HOLE: SAVAGERY OF THE WHITES

(5)   CHIEF WHITE BIRD THE YOUNGER (died Jan. 27, 1927)

*A sidelight on the question of spies in the Indian camp, and the
terrible straits to which the women and children were driven in an
effort to escape the holocaust of death, is given in this narrative of
the late Chief White Bird the younger, then a 10-year-old lad.*

I was born about 1868, and was with my parents through the
war of 1877. My mother was sister to Chief White Bird, and,
according to an old tribal custom, I inherited his title, took his
name after reaching manhood.

I could not understand why the fighting. I saw bad happenings
at different places, and I remember too well the one battle in which
I was caught. I now know it was fought at the Big Hole.

We came to that place in the afternoon, toward evening. We
stayed that night and next day. Evening came on again. It was
after sundown—not too late—lots of us children were playing. It
was below the camp, towards the creek, that we boys were playing
the stick, or bone, game. Having lots of fun, we were noisy. We
were young, and I do not want to be understood we were gamblers.
Only having a good time. Finally dark came, and we had fire for
light and warmth.

Two men came there wrapped in gray blankets. They stood close,
and we saw they were white men. Foolishly we said nothing to the
older people about it. We ran away, and then came back to our
playing. The strangers were gone. We resumed our game, having
great sport.

Just about this time I became tired, so I went to our tepee.
Though I noticed the men in gray blankets had gone, I said nothing.
I went to bed and slept till morning. Of course I was in the same
tepee with my father and mother.

My father got up early to go look after horses. Another man
was perhaps forty steps ahead of him, going for his horses. The
soldiers shot him down. They did not try to capture him, but
killed him first thing. My father saw the gun flash, heard the report,
and turned back to camp.

Right away the troops began shooting. Bullets fell like hail on
camp, on tepees. The noise was that of Gatling guns as I have since
heard them. The sound awoke me. I heard bullets ripping the
tepee walls, pattering as raindrops.

My mother jumped up. She caught my hand, pulling me from the
blankets. She took me out the doorway with her. My mother said
to me, "Go that way! Get away as fast as you can!"

139

I did as my mother told me. Horses hitched overnight, ready to go caring for other horses, were all killed. I ran only a little ways and saw a low place in the ground. I stopped and lay down. Several women were there, and my mother came fast after me. I heard the voice of a man speaking very loud. He came where we were lying and called, "Soldiers are right on us! They are now in our camp! Get away somewhere or you will be killed or captured!"

My mother picked me up, saying, "Come, Son, let us run from here." She took my right hand in her left, and we ran. A bullet took off her middle finger, the tip of her thumb, and my thumb as you see. The same bullet did it all. My mother pointed to the creek and said, "Get down to the water. There we may escape away!"

I started. She told me to go up the creek to some bushes, to get out into the stream. I noticed one woman digging in the bank where she could hide. One soldier was shooting at everybody. We reached the bushes and my mother sat down, her head only above water. I stood up, the water almost to my shoulders. While there was a little brush, we could be seen. Five of us were there, and two more came, all women and children.

One little girl was shot through the underpart of her upper arm. She held her arm up from the cold water, it hurt so. I could see through that bullet hole. It was not full day when we ran to the creek. But it grew light as the sun came up.

An Indian who was shooting fast at the soldiers was killed. The woman I saw digging in the bank was shot in the left breast. She pitched in the water, and I saw her struggling. She floated by us, and my mother caught her and drew her to her side. She placed the dying woman's head on a gravel bar just out of the water. She was soon dead. A fine-looking woman, and I remember the blood coloring the water.

Some soldiers leveled their guns at us. My mother threw up her hand and called, "Only women! Only women!" as she jerked me entirely under water. An officer spoke to the soldiers, who let down their guns and went away.

(6) RED ELK (died Oct., 1930)

This story of the Big Hole fight as seen by a lad of strong, native talent, was secured by interview in October, 1926, our only meeting. On January 13, 1931, interpreter Many Wounds wrote me: "Red Elk died last October; the Noisome Night, you know"—alluding to Halloween. The narrative follows:

AT THE BIG HOLE: SAVAGERY OF THE WHITES

I was ten years old in 1877. My father, Red Elk, was a brother to Chief Yellow Bull, and we were with him. We were native to the White Bird River. My brother, who did fighting, told me considerable about the battles, but I saw something of two of them.

The first was at the Big Hole. Sun was going down. I heard someone say he had seen a *shoyahpee* [white man] cross the canyon, riding down horseback. A second time they saw him, this time going back. Some thought he must have been a spy. It was now nearly dark. I heard some of the older people talking that the white man must be working a mine somewhere. He might have quarreled with the others. He might have been a spy locating our camp.

After dark we small boys had a bone game near the end of the camp. After playing awhile, I was ready to go home and sleep. I heard someone say that a *shoyahpee* was approaching. I saw a man standing wrapped in a blanket. Standing in the firelight, I saw white on his forehead under his hat. I went home and all were sleeping. I did not wake them but went to bed and fell asleep.

About early morning I was awakened. My father and Chief Yellow Bull were standing, talking low. They thought they saw soldiers across the creek. Next instant we heard shots from above the creek across the canyon, maybe a quarter mile away. I heard the loud call, "We are attacked!"

Then I heard two shots, and another loud shout, "We are attacked! We are attacked!"

After these two or three shots there broke a heavy fighting. Soldiers soon came rushing among the tepees. Bullets flying everywhere. Of course I jumped up and ran outside, down below. It was like spurts of fire, lightning all around.

When I ran away, Sarpsis Ilppilp and Tipyahlanah Kapskaps were still sound asleep. They woke up, and these two brave men ran across to meet the enemies. I crossed the creek. It was becoming more light. I gained a point where I could see the soldiers plainly. We watched from there, myself and other boys.

We saw the camp deserted by Indians. Soldiers still crossing the creek. Seemed to be surrounding the camp. One man, Wahlitits, remained there fighting, and was killed. He was fighting from behind a small, decayed log. His wife was a few feet back of him. When he was killed, she snatched his gun and shot the soldier who had done the deed. She was then killed by shots from several soldiers. A fine-looking woman, the only woman known to do fighting. After soldiers were driven to the hill, there lay Wahlitits and wife dead. Several mothers and their children were killed.

141

Nobody to hold the soldiers back, they set fire to some tepees. I saw desperate fighting among the tepees. Only a few Indians with guns. Sarpsis and Tipyahlanah seemed to drive the enemies back lonehanded.

It was about sunrise when the soldiers gathered on the flat and dug hiding places. The fighting then stopped for a while, and the Indians returned to the partly ruined camp. They all cried when they saw what had been done. Boys, girls, women, and children, and men who had no guns, no arms, lay scattered among dead soldiers, burned tepees, and bedding.

(7) EELAHWEEMAH (died Nov. 2, 1920)

The late David Williams, successor to Joseph as chief of the Nez Perces on the Colville Indian Reservation, whose native name was Eelahweemah (About Asleep), was a lad of twelve or so at the time of the war. He gave me the following reminiscences of the Big Hole:

It was just breaking day and everybody was in bed. I heard gun reports, about twice. Then followed rapid firing into our tepees. A warrior yelled:

"Wake up, people! Soldiers right up against us, shooting at us!"

Before the sun was up, Indians and soldiers came together in a close war. My father, Likinma [Last in a Row], showed us where to go and told us not to go anywhere else. He then made some shots at the soldiers.

Seven of us—five women, my little brother, and myself—were in the shallow gully where my father had directed us. It was not deep, and when the soldiers saw us they began shooting at us.

I saw one woman killed—my mother, Tumokult [I Block Up]. She was the first to be killed. I saw my father shoot and drop a soldier. I do not know if it was the one who killed my mother.

Then I looked around. All the other four women lay dead or bad wounded! I said to my little brother,* "We must get out of this place!"

The bank of our shelter was on the wrong side and did not hide us from the soldiers.

We jumped from there, and soldiers fired at us. I do not know how many shots. As many as they could while we were in sight. There was a creek, and we got under its bank. I saw one Indian

---

* Eelahweemah's smaller brother was one of the many who succumbed to malarial fever in the swamplands of Fort Leavenworth district, Kansas, whither the war prisoners were exiled before being sent to the Indian Territory.

lying there dead. He did not have a gun. Very quickly I heard someone call:

"Soldiers now running from the warriors!"

It was true! Looking, I saw soldiers running and Indians after them, shooting. Not many Indians in the chase.

The soldiers ran toward some timber on a bluff where was a sloping flat. There they dug trenches for hiding. There the warriors kept them all that day and all night. Some were killed in their trenches.

The camp soon moved and I went with it.

(8) PAHIT PALIKT

Pahit Palikt, still living (1940), is the son of Uwhee Tommoset (Heyoom Pishkish) (died 1926), a warrior later known as Lame John, from a sprained foot received in a sawmill accident while a prisoner in the Indian Territory. The son, a fine specimen of his tribe, gave the author these war recollections:

I remember only one time in that war. I was so small. It was early morning the soldiers came. I did not hear the first shooting. My father and mother ran from the tepee, leaving me, my brother twelve years old, and a cousin thirteen, sleeping under blankets. We would be safer there. Bullets would go over us.

Soldiers came and shot my dog in the tepee. I did not hear. They must not have seen us, all covered feet and head. When the soldiers left, my brother shook me and said, "Wake up! Bring that blanket and come!"

I grabbed my blanket, and we all three ran from the tepee. Guns were going fast, popping loud! We ran maybe thirty steps, when my brother leaped over the creekbank and called to me, "Jump down here!"

I jumped to where he was. We stayed there maybe half hour, maybe one hour; I do not know. I heard terrible gun noise. Lots of smoke. Plenty of powder smell. Indians yelling, soldiers shouting, cursing. I was scared! Bad scared! Soldiers seemed shooting at me. I heard bullets going past my head. My brother was killed there under the bank. I missed my blanket. I thought, "Where is my blanket?"

I had dropped it while running for the bank. I ran back and got my blanket. I saw Indians going up the hill. I saw my father, horseback, coming down the hill to where the Indians were. In the wrecked camp I saw and heard lots of Indian men and women crying.

Oh, lots of them crying! Crying loud, mournful. I could not understand. I did not know. I saw many soldiers, many Indian men, and oh, so many women and children lying on the ground. I wondered if they were sleeping so. Afterward I understood.

This is all I remember of that war my parents carried me through —the only things I can recall. It must have been the Big Hole battle, from what I now know. There is nothing more I can tell.

(9) KOWTOLIKS

Kowtoliks (Charley Kowtoliks), a lad of fifteen at the time of the Big Hole battle, gives the following recollections:

When I first heard the firing of guns, I jumped from my blankets and ran about thirty feet and threw myself on hands and knees, and kept going. An old woman, Patsikonmi, came from the tepee and did the same thing—bent down on knees and hands. She was to my left and was shot in the breast. I heard the bullet strike. She said to me, "You better not stay here. Be going, I'm shot." Then she died. Of course I ran for my life and hid in the bushes.

The soldiers seemed shooting everywhere. Through tepees and wherever they saw Indians. I saw little children killed and men fall before bullets coming like rain.

One young man, Kahwitkahwit [Dry-land Crane], had two wives. When the attack came, all three hurried to the river and sprang in. They swam downstream, side by side, the man in the middle. Coming to some willows, they landed, the man lying flat, the women sitting on either side. They stayed hidden until the fighting quit the village.

At the last battle Kahwitkahwit cried when Chief Joheph returned from the soldier camp and ordered fighting renewed. Said he would go surrender himself.

Later, Joseph was forced to surrender. Many Nez Perces were scattered in the hills and canyons. Women and children as well as men—without blankets or food. Joseph wanted to save them.

Kahwitkahwit, the cowardly, was taken to the Territory with others. He was returned and placed on the Colville Reservation, where he died. He was not a warrior.

(10) BLACK EAGLE

Black Eagle, Wottolen's son, aged sixteen at the time, gives the following graphic account of what he saw and experienced at the Big Hole struggle:

144

AT THE BIG HOLE: SAVAGERY OF THE WHITES

Our tepee stood at the very lower end of the village. When I was awakened that morning by guns, I sprang up and ran out the doorway into the river. It was cold! Remembering a horsehair rope, I ran back to get it. While doing this, bullets passed through the tepee. Guns were barking, and I heard someone yell, "We are attacked!" Must have been somebody just aroused from slumber.

But the soldiers did not get through the brush to our part of camp. Only a very few warriors with guns, maybe three, held them from crossing the river.

With others I ran for the horses. They were bunched farther down the river, badly scared. We had trouble getting around them. A distance from camp I heard the cry go up, "Soldiers are defeated!" The soldiers, driven from camp, were running for the woods.

Chief Joseph's horses with many others were on the open hillside to the west. The herd was back of and above the soldiers when they first charged the camp. I saw Chief Joseph and No Heart, a young man, up the hillside going afoot after the horses. Both were barefooted, and Joseph had no leggings. Only shirt and blanket. Reaching their own horses, they mounted and drove the herd farther up the hill. Out of sight of soldiers and the fighting.

Up there No Heart was killed. Shot through mistake by a friend. Word had gone out that Flathead Indians were driving the horses away. This was not true, and cost the life of a good young man. Afterward the Indian who shot No Heart went back to bury his body, but it could not be found. Nor could No Heart's horse be seen anywhere. Maybe No Heart came back to life soon after he was shot, and went away and died.*

The horses were brought to camp by Joseph and others after the soldiers were driven to the timber flat, where they dug holes for hiding. That night the warriors heard soldiers crying like babies.

I did not see all the dead buried. When I got back with horses, many bodies had been taken away. Some carried on horses were buried secretly. I saw dead soldiers lying about, but did not count them. They killed forty-four Indians before being driven from the camp.

I knew two little boys who were sleeping in a tepee that was burned. Their mothers covered them with blankets and a buffalo robe, and they escaped unhurt. Peopeo Tholekt was the father of one, and the other was Peo's wife's brother. Another brother sleeping in the same tepee was Jackson Sundown [late champion horseman of

---

* Mr. Andrew Garcia, who was over the Big Hole battlefield in 1879, told the writer that he had found an Indian grave on the hill where No Heart was last seen with the horse herd.

the Northwest]. Peo's wife and child escaped when the attack was first made at the last battle, but the family was never again united. I do not know what became of her. Her child and Sundown were of the same age.

Camp was packed. All us young boys with women and children and old men left with horse herd on the trail. Warriors were along to protect the families against enemy attacks. Tepee poles were used for travois for bad wounded. Chief Joseph and Chief White Bird went with the families.

All along that trail was crying. Mourning for many left where we thought no war would come. Old people, half-grown boys and girls, mothers, and little babies. Many only half-buried—left for wolves and coyotes. I can never forget that day.

(11)   SAMUEL TILDEN

Samuel Tilden, Nez Perce of high standing, writes briefly of his experiences in the Big Hole horror:

At the Big Hole I was sleeping with my grandmother, Martha Joseph, a close relation to Chief Joseph. She was shot through the left shoulder as she lay there, and she told me to skip for my life. I ran for the brush with other boys. I heard the bullets as they cut leaves and twigs down about us. I saw tepees on fire, where warriors mixed with soldiers in dreadful fight, and drove them to the hill. About ten years old at the time, I remember all very well. Sometime when I see you I can tell you more.

(12)   THE FATE OF WHITE FEATHER

During the Big Hole battle White Feather, a comely Nez Perce maid of seventeen or eighteen snows, was struck in the left shoulder by a bullet and knocked to the ground. Dazed and half blinded by the shock, she mechanically caught at the boot of a soldier or volunteer in an attempt to draw herself up. That gallant defender of his flag and country's honor dealt her a blow on her right shoulder with the breech of his gun, followed by a vicious jab on the mouth with the metal-plated butt of the piece, bruising and cutting her lip, and breaking out an upper front tooth.

Gray Hawk, White Feather's father, mortally wounded, died at the second night's camp from the Big Hole, leaving her with no blood kin. With no care and nursing throughout the long retreat, her misery and suffering were increased by the cold winter spent in the camp of the unfriendly "Walk-around" Sioux, where she was left because of her inability to continue the flight to the haven of Sitting Bull's camp.

The story of the unfortunate White Feather as written and held in manuscript by Andrew Garcia, to whom she was later married, is short but fraught with pathos; it ends with her death in 1879, at the hands of the implacable Blackfeet in the wilds of the cheerless Marias Mountains.

(13)   AN UNSUNG HEROINE

More fortunate, perhaps, than the Nemesis-pursued White Feather was Halpawinmi (Dawn). Eighteen or twenty years of age, strong and handsome in form and physique, and endowed with a beautiful personality, she was the recognized belle and favorite of her tribe.

Though her brother was killed in her presence, she did not give way to unavailing grief and lamentation. Disdaining to flee the awful holocaust about her, she fell while ministering to the wounded and dying about her. She survived her mortal wounds two days, and was buried on the trail.

Closing Scenes at the Big Hole

An outstanding occurrence of the Big Hole battle was the capture by the Nez Perce warriors of Colonel Gibbon's only piece of artillery. When Gibbon started moving toward the Nez Perce camp before daybreak, he discovered that his howitzer could not be brought along, on account of the noise it would make in negotiating the fallen timber in the trail. He therefore ordered that it should be brought on by six men shortly after daylight, accompanied by a pack mule loaded with two thousand rounds of ammunition. But the howitzer, Colonel Gibbon writes, did not reach its destination:

"Just as we took up our position in the timber two shots from our howitzer on the trail above us were heard, and we afterwards learned that the gun and pack-mule with ammunition were, on the road to us, intercepted by Indians. The non-commissioned officers in charge, Sergeants Daly and Fredrics and Corporal Sales, made the best resistance they could, whilst the two privates cowardly fled at the first appearance of danger and never stopped till they had put a hundred miles between themselves and the battlefield, spreading, of course, as such cowards always do, the most exaggerated reports of the dire calamity which had overtaken the entire command. The piece was fired twice, and as the Indians closed around it the men used their rifles. Corporal Sales was killed, the two sergeants wounded, the animal was shot down, and Private John O. Bennett, the driver, entangled in their fall, cutting himself loose, succeeded in reaching the brush and escaped to the train, which the two sergeants, Blodgett, the guide, and William, a colored servant of Lieutenant Jacobs, also reached. In the meantime, our fight in the timber continued with more or less activity all day. . . . " ("Report of the General of the Army, 1877," pp. 69-70.)

After giving the Indian version of the taking of the gun, Yellow Wolf describes how the Indians packed camp and silently moved away from the battlefield after hastily burying the dead.

I WILL tell how we got this gun. Six of us were mounted and this side [southwest] of the entrenched soldiers. They were my uncle, Old Yellow Wolf, brother to my mother, Tenahtahkah Weyun [Dropping from a Cliff], Weyatanatoo Latpat [Sun Tied], Pitpillooheen [Calf of Leg], Ketalkpoosmin [Stripes Turned Down], and I, Yellow Wolf.

We were scouts on the lookout. Scouts everywhere that enemies might be coming. From across the valley south of us, I heard a voice—a Nez Perce voice—call a warning, "Look this way!"

Looking, we saw three scouts riding fast toward us. Drawing near, one of them yelled, "Two white men riding on trail towards you!"

We ran our horses in that direction. Soon we saw them! We chased those two white men back the way they came. We fired at them. Up there we found the cannon. We saw the big gun on a wagon with men. Four, maybe six, mules hitched to that gun wagon. While we charged this cannon, the men having it in keeping fired it twice. But some distance away, we scattered, and nobody hurt. I saw a warrior off his horse running afoot towards this cannon from the opposite side. This was Seeyakoon Ilppilp [Red Spy], a brave man, a good fighter. He came running, dodging, getting closer and closer to the main cannonman.[1] That soldier

---

[1] Of the killing of the cannoneer Wattes Kunnin (Earth Blanket), known as "Big Joe," a half-Umatilla who was born on White Bird Creek and belonged to Chief Joseph's band, in an interview said:

"Riding up the hill I came to a kind of small canyon forks. From there I saw the big gun and soldiers running away from it. Two Indians afoot came down the hill towards the cannon. I galloped up the hill a short way, and when I came again where I could see, just one white man was there. Only one left. He was shooting back; sort of back of himself and not ahead.

"The two Indians were getting closer. I saw the white man sinking down. I thought he was going to shoot at me. No! he was dying.

"When I saw him go down, I galloped faster. When I reached the cannon, there stood not far away a bay horse with packs on his back. Those packs were gun cartridges. Lots of them."

Without a gun, Earth Blanket made no claims of having taken part in the Big Hole fighting.

did not see him. Then Seeyakoon, still at good distance, shot him in the back, killing him. At the same time Tenahtahkah dropped the right-hand lead mule. The cannon was completely stopped. Some other soldiers with it skipped to the brush, escaping with their lives. But the main warrior in its capture was Ketalkpoosmin, a young man afraid of nothing.

This little fight over, we again heard one scout across the creek calling, "Coming down this way leading one pack horse, about ten soldiers!"

We mounted in a hurry and went to meet these new enemies. As far as to our camp [600 yards] one of the soldiers was leading the pack horse. My uncle, Espowyes [Light in the Mountain][2], was some distance ahead of us. I saw him head this soldier off and take the pack horse. That soldier put up no fight. He skipped for his life. We fired at him, but did not stop him. Espowyes was brother [relation] to Chief Joseph. Those ten or eleven soldiers ran their horses fast back up the trail. When we got to that pack horse, we cut the rope holding the packs, dropping them to the ground. With rocks the boxes were broken open. It was ammunition, more than two thousand cartridges.[3]

I paid no attention, but about thirty Indians were there by this time. We all piled after that ammunition. Some got only few cartridges, some got more. Later it

---

[2] Espowyes, according to some of the interpreters, is a name apparently foreign to Nez Perce proper. He was the full brother of Yellow Wolf's mother, and was a warrior of note, having engaged in previous tribal wars in the buffalo country. Shot in the hip by an Assiniboin Sioux, he walked with a slight limp ever afterwards.

[3] In a field dispatch dated August 14, 1877, sent from Camp William Logan and directed to the Adjutant General, Military Division Pacific, San Francisco, General Howard stated:

"They [the Indians] captured on last battle field not less than thirty-five hundred (3,500) rounds and fifteen (15) muskets, caliber forty-five (45)." ("Report of the General of the Army," 1877, in *Report of the Secretary of War*, 1877, Vol. I.)

was divided evenly by the chiefs. Just one kind of rifles it fit—those we took from the soldiers.

Most of the warriors now went back to fight the soldiers in their trenches, while several scouted the woods above us, the mountainside. Might be soldiers coming through that way.

Only my uncle and I rode up the trail where the ten soldiers had fled. We went quite a way and decided those soldiers had left for the Bitterroot Valley. We turned back. Had we found them, one would have watched them, while the other returned to bring warriors for the fight.

While we chased those soldiers and captured the ammunition, other Indians knocked out whatever was used in firing the cannon. Took off the wheels and rolled them down a steep place to the swamp or creek brush. We could have fought the soldiers with that gun had we known how to use it. I understood Peopeo Tholekt shallow-buried it, digging with his hunting knife. He came there as the fight ended. Poker Joe afterwards rolled it down the bluff to thick brush. I knew Poker Joe very well. He was a great leader—a brave warrior.[4]

I am telling the facts. What I saw, and what was told

---

[4] Poker Joe derived his name from his supposed addicition to that card game. His Nez Perce cognomen was Wahwookya Wasaäw (Lean Elk), often abridged to Wasaäw, "Weak" or "Poor." Slightly undersized, he had a wonderfully strong voice. This served him well in his role as chosen commander of the retreat from the Big Hole disaster. This he successfully conducted until after the Missouri River crossing, as will be seen in Chapter 16. How Poker Joe happened to be with the retreating Nez Perces is explained in the following letter from interpreter Williams, dated March 21, 1938:

"Mrs. Phillip Williams who knew Poker Joe well, says that his surname was something like 'Alexs,' and that the true name should be found recorded at the Catholic Mission, Flat Head Indian Reservation. Joe was a half-blood French.

"Returning from the buffalo country, Poker Joe and his little band went on to Idaho. When within six miles of Kamiah, he heard of the war; so he started back to Montana from Lolo Creek. In some way he cut his leg with a knife on the way, and reached home quite lame. White people thought he had been wounded by soldiers in Idaho, and would not believe Poker's explanation. Not liking to be accused of something he had not done, he joined up with the war party."

Poker Joe's little band consisted of six tepees; but these were transformed, in General Howard's dispatch of August 14, previously quoted in part, into "twenty lodges": "Indians have had reinforcements of about twenty (20) lodges from buffalo country."

me about the big gun hiding. I am telling to hurt nobody. The true history must be given.[5]

With my uncle I now rode up the open mountainside to timber where other scouts were watching. They were guarding against any new enemies who might come. Hiding up there, we would be ready to head off any soldiers coming along the trail below. The fighting at the soldiers' trenches was going on. The gun reports did not grow less.

From the scene of the capture of the howitzer, Yellow Wolf led us northwest up the open hillside to the timber. He passed over the shoulder of the ridge point with unerring accuracy, and proceeded to a small parklike opening on a slightly sloping flat facing the northeast.

This place was headquarters on this side of the creek for the scouts and guards who were watching for any new enemies who might be approaching over the trail. A good bunch of men were standing here, I, Yellow

---

[5] This manifest digression by the narrator was made in anxiety lest he be construed as antagonistic to Peopeo Tholekt's claim of burying the howitzer, which was questioned by some of the warriors. Peopeo, in his unpublished war narrative, states that he was mounted and in another part of the field when attracted by the cannon shots, and that by hard riding he arrived on the scene before the unhurt mules were yet detached from the carriage. In vain he urged moving the gun to position and using it against the soldiers. The warriors, claiming the animals by right of capture, unhooked and took them away. Peopeo then proceeded with an attempt to conceal the gun by burying it.

Duncan McDonald in his "Nez Perce War of 1877" says of this occurrence: "After capturing the howitzer they damaged it so that, as they believed, it could not be used. A few minutes later an Indian reached the gun and expressed great regret that it was rendered useless. He said: 'It is a great pity. I know how to use this kind of gun. I learned when I was with Col. Wright fighting Cayuses and Yakimas.' "

Perhaps no unalloyed version of the Indian disposal of the howitzer can ever be obtained. An unsupported claim among the younger members of the war party has it that a certain "Tababo," a half blood, was the one who consigned it to the swamp thicket. The name is obviously a corruption of "Tabador," a French half blood who figures prominently in later parts of Yellow Wolf's narrative but who had no part in the capture of the howitzer or its disposal. Poker Joe was the only half blood who was connected with the incident.

Of the recovery of this gun Colonel Gibbon says: "Parties were sent out on the 11th to bury the dead, all of whom were found, recognized, and decently interred, and to recover the howitzer, which was found concealed in the brush, the carriage-wheels being carried off." (Idem., p. 71.)

Colonel Gibbon clearly indicates that the wheels were completely missing, which is erroneous. The wheels (at least one of them minus a few spokes) were recovered, and the howitzer was remounted on its carriage and taken to Deer Lodge. The entire outfit, with two unexploded shells found in the proximity of the capture, now rests under cover within the small National Park in proximity to the still well-preserved rifle pits where the remnant of the harassed troops found precarious refuge.

COLONEL GIBBON'S ILL-FATED HOWITZER

Wolf, among them. Our horses were tied just back of us.

Word came that Sarpsis Ilppilp [Red Moccasin Tops][6] had been killed. He was lying dead near the soldier trenches. Chuslum Moxmox [Yellow Bull], his father, made announcement, "We do not want to leave him there. We do not want to leave him for crazy white people who might cut him in pieces to make fun of brave warrior. Who will go bring his body away, bring him to this place?"

Then the word went around, "We are bringing Sarpsis Ilppilp away from there!"

Seven or eight of us started down that way [northeast]. We had to keep away from the soldiers' aim, stay hidden in the timber. Tipyahlanah Kapskaps [Strong Eagle], cousin of Sarpsis, was our leader. I can not recognize every place as then. Young trees have grown up, changing looks of woods and land. But I will explain best I can.

When we came down above where the ranger station now stands, we tried avoiding shots from the soldier trenches. Weweetsa [Log], who had been wounded in the right side earlier in the fight, was the rear man. He became exposed and was killed [wounded] by a bullet from the trenches. It struck at the collarbone and came out at left shoulder. Weweetsa soon regained life and remained with us two weeks. Then, with three other wounded men, he went to the Flathead Reservation. He got well of the shot but was killed soon afterwards by Flatheads in a quarrel.

Hardly three minutes after Weweetsa was shot,

[6] Sarpsis is the upper, or ankle-wrapping, part of the moccasin. Ilppilp is "red," and from his decorating thus the tops of his moccasins was derived the name of the meteoric though short-lived warrior, Sarpsis Ilppilp. For a sadly confused description of his death—apparently plagiarized from Duncan McDonald—see Shields, *Battle of the Big Hole*, p. 52, and Brady, *Northwestern Fights and Fighters*, p. 176.

Quiloïshkish had his right elbow shattered. His name is Flathead language. At Bearpaw Mountain fight he escaped to the Sioux. Never did surrender. Finally returned to Lapwai where he died. At the wounding of Quiloïshkish, we all returned to this place.

We thought to try again. Six or seven of us went this time. A shallow draw led down where Sarpsis lay. We worked down it quite a ways, within about twenty steps of where he lay. Then Tipyahlanah sprang forward and caught up Sarpsis, who was still breathing. Only ran with him a few steps when he was shot through right side just below short rib. Wounded, he carried his brother [cousin] part way to safety, then fell. Sarpsis there died. Tipyahlanah crawled back up to the benchland. We came back up here, our hearts feeling bad. After another council, we said we would try again.

A third time we were ready to go. My uncle Yellow Wolf told me he would go in my place. As I have told you, he was my mother's full brother and first cousin to Chief Joseph. This is why I stayed in Joseph's tepee, by his campfire. Relations always stay together.

They went down. The dead man had a white wolf-skin over his shoulders. His father, Yellow Bull, kept shouting from the wooded bench, "Who saves the body can have the wolfskin!" That wolfskin was strong medicine.

I do not know only as they told when they came back. While the other warriors kept firing at the trenches from hiding places, Tahwis Tokaitat [Bighorn Bow], a strong man, crawled down to the body and pulled it away. The soldiers did not see him. As he brought the body behind a tree, Yellow Bull called to him, "You have done what you wanted! Come away!"

They brought the body of Sarpsis Ilppilp up here and buried it secretly. I saw the bullet mark. He was shot in the throat. The bullet cut one strand of his wampum beads.[7]

Yellow Bull did not keep his promise to give the white wolfskin for bringing away the body of Sarpsis. The mother, a magician, got the skin. It was taken from her by Tahomchits Humkon, a medicine man. At the last battle, wearing this wolfskin, Tahomchits was shot across the back of neck. He always shook afterwards—hands shaking.

Not many warriors stayed at the fighting. A very few could hold the soldiers, while if any new enemies came, warriors must be to hold them back. Where the soldiers buried themselves, one warrior, going from tree to tree while shooting, could be as three, maybe as five or seven, rifles.

That same afternoon of the attack on our camp, all women, children, old men, and wounded left, going forward on the trail. Chief Joseph, White Bird, and fighting men also went. Many had wounded friends and relations to care for. The families must be protected if new enemies appeared.

It was the women and children we must fight for. So, in the evening all warriors, all but thirty, left to join the camp, to be there before darkness came, to watch for soldiers through the night. We remaining would fight as we could, and bring news if other soldiers came.

Night drew on. We then went after the fighting strong. Scattered among trees, lying close to the ground. In low places hard to see, we crawled close to those

---

[7] See Appendix I, this chapter.

trenches. We heard the soldiers talking, swearing, crying.[8]

Late in the fore part of the night, we heard noise in the willows under the bluff below the trenches. We heard one talking loud in the trenches. Then we heard him crying! When we heard this, we understood. Must be some young man [a volunteer] escaped us to the willows, and the old man [his father] could not go. Probably he was wounded. Then the escaping soldiers seemed all returned to the trenches. That was what we thought, hearing such noises.[9]

The night grew old, and the firing faded away. Soldiers would not shoot. Would not lift head nor hand above their hiding. We believed they had but little ammunition.[10] Of course, they must have some few cartridges, but shots slowed. Then they stopped entirely. We knew then they were holding cartridges for maybe a charge by us. We did not charge. If we killed one soldier, a thousand would take his place. If we lost one warrior, there was none to take his place.

We then held council to know what best to do. The older warriors always decided. They talked this way:

---

[8] The plight of the wounded soldiers was indeed pitiful. Their clothing was still damp from twice splashing through the cold mountain stream. The pangs of hunger and thirst as they cowered in their inadequate shelter trenches were nerve-wracking, and some of the boys became half delirious. Peopeo Tholekt, one of the more active young warriors, crawled within a few feet of a trench and heard the following remark. "Charley! Charley! Hold on there! Hold on! G-- d--- you, wait!" From some of the trenches came raving, from others weeping. Sergeant Loynes speaks of this condition in one of his letters.

[9] This was evidently the party sent out from the trenches for water, of which Shields says:
"Not until nightfall did the commanding officer deem it prudent to send out a fatigue party for water. Then three men volunteered to go, and under cover of darkness and a firing party, they made the trip safely, filling and bringing in as many canteens as they could carry." (Shields, *op. cit.*, p. 72.) Colonel Gibbon makes no mention of this occurrence in his official report.

[10] In regard to the supposed dearth of ammunition, Sergeant Loynes states in a letter (January 7, 1935):
"The claim is absolutely correct. We certainly were getting down to our last cartridges. We were cautioned by the officers to waste no ammunition. But, as to us receiving a supply of ammunition—just imagine someone leading a horse or mule to our relief with a pack of cardtridges when you could not lift your head above our small protection of dirtwork without getting a bullet somewhere in your body if not head—surrounded as we were at all times by Indians."

"Those soldiers can no longer be dangerous to the families. They are afoot, all badly scared. Our best warriors are gone. No use that more of us get killed fighting so far from families. A few young men will stay and watch these soldiers. See if others come. They will follow the camp later. Must now be near middle of night."

The camp then packed and left.[11] Only eight or nine of us young men who had swift horses remained behind. Only a few of us, we did not try rushing the soldiers. Why get killed? The soldiers were safely corralled. Families good distance away.

We just settled down to watch those soldiers.

Late in after part of night we heard a white man's voice. He shouted up on the mountain. Might be some soldier lost! Maybe guiding in other soldiers? We did not know what might be doing up there.[12]

It was almost dawn when we heard the sound of a running horse. Soon a white man came loping through the timber. He was heading for the trenches.[13] We did

---

[11] Various writers have stated that the Indians' camp was packed under fire from the soldiers (e.g., Gibbon in *Harper's Weekly*, Dec. 28, 1895; Woodruff in *Contributions to the Historical Society of Montana*, Vol. VII, p. 110). Shields (op. cit., p. 64) states that the Indians "had hot work breaking camp, and several of them and their horses were killed while thus engaged. Two of Joseph's wives and a daughter of Looking Glass were among the slain." This is denied by survivors. Black Eagle declared: "No! The horses were packed without enemy firing. Soldiers were then in the woods entrenching. They could no longer see our camp, what we were doing." This is confirmed by Sergeant Noyes, of Captain Rawn's company, who writes me, "You are right in your surmise that this is a mistake, for, from where we were entrenched, the camp could not be seen, consequently, there was nothing visible to shoot at. But it was near enough for us to hear the cries of our wounded when the Indians finished them."

[12] It was claimed by a surviving citizen volunteer who participated in the Big Hole battle that just when the besieged force had exhausted their ammunition, holding in reserve only one or two rounds each, the Nez Perces suddenly ceased activities and decamped within five minutes. He said this mystified the soldiers until they subsequently learned that the Indians thought the halloo of a straggler on a distant ridge signaled the approach of enemy troops. However, according to both Yellow Wolf and Peopeo Tholket, it was not the voice of this unknown straggler in the night that caused them to "decamp"; rather it was their knowledge that the Nez Perce families were by now so far ahead that they were out of danger of immediate pursuit. This was the primary reason for the sudden cessation of firing.

[13] This was Sergeant O. Sutherland, Company B, First Cavalry, courier from General Howard to Colonel Gibbon. (Howard, *Nez Perce Joseph*, pp. 185-89). For an interesting, though overdrawn, picture of this courier's achievement, see "Sergeant Sutherland's Ride," by Garrett B. Hunt in the *Mississippi Valley Historical Review*, Vol. XIV, No. 1, June, 1927, pp. 39-46.

not try to kill him. Had they wished, some warriors where he passed could have shot him. They said, "Let him go in! We will then know what news he brings the soldiers!"

When that rider reached the trenches, the soldiers made loud cheering. We understood! Ammunition had arrived or more soldiers were coming. Maybe pack horse of cartridges left in the woods with soldiers guarding? Some of us went back over the trail looking for any horse there. We found none. Had we gone two hundred steps farther, we would have captured their cavalry horses. All their supply train! We did not look in a gulch where concealed.[14] This we learned after the war was quit.

I was watching from south side of hill. When all returned from hunting for pack horses, we assembled south of trenches. There was a short council. Chief Ollokot was our leader. It was thought to quit the watching, and follow after the families. Soldiers must be coming. They might overtake the camp. Might capture or kill the rest of the old people, women, and children. Our camp was only a half-sun's travel ahead. Our business was now to warn them. If fighting was to be done, we would all be there.

We gave those trenched soldiers two volleys as a "Good-by!" Then we mounted and rode swiftly away. No use staying. Those soldiers buried, hiding from further war. We quit the fight. They were brave when attacking our sleeping village, firing into our tepees! Eight women had been killed, eight more wounded. One

---

[14] At least one chronicler contends that Colonel Gibbon's supply train was found and attacked. (Fuller, *History of the Pacific Northwest*, p. 269.) Other warriors agree with Yellow Wolf that the train was not found; and Colonel Gibbon in his official report says nothing of any attack, but tells of its arrival intact, "just before sundown" of the day following the battle.

of these died next morning. Another died still later. That was ten women to lose their life at the Big Hole. Many children and old men were killed. Killed in their tepees or when running for shelter places. A few bad wounded were buried on the trail.

Only twelve real fighting men were lost in that battle. But our best were left there.[15]

Traveling was hard on the wounded. So bad that when we reached more safe places, several of them stopped. Remained scattered and hidden away. A few of these were never afterwards heard of.

When Yellow Wolf was informed that Colonel Gibbon states that the Nez Perces were seen throughout the day following the first day's battle, and that the parting shots from the warriors came about eleven o'clock that night ("Report of the General of the Army," 1877, p. 71) the usually impassive narrator smiled, but earnestly protested:

Not true! Badly scared, that commander and his soldiers maybe saw ghost Indians in the woods. They were brave when killing women and children, crushing newborn babies' heads while in the mothers' arms. Shooting men who had no guns! Afraid of armed warriors, they lay too close in dirtholes to know when we left!

---

[15] Of the casualties suffered by the Nez Perces, Colonel Gibbon in his official report states: "Captain Comba, who had charge of our burial party, reports eighty-three dead Indians found on the field, and six more dead warriors were found in a ravine some distance from the battle-field after the command left there." ("Report of the General of the Army," 1877.)

Wounded Head, a participating warrior, tallied on his buffalo drinking horn the number of his tribesmen killed; his figures were: ten women, twenty-one children, and thirty-two men, a total of sixty-three in all. Yellow Wolf remarked, "There were not as many killed as reported by the whites, and Wounded Head could make correct number, knowing the Indians so well as he did."

Duncan McDonald informed the writer that during his visit to Sitting Bull's camp in the summer of 1878, Chief White Bird with stick tally made the number killed at the Big Hole eighty-seven. Doubtless the correct count would fall somewhere between the foregoing enumerations.

Shields (op. cit., p. 101) states that Joseph "is said to have admitted that 208 of his people were killed in the Big Hole fight." Likewise, Colonel J. B. Catlin, commander of the volunteers, specifies unqualifiedly: "Chief Joseph admitted the loss of two hundred and eight warriors [sic] killed in the battle, so there were a larger number of Indians killed than of white men engaged." (Society of Montana Pioneers. Historian's Annual Report, p. 14.) It need only be pointed out that the Nez Perces did not muster one half of 208 "warriors" or fighting men.

No Nez Perces were there after those good-by morning shots. We were not there to see the new soldiers you say came. They must have arrived after we followed the camp. In all the war, General Howard never came where we could see him.

✳　✳　✳

APPENDIX I

Chief Peopeo Tholekt says of the death of Sarpsis Ilppilp, his partner in arms on that day:

"My partner and I were about eighteen steps apart. A soldier shot him after I had left him at the little barricade we called our fort. I thought we had got the last soldier in a certain trench, but we must have left one. Sarpsis wore a close-fitting wampum necklace of five strands. The upper strand was cut by the bullet that killed him. He spoke after being struck, 'I am done! I will not live!' "

Red Elk adds the following confirmation:

"Sarpsis was killed near the enemy trench. Killed the forenoon— this brave young man. His brother [first cousin], Tipyahlanah, tried to bring his body away. But he was shot in the side of the hip, and had to drop him."

Penahwenonmi (Helping Another), an elderly woman who passed through the rigors of the war, speaking on the subject of warrior immunity to bullets, declared:

"There were seven Nez Perces whose bodies from shoulders down were bulletproof. All were killed by shots in the neck. One of these warriors was Sarpsis Ilppilp, son of Chief Yellow Bull, killed in the battle of the Big Hole. A strand of the wampum necklace he wore was cut by the bullet that killed him. One of these men who received bullets on his body showed black spots the size of a dime."

Two Moons also held faith in this immunity against enemy bullets. He tells how he saw Sarpsis Ilppilp and two companions, Wahlitits and Strong Eagle, ride the battle line at White Bird Canyon without incurring any injury from the shots rained upon them by the soldiers. On another occasion, he said, Sarpsis loosened his belt and permitted several bullets, some of them misshapen as if they had hit an impenetrable surface, to fall to the ground. His red flannel shirt showed perforations, but no bullet had broken the skin.

YELLOW WOLF:
His Own Story

❊

CHAPTER 12

From the Big Hole to Camas Meadows

Yellow Wolf has told how, before starting over the Lolo Trail, rules regulating a peaceable and law-abiding passage through all the country beyond the mountains were proclaimed by the chiefs.

Prior to the Big Hole battle, there was but a solitary violation of these rules, wherein a negligible amount of foodstuff—mostly flour and dairy products—was taken from a vacated ranch house. But horses of greater value, first branded by the rancher's own iron, were left in the corral as pay.

It was not until after the shambles ordered by Gibbon that the warriors indulged in retaliatory raids of killings and plunder. But in none of these can it be said that there were victims other than adult men who might well be regarded as enemies. By the code of war the destruction of property, as depicted in this chapter, was legitimate, as was also the purloining by the playful warriors of General Howard's pack mules. Yellow Wolf concludes the chapter with his account of the battle of Camas Meadows (Idaho), on August 20, 1877, after which the Nez Perces moved on to Yellowstone Park, followed at a considerable distance by the outmaneuvered soldiers.

THAT ended the Big Hole battle—a hard, desperate fight. Had some of the chiefs not thought all war ended for sure at Lolo peace treaty, we would not have been caught as we were. Looking Glass made us believe we were safe.

After bidding those soldiers a rifle "Good-by," we left, following on the trail of the families. Riding hard, we overtook them that same morning at their first camp from the battle. But some had already left, and others were packed to start.

The name of this camp place is Takseen [Willows].

The people had been a long half-sun reaching there. Could not travel too fast with some bad wounded on travois. They had gone scattering from the Big Hole.

At this camp died Aihits Palojami [Fair Land], wife of Ollokot. Died of wounds, leaving a boy baby.[1] Of course she was buried secretly.

We now kept moving for three suns, watching always for horses. While we had many horses, it was good to have fresh ones. Best, too, that none be left for soldiers. It was aimed that no horses could be found by soldiers anywhere we passed.

We took many horses at places I do not know by white names. Some fighting and a few white people killed where horses were captured.[2] Of course citizens did not like to lose their horses, many of them good horses.

It was during this time, the second sun from the Big Hole, that what I now tell you took place. Came morning, and the families moved, a guard of warriors following at a distance in the rear. I held far back of the guard, to be a scout, a lookout, for pursuing enemies. It was a

---

[1] This was the older of Ollokot's two wives. The orphaned infant was cared for by relatives throughout the remaining retreat, and through the long, sickening years of exile. The lad appears to have been the solitary infant to survive the deadly malarial plague. He later died on the Colville Indian Reservation at the age of about sixteen. He took his father's earlier name, Tewetakis, an old name of uncertain meaning.

[2] The principal killing was at the Montague-Winter ranch, now owned by the Brenner Live Stock Company, some twenty-five miles from Bannock City. The Brenner dwelling is built on the identical spot where the Montague-Winter house stood, in which W. L. Montague and William Flynn were killed. William Smith and William Farnsworth were shot to death while fleeing with three others on a wagon they were loading with hay in a near-by field. The bodies were found next day unscalped and unpilfered; Montague's purse, containing two hundred dollars, was still in his pocket. The dead were covered with blankets. (See *Progressive Men of Montana*, p. 1609.)

It is claimed that the Nez Perces were only seeking bandage material for their wounded, and had this request been complied with, probably no fight would have occurred. Mr. Charles Brenner writes me that M. S. Herr, one of the hay haulers who escaped, was authority for the report that Flynn was an impetuous, hot-tempered man, who loaded a double-barreled shotgun with buckshot, and declared that he would "settle the d——d Injuns" if they put in an appearance. Whether the first shot was fired by Flynn is conjectural, but the gun lay on the floor with its owner's lifeless body, both barrels showing that they had been but recently discharged. The table and chairs were overturned, and the bloody imprint of a hand showed clear around the room walls. All fabrics that could be used for bandages had been carried away.

sure fact that in those times I was as a watching eye, missing nothing that was danger.

All the people knew what I could do. That I could smell white people, the soldiers, a long distance away. I would then tell the boys: "Get ready your arms!" My guardian Spirit instructed that I scout mostly alone.

As I now look back, I was lucky to come through that great war. I thought that I might die in a war somehow, but not by the bullet. I knew from the promise given, no gun would ever kill me. I am now getting old, and I think that I will die from sickness sometime. But I am still well and in good condition.

It was just mid-sun when I mounted my horse and followed after the camp. None of the enemies had appeared coming on our last sun's trail. Alone, I loped along, not too fast! I watched everywhere. If antelope acted curious, it might be danger. If prairie birds flew up in distance, it might be buffaloes stampeding, getting away from something—maybe soldiers!

I looked ahead about a quarter mile. Something must be there? I checked my horse to a trot, then to a walk. I took a good look. The sun pictured something against a big rock. I thought it must be the shadow of a man. I did not stop my horse, but I made a strong look.

Yes—a white man!

I did not act differently—did not show surprise. I looked another way and turned my horse slightly. Watching me, that shadow-man saw and raised up from his hiding. *Eeh!* Eight of them! They began firing at me. I was on good ground, and ran my horse at his fastest. I did not return their fire. Too far to shoot with horse running. Quartering away, I thought to save my cartridges. I did not look back what they were doing.

I laughed at those men. Eight white men—maybe citizen scouts—waiting for one Indian to ride close and be killed. That shadow was not a lie.[3]

Those white men did not follow me. They were afoot. The warriors had gathered up all their horses.

It was dark when I reached camp. I reported to the chiefs what I had seen, what I knew. If soldiers following, they were far behind.

I walked through part of the camp. Some people had lain down, others were fixing blankets for sleeping. One woman lay on a buffalo robe, moaning, with many around her. Badly shot through the stomach at the last battle. They told me she could not live. Next morning the woman on the robe was dead.

We continued traveling. During this time a train of eight wagons was captured. I was back as a scout but came up as camp was being made. Those wagons formed three teams, drawn by mules and horses. Loaded with different kinds of goods, and lots of whisky. That whisky was mostly in barrels. That whisky was soon opened up. Some Indians got bottles and rode away; but many began getting drunk there at the wagons. In the meantime three of the white men were killed in a fight.[4]

---

[3] This exploit Yellow Wolf described with stolid satisfaction. The safety of the moving camp depended greatly on the ability and alertness of the rear guard. That the keen-eyed warrior at such a distance could, by the mere contour of a shadow cast by the sun against a cliff or rock, determine the lurker to be a white man and thus escape the ambush has, perhaps, no parallel in Indian annals.

His would-be interceptors were doubtless citizen volunteers, a community guard, for the settlers and mountain rovers were armed and aggressive wherever the patriots passed. They could not have been General Howard's advance scouts, for never during the entire pursuit was he within forty-eight hours of the Nez Perce rear save once, and that proved most disastrous to him, as will be seen.

[4] This was the destruction of a freight wagon train on Birch Creek, Idaho, which can well be regarded as an aftermath of the Big Hole. Mr. Phillip Rand, of Salmon, Idaho, writes me in part:

"The outfit was in charge of its owners, Albert Green with one wagon and a trailer drawn by eight horses; Jim Hayden and Dan Combes with two wagons and a trailer each, drawn by sixteen mule team each, all handled by 'jerk line.' The train was loaded with merchandise, clothing, groceries, general merchandise and whiskey; consigned to George L. Shoup & Company, Salmon, Idaho. Two Chinamen, 'Old Dr. Charley' and companion, and two, possibly three outside whites. One of these, a Mr. Loynes escaped, and the Chinamen turned loose, carried news

Two Chinamen with the wagons were not hurt. They cried, and were left to go see their grandmother [Yellow Wolf here evinced unusual amusement]!

The Indians were getting bad. Ketalkpoosmin called out:

"If soldiers come they will kill us all!"

He and all the sober warriors were then appointed by the chiefs to spill the whisky on the ground. Peopeo Tholekt was one who helped, and I, Yellow Wolf, helped.

Two drunk Indians shot at each other, one getting head grazed by bullet. Itsiyiyi Opseen [Coyote with Flints] stabbed Heyoom Pishkish, an oversized man later known by whites as Lame John, under right arm. Heyoom did not grunt, did not lie down. He had a strong Power and became well.

Ketalkpoosmin was shot by Pahka Alyanakt [Five Snows (Years)], who was mad drunk. Of course, drinking Indians did not want the whisky spilled. Ketalkpoosmin after two, maybe three, suns' travel, was left at camp to die. He asked to be left. He could not hold to life. A good warrior, he had much in capturing the cannon-gun at Big Hole fight. Pahka Alyanakt was killed at last battle.

It was about the tenth sun from Big Hole that a report came. Perhaps ten o'clock in the morning, and camp had not broken. We heard the shouting, "Soldiers close! Soldiers right upon us!"

Then came call from the chiefs, "Come, all you warriors!"

When the warriors gathered, the chiefs gave order, "Get horses!"

of the disaster to the Lemhi settlement. The wagons, harness and what goods that were not carried away, were burned. All of the team animals were added to the Indian herd."

Horses ready, the chiefs said, "We are going to meet the soldiers! All warriors will go!"

A scout came riding and reported, "Soldiers making camp!"

The chiefs now made arrangements to arrive at the soldier camp in darkness of after part of night. Warriors now staked their horses to graze, while scouts closely watched the soldiers.

After sundown, and darkness growing, we started, riding slow. The chiefs said, "If we get to where the soldiers have stopped, and it is afterpart of night, we will take their horses."

We traveled slowly. No talking loud, no smoking. The match must not be seen. We went a good distance and then divided into two parties—one on each side the creek. I was on right side of this creek, called Wewaltolklit Pah. Its name is because it flows some distance, and then drysinks—disappears. I do not know the white men's name for this creek. It is not large.

Chiefs Ollokot and Toohoolhoolzote were the outstanding leaders of my company. These men were always in lead of every fight. Teeweeyownah and Espowyes led the other company. Brave men with swiftest horses were always at the front in war movements.

We rode on through the night darkness. Before reaching the soldier camp, all stopped, and the leaders held council. How make attack? The older men did this planning. Some wanted to leave the horses and enter the soldier camp afoot. Chief Looking Glass and others thought the horses must not be left out. This last plan was chosen—to go mounted.

Chief Joseph was not along.

Then we went. It was not yet daylight when we ran

into soldiers. They must have been the guard soldiers. I heard a white man's voice call, "Who are you there?"

Then a gun sounded back of us.[5] It was one of the guards who called, and after that first gun, we fired at where the voice came from. Then we heard guard-soldiers speaking, calling to their headman. Some were crying. They ran, and one voice called loudly for them to come back to their guns. But those guard-soldiers did not mind him.

"Where were the guns of those soldiers who were standing on guard?" I interposed.

Their guns were stacked.

"You did not really hear the soldiers crying, did you?" I asked.

I heard them cry like babies. They were bad scared.

The soldier camp was alarmed. The bugle sounded quickly. The warriors were yelling and shooting fast. They had circled the soldiers' horses, stampeding them. The soldiers were now also firing in every direction. Some young men had gone in to cut loose the horses tied, and I, Yellow Wolf, was one of them. I found three horses staked on long ropes. I cut them loose. At this time the Indians were driving the horse herd rapidly away. I could see no Indians. Mounting, I followed silently as I could with my three captured horses. When I got out from the soldier camp, I turned the horses free. Lashing them, I fired my six-shooter, yelling loud. Frightened, those horses soon ran into the herd the Indians were driving. We kept going, did not stop.

[5] This shot was fired by the irascible Otskai, whose incentive is best defined by Yellow Wolf's explanation in Chapter 10 that "at times his head did not act right." Chief Peopeo Tholekt, who was in the raid, declared, in reference to the incident, "Otskai was always doing something like that." The only comment which this premature gun report elicited from the silently moving cavalcade was the low spoken protest: "Ise tanin kenek kun nawas kunya tim onina padkuta? (Who in hell fire that gun?)" Interpreter Williams is doubtful about such language being used by any Indian in that band. While Yellow Wolf did not state the strength of the raiding party, other reliable Indian informants placed the number at twenty-eight warriors.

After traveling a little way, driving our captured horses, sun broke. We could begin to see our prize. Getting more light, we looked. *Eeh!* Nothing but mules —all mules! Only my three horses among them. I did not know, did not understand why the Indians could not know the mules. Why they did not get the cavalry horses. That was the object the chiefs had in mind—why the raid was made. The place where we took General Howard's mules is called Kamisnim Takin [Camas Meadows].

We looked back. Soldiers were coming! Some footrunning, others mounted. Then we divided our company. Some went ahead with the mules; others of us waited for the soldiers. Then we fought, shooting from anywhere we found hiding. A few warriors made a flank move, and from a low hill did good shooting. Peopeo Tholekt was one of those flankers. Soon those soldiers ran for a bunch of small timber not far away. They went fast. It was then we crept close and shot whenever we saw a soldier. What I saw of soldiers falling, I do not know. Earlier in the fight, a soldier with a bugle was shot from his horse at foot of a small bluff and killed.[6] Indians were on that bluff, protected behind rocks. It was a sharp fight for some time. After a while I heard the warriors calling to each other, "Chiefs say do no more fighting!"

Then we quit the fight. Of dead soldiers I saw I know not how many.[7] No Indian was bad hurt, only one or

---

[6] The soldier with the bugle was Bernard A. Brooks, of Jackson's company, First Cavalry, Major George B. Sanford, battalion commander. Brooks was buried amid the sagebrush near the rocky butte where he fell. For a touching tribute to him, see Colonel J. W. Redington's "Story of Bugler Brooks," in Brady, *op. cit.*, pp. 198-202.

[7] General Howard gives the casualties suffered by his troops engaged in this fight at Camas Meadows as one killed and one wounded of the enlisted men of the First Cavalry. ("Report of the General of the Army," 1877, p. 130.) Captain R. Norwood, commanding officer of a troop of the Second Cavalry in Colonel Gibbon's military zone—which practically bore the brunt of the engagement—gives his loss as seven wounded, two of them mortally. (*Idem*, p. 573.) Sergeant H. J.

two just grazed by bullets. We followed after the mule herd to camp. When we all reached there, the Indians made for those mules. Some took two or three, others took three or five.[8] I did not know how many mules we got. All were kept for packing and riding, but the warriors did not ride them.

General Howard could not take those mules from us.

We stayed the rest of that sun and all night at the same camp. Not until next morning did we move to another place. Scouts watching General Howard, we kept moving every day. The soldiers did not hurry to follow us. They slowed after losing their pack mules.

Davis, of Norwood's company, in his graphic description, "The Battle of Camas Meadows," names eight men who were wounded, two of them fatally. (Brady, op. cit., pp. 196-97.) Doubtless it was these wounded whom Yellow Wolf seemingly mistook for killed.

[8] Owhi, the Yakima, in his manuscript war story, speaks of the distribution of the captured mules according to the needs of the various families. Of his own case, he says:

"I didn't have any family and didn't have very much to pack, so they gave me two mules. They thought much of me in those days because I was a good fighter."

Into Yellowstone National Park

Perhaps no phase of the Nez Perce retreat drew such wide attention as did their passage through the Yellowstone National Park during the last week of August, 1877. Their contact with the tourists was unprecedented, as was also the scare thrown into Army circles because of the fears that General Sherman, who was "doing" the Park, stood in grave danger of receiving a chance call from the warrior outriders.

It is an egregious error to contend, as some historians have done, that the Nez Perces became badly bewildered in the Park. They had entered it over a trail with which they were not too familiar, knowing only that it was a shorter route to the region for which they were heading. Scouts could have determined the correct trail, but at a cost of valued time. The capture of a qualified and willing prospector solved their problem. During this period General Howard's forces were lagging far in the rear.

IT WAS, I think, twelve suns from the Big Hole that we camped on the southwest side of a fine lake [Henrys Lake]. Camped for about one sun. Then we went through a gap [Targhee Pass] into the Yellowstone Park. We did not follow the usual Nez Perce trail. We traveled over a hunting trail instead.

We were troubled about direction for a short half-sun, but soon found the right way. No help from Crow Indians![1] No help from anybody but one white man. He acted as guide once. It was like this:

One noon camp while the families were getting ready to go, I took my horse and went ahead quite a way—five,

---

[1] In regard to alleged aid given by the Crows to the Nez Perces, see Note 9 of following chapter.

maybe six, miles. The sun was about there [four to five
P. M.]. I heard someone coming behind me. I looked
back. It was my brother [cousin] Otskai. I told him, "I
am glad you have come."

We traveled on. We heard chopping. Maybe it was
soldiers? We went there where we heard the chopping.
It was a white man doing cooking. We went up to him,
one on each side, in back of him. We grabbed him! He
was armed but did not offer fight. Otskai understood a
little English and talked with him. We stayed there quite
a while, and then a lot of Indians came—just to be
friendly with him.

We did not want to do him harm. Only if he had
horses or things needed, we might take them for ourselves. One warrior, supposed to be bad, came up. He
was Teeweeyownah [Over Point of Hill]. He asked,
"Can any one talk to him?"

They found Heinmot Tosinlikt. Henry Tabador was
another name he had.[2] A half blood, he was bad, but
could interpret. This white man was asked if he knew
the way to the head of Yellowstone Park, toward the
Crow Indian lands about Elk Water, as the Crows call
it. He said he did and would go with us. Said his horses
were lost, and he was on hunt for them. The warrior told
him he would give him a horse to ride, and that it would
be a gift for him to return on.

Then I said to my brother, Otskai, "Take him down
to the chiefs. They will make him tell about this trail,
where this trail will take us." Then I left.

The Indians were partly lost for a short time. Not sure
of their way. This man who was oldlike, this white
prisoner, was all the guiding they had. Showed them for

---

[2] For sketch of Henry Tabador, see Appendix C, end of volume.

half of one sun. He was kept for a few suns, but we did not try holding him longer.

In meantime I kept going. I did not tell anyone where I was going. It was to watch ahead, and this half blood, Henry Tabador, overtook me. He asked where I was going. I told him I was watching for more white men, and he said, "I will go with you."

We did not go far until a horse was heard coming behind us. Another fellow came up. He was Tiskusia Kowiakowia. He asked where we were going, and Tabador said, "Heinmot Hihhih is out looking for white men. I am going with him."

Tiskusia Kowiakowia said he would go, and he came with us. Soon another young fellow, Towassis [Bowstring] overtook us. He was followed by Nosnakuhet Moxmox [Yellow Long Nose]. We now were five, and the four said to me, "You are supposed to be our leader."

We rode on, always watching for enemies. We went up a meadow, and our scouting took us to a swampy place about three miles long. The sun had gone down, and darkness was coming on. I told the men we were going to stay there all night. They already were staking their horses. I was going to stake mine when one of them said, "Let me stake your horse. I will do that for you."

He took my horse, and as I turned back, I saw a light at some distance, a small light. I called the others to come. Pointing, I said, "Look that way!"

Nosnakuhet Moxmox said, "That is fire burning!"

"Yes," I answered. "It may be soldiers or other white people. We will go see why it is."

But one boy thought different. He warned, "We better not go there. It is a swampy place. Our horses might mire down, for we cannot see good."

I replied, "We will lie right here till morning. Then we are going to have a fight with them."

All agreeing, we took our blankets, but built no fire. No fire when scouting. I did not know if they meant true when they answered, "All right," to what I said about fighting. Some of them were afraid, I was sure. Only two, Tabador and Towassis, were brave. The others were not fighters. I knew not why they had come with me.

Early, at breaking light, I awoke the boys. All got ready. We saddled horses and rode on a swift gallop along a draw. It was quite a ways to where we had seen the light.

When we got there, we saw four persons lying close to the fire. Then we saw two more not so close, and a little apart was a small tent.[3] These people were not soldiers, but all white people seemed our enemies. We talked what to do with them. I said we would kill them. But the half blood, Heinmot Tosinlikt, said, "No! We will capture them. Take them to the chiefs. Whatever they say will go."

Then some of us, not all, went close to the fire. Two boys stayed back. The white men were getting up. Henry, our interpreter, told them we would not hurt them. The leader was a fine looking man. He shook hands with us. He asked, "Who is the leader of this bunch? I see five of you."

Heinmot Tosinlikt pointed to me. He said, "There is our leader!"

---

[3] This was the Carpenter-Cowan tourist party. For a vivid description of the whole affair by one of the captives see Guie and McWhorter, *Adventures in Geyser Land*—a reprint, with annotations, of Frank Carpenter's *Wonders of Geyser Land*, originally published in 1878.

Because I shook hands with him put me in mind not to kill him. He looked at me and said, "I am going to ask you. Why you come here? I hear a little about you."

I answered by the interpreter, "Yes, I am one of the warriors."

Then these white men got afraid. The leader asked, "Would you kill us?"

"They are double-minded," I told him.

It was hard work, this talking to the white man. Not understanding many words of his language made hard work. At the end he asked, "Can we see the Chief Joseph? Will you take us to him?"

"Yes, but some boys are very bad," I told him. "They might kill you." That is what I told the good-looking white man. I wanted to be a friend to him.[4]

Then he said, "Will the chiefs do anything to us?"

I answered, "I guess not."

"All right," said the white man. "We want to see Chief Joseph. We will go." That was the white man's answer.

I stepped to the tent doorway. I threw back the flap. A white man was standing there. He spoke. What he said, I did not understand. Two women had been in the tent, but they had run away.[5] The white man called

---

[4] Yellow Wolf was reluctant to conduct this "good-looking" white man to the Nez Perce forces. "They are double-minded" was an allusion to the marked diversity of temperament found among his compatriots, and the uncertainty of the safety of the white people in their power. His own fidelity of friendship had been pledged in the earlier handclasp. Although his intention of shielding them was endangered by the insistence of the white man that they be conducted to the chiefs, racial courtesy demanded that this request be granted.

At this point in the recital the small group of contemporary warriors present conversed together earnestly, lamenting the tragic sequel of the occurrence. They attributed it all to the ill-timed insistence of the white leader that he meet Chief Joseph in person. The interpreter explained, "These warriors all know how it was. Those white men wanted to see the chiefs. Should they see Joseph, he was a good man. If they should see White Bird, his band might kill them."

[5] Yellow Wolf later related that the presence of the women, Mrs. George F. Cowan and Miss Ida Carpenter, sisters was not discovered by the Indians until a few minutes before the camp was ready to move. Mrs. Cowan, the last survivor of the historic tourist party, died at her home in Spokane, Washington, December 20, 1938.

them, but they did not answer. Six times he called, then the two women, one smaller than the other, came from the brush.

While we were there, the leading white man gave us sugar, flour, and two good pieces of bacon. The food made our hearts friendly. Heinmot Tosinlikt said, "Take it. I will put it on my horse and pack it for us."

But the white man from the tent showed mad. He said something to the leader, who then stopped giving the food.

The white men harnessed their team and saddled their horses. They had eight head, and I saw one good roan among them. Two men and the women rode on the wagon, the other men rode horseback. When they were ready, we mounted our horses. We took the lead, white people following.

Whatever now happened to their lives, I could not help. I did not tell them go see the chiefs. It was their own mind—their own work—that they were going. They heard me say the Indians were double-minded in what they can do.[6]

At last, after we traveled part of that sun, I heard a great noise ahead of us. The other Indians had seen us. Not the chiefs, only the warriors. Quickly they made for us. The warriors mixed us up. They did not listen to anybody. Mad, those warriors took the white people from us. Going on, I saw them no more for a time. But I saw their wagon where left by the trail. When we camped for noon, I saw those prisoners. They were all alive. Wattes Kunnin [Earth Blanket] was first to grab the good roan horse.

---

[6] Yellow Wolf's version of this episode, up to this point, has already been published in Guie and McWhorter, *op. cit.*, pp. 275-80.

After dinner the chiefs called, "We will move! All get ready!"

Those nine [there were ten] prisoners the warriors bothered. The chiefs took the two women away from them. One was full grown, the other young and small. Both good looking. I saw everybody making to travel. Soon all were ready, some already gone. I did not see the white people at this time, but heard they were being treated right. Then, soon, I heard some gun reports.

It was the bad boys killing some of the white men.

But one they did not kill, and two escaped into the brush.

When asked why they were shot, Yellow Wolf replied:

Some ran into the brush. It was for trying to escape.[7]

The man Otskai and I captured the day before was on ahead as guide. He knew the trail. The other man and two women came on with the families.

That night camp was made late. There was some rain, but not hard. Next morning we traveled on, and at noon the chiefs said, "We will camp." Place of this camp was Koos Kapwelwen [Swift Water], which joins the Yellowstone River. At this camp I saw the chiefs turn loose the young man and the two women, the three together. The chiefs had agreed and said, "We free these white people to go home."

The women were given horses, the man was made to go afoot. They must not travel too fast. Food was given

---

[7] This sudden attempt to escape meant to the Indian mind that, if it were successful, news of the location of their camp would immediately be relayed to General Howard's forces. This was an evil particularly to be guarded against, inasmuch as they were uncertain of their bearings at this time. None of the tourists were killed, as Yellow Wolf thought, and Cowan alone was seriously wounded. It was he who had incurred the displeasure of the warriors not only by his marked animosity towards them, but also by his refusal to let further food be distributed to them.

for their living while going to some town or wherever they lived.

We did not want to kill those women. Ten of our women had been killed at the Big Hole, and many others wounded. But the Indians did not think of that at all. We let them go without hurt to find their own people. The man captured by Otskai and me, the one who had guided the families, went later. None of them were hurt. Only those who tried to escape.

There were two other small scouting bands in the Yellowstone Park country besides mine. One was headed by Kosooyeen, the other by Lakochets Kunnin. I do not know which of these made attack on some hunters or visitors, but I have heard they killed one man. Each party did scouting every sun.

It was a few suns after the chiefs turned the white man and women loose that what I am telling you happened. It was coming towards sundown when we saw a white man standing in the doorway of a house. We stopped not far from him but did not dismount. We sat on our horses, six or seven of us, thinking. Chuslum Hahlap Kanoot [Naked-footed Bull] said to me, "My two young brothers and next younger brother were not warriors. They and a sister were killed at Big Hole. It was just like this man did that killing of my brothers and sister. He is nothing but a killer to become a soldier sometime. We are going to kill him now. I am a man! I am going to shoot him! When I fire, you shoot after me."

Chuslum Hahlap Kanoot then fired and clipped his arm. As he made to run, another warrior, Yettahtapnat Alwum [Shooting Thunder] shot him through the belly.[8]

_____

[8] This occurrence was at McCartney's cabin, and the man killed was Richard Dietrich, a German music teacher from Helena, Montana. He was a member of a

At this point I interposed, "You know General Scott? He was a lieutenant in the Seventh Cavalry at that time, and says that with ten men he chased eighteen of you Nez Perces so closely that he recovered nineteen head of horses abandoned by you, which you had stolen. In that chasing he found the man you killed at the house while the body was yet warm."

Yellow Wolf smiled gimly as he replied:

Those soldiers did not let us know they were chasing us. We would have been glad to see them! Only six, maybe seven in our band. We had no captured horses.

We rode into the woods looking for anybody getting away. Finding no one, we decided to remain concealed there until after dark. When came the dusk, we went back to the house, all going inside but two men. With matches we looked around, taking arms or anything wanted. Soon somebody outside called, "Soldiers attacking us!"

All ran out as crazy. I was last to get out the door. My horse near by was rearing on the rope. I could not get him loose, I jerked up my gun and fired twice toward the soldiers. I heard horsefeet to my left. Hemene Moxmox, my uncle, called to me, "My son, do not lose your head. Have clear mind. Do not miss any of them. Shoot straight!"

I heard another noise coming. I glanced that way, and saw Watyahtsakon. The three of us made for those soldiers. I went around the house where lots of willows grew. The soldiers went through those willows. One was wounded on a white horse. He and Watyahtsakon both drew up their guns. The Indian beat him, and he fell from his horse. This warrior was a great hero with a

---

tourist party which met with rough handling by one of the other two groups of Nez Perce outriders scouring the Park. Second Lieutenant Hugh Lenox Scott found a white man lying dead at McCartney's door, "not yet cold." He had apparently "been shot a second time after falling on his face . . . the bullet going the length of his body." (Scott, *Some Memories of a Soldier*, p. 62.)

strong Power. Nobody could get him. I do not know if the soldier was killed. We found his gun and ammunition. The horse we did not get.[9]

We chased the soldiers, or whoever they were, into the brush. My uncle said we would not go in after them. They might be too many for the few of us.

We now started for home. But I thought to get horses from white men where I knew. The others did not agree to this. A little council was held, and they said, "No! We are all alive after the fight. We better go home. Not try taking any horses."

I did not listen. I went back toward where some white men were staying. I did not hurry. Just breaking day, I started the horses, bunched together, the way I wanted to go. I saw about five or six white men in the house watching me from the windows. When they saw the horses going, they fired two or three times. The guns scared the four horses I was driving, and they ran away. There were two bays, one buckskin, and a roan. The gun reports helped me get away with their own horses.

I was glad to take four horses from six men. I looked back and saw there were no more horses. They could not follow me.

Driving my captured horses, I started over a hill to-

---

[9] Chroniclers in general do not speak of any clash between the military and the Nez Perces at this time, but evidence is not lacking that such a skirmish took place. We read in General Howard's report:

"My scouts brought me intelligence of depredations, burning, and murdering done by foraging parties of the enemy, one of which, probably not more than ten in number, had recrossed the Yellowstone at Barronett's bridge, descended the river on the left bank for twenty miles to the vicinity of Mammoth Springs, where they burned a store, killed a citizen, had a slight skirmish with Lieutenant Doan, and then returned, murdering another citizen *en route*, and, after recrossing the bridge, burned the stringers sufficiently to render it impassable. They had recrossed this bridge just before our arrival." ("Report of the General of the Army," 1877, p. 621.)

Yellow Wolf throughout vehemently declared that there was no bridge across the Yellowstone that he ever saw, much less crossed. Nor did he know anything about various other chronicled episodes, such as the attack on Goff, Leonard, and a young Warm Springs Indian, scouts for Colonel Sturgis, in which they all lost their horses. Goff and the Indian boy were wounded. The boy disappeared and was never found. Later both Goff and Leonard were killed. (Scott, *op. cit.*, p. 64.)

ward the river. In time I overtook my friends. They had camped where I left them and were riding slowly, holding back for me. About one-fourth mile off we saw a bunch of Indians breaking camp. They were Crows and Bannacks, packing up to leave. Scared of us, they were hurrying fast to get away. We did not try catching up with those coward Indians.

In the distance were several horsemen approaching, bringing many horses. We had no glass. Some boys thought they were soldiers. But I knew differently. The wind was from them, and I could smell. I said, "No! I know our people. No soldiers there."

It was true. Our camp was on the move. No enemy in sight, but in wartime we are like children—afraid of the whip!

We halted and when the camp came up, the others of our party fell in. All soon passed over a small hill.

I remained behind. Obeying my Spirit Power, I watched for any pursuing enemies. I saw none, and reached camp soon after dark.

YELLOW WOLF:
His Own Story

✿

CHAPTER 14

The Canyon Creek Fight

Having proceeded about one hundred miles after leaving Yellowstone Park, the Nez Perces again crossed the Yellowstone River. There, on September 13, 1877, occurred the "battle" of Canyon Creek— derided by the Nez Perces as no more than a skirmish, for Colonel Samuel D. Sturgis with six companies of the Seventh Cavalry, numbering "about three hundred and sixty men," reinforced by Lieutenant Otis "with two mountain howitzers on pack mules," and by "about fifty of Sanford's cavalry" under command of Captain Bandire, of the First Cavalry, signally failed in an attempt to stay the flight of the Nez Perce cavalcade. ("Report of the General of the Army," 1877, pp. 507-11.)

The usual assertions that topographic hindrances excuse Colonel Sturgis' failure to halt the Nez Perces is decidedly open to question. Certainly no just conception of Canyon Creek can be formed from the military accounts. The canyon itself is far from being a narrow, rock-walled gorge. On the contrary, its lower reaches comprise a broad, open country of no mean extent, and the trail leading to its very head, though among rolling hills, is nowhere cramped and winding among cliffs or disjoined boulders.

In the latter part of the chapter Yellow Wolf shows how bewildered and resentful the Nez Perces were to discover that their supposed friends, the Crow Indians, were aligned with General Howard.

MORNING came, and soon the families were on the move. After starting, one of the chiefs told some of us to go ahead about one sun to see if soldiers were in the way. All knew General Howard was good distance behind. No danger there, so a few of us went ahead as the chief ordered. We traveled, keeping a strong lookout for

181

enemies. None were seen. No signs discovered, and night drawing on, camp was made.

Next morning early, we were riding. More must be seen of what was in that wild country. Our party was slightly scattered. Soon we saw it—a fire! Just a short distance, and we started to go there. Then he was seen— a man—leading a buckskin horse. He saw us, and sprang to his saddle. A tall fellow, wearing a buckskin suit. He went! After him came another man, leading a gray horse. He, too, jumped on his horse and went; but he proved a fearless man.

The fellow on the buckskin was shot and fell to the ground. The man on the gray ran swiftly ahead. Otskai and I went after him. I had a fast horse, and soon Otskai said to me, "My horse is giving out. Go on, brother! Grab that fellow's neck! Jerk him off his horse!"

I kept running my horse to his best. But just beyond my reach, this fellow jumped to the ground. His horse knocked him over, and I, going fast, passed him a few steps. I was off my horse as the man regained his feet. We both drew up rifles and fired. I did not know if I hit him. His bullet glanced my head, shaving through my hair. I was brought to my knees, blinded. Nearly knocked out, but did not know I was hit. I was partly out of sense. The enemy was trying to work his gun when Otskai killed him.[1] Then was seen why his gun would not work. The hammer had been knocked off by a bullet—my bullet, for the other warriors were a good distance away. Had this not been done, he must have killed some of us. He was a brave man.

I know not why the big rifleshot did not go through

---

[1] These two scouts were prospectors hired by Colonel Sturgis, because of their intimate knowledge of that wild, mountainous region.

my head. It only put me out of sense a short time. It must have been some help saved me from death. But no bullet was to kill me.

When I came back to sense, I heard Heinmot Tosinlikt say, "That other white fellow is not dead!"

We both went down to him, and Heinmot said, "I am going to finish him!"

I told him, "Do not do that! His wound is bad. He will soon die. It is not good to waste ammunition."

There was no more fighting that sun.

I guess maybe the soldiers heard our shots. They came afterward—not that sun—but missed us. We had gone down the creek while they came along the hillside. That is why they found that wounded fellow. He had not died.

In the meantime, we had gone up the hill. Looking around, we saw their camp. We saw them taking that wounded fellow back, traveling along the hillside. We could see the Crows and the Bannacks together. All bunches going back to camp. We did not make ourselves seen to the enemy.

That night we stayed close to the main families' camp, guarding during all the darkness.

Next morning all soldiers went north over the hill, not seeing us. We saw five citizen men start back with the wounded fellow toward the Crow Indian Agency. We watched and followed them. It was about noon, when they stopped for food, that we charged them. But they saw us coming, and the five men mounted and skipped for their lives. They might have escaped from us, for they had good start in the race. But other Indians were crossing below. They were the ones to head them off. Siyikowkown [Lying in Water] shot one fellow from his horse; the bullet cracking his head. It was Otskai again to do the finishing.

The other four men got away. Of course, that first wounded fellow on the travois was killed after the four men escaped. It was Peetomyanon Teemenah [Hawk Heart] who killed him. Every white man in those mountains could be counted our enemy.

We had no more fighting that sun.

Three suns after I was scalp-wounded, there came a close call for my life. I went for my horses and while letting them drink, I sat down on the creek bank. Scouting and night guarding, I must have gone a little asleep. I must not have been full awake when I heard, as dreaming, "Look out for *hohots!* Look out for *hohots!*"

Still I was sleeping. I did not understand with good sense. I heard again, away off like dreaming. "Look out for *hohots! Hohots* coming close to you!"

I was partly awake now. I turned my head where was a noise. *Eeh!* I saw it—a big *hohots* [grizzly bear]. My rifle was in my hand. I sprang up as I threw back the hammer. That *hohots* made for me, a bad sound coming from his mouth. As he stood up, I held my rifle ready. That bear came stepping to the muzzle of my gun. Just touched it when I pulled the trigger. He fell, and I finished him with my war club. Struck him on the ear.

You ask if I was afraid? No, I was not scared. The bear had no gun. Did my heart travel fast after it was all over? [Laughing] No! I could not save myself by running. I must hold my ground. Must stand face to face with that *hohots*. After I had killed him, why, I thought about it. I had been close to death.

From fighting the grizzly, I drove my horses and that night camped with the families. Next morning everybody got their horses ready. They packed up. I saddled my horse. I was to go one way, alone. I traveled only a little distance when I saw a blanket signal.

I understood that warning. It meant, "Soldiers coming close!"

I ran my horse to where the blanket was calling. When I reached that warrior who was riding in short circles, I saw soldiers near, and across the valley from us.

The traveling camp had nearly been surprised. Soldiers afoot—hundreds of them.[2] I whipped my horse to his best, getting away from that danger. No more warriors to signal, the blanket waver also left. His signal had been mostly for me.

But we did not go together from there. We had our warrior ways. We did not line up like soldiers. We went by ones, just here and there, entering the canyon.

I came to one place at the mouth of the canyon. Only one warrior there doing the fighting. His horse hidden, he was behind rocks, holding a line of dismounted soldiers back.[3] He was shooting regularly, not too fast. As I approached, he called to me, "My boy, run back from here! Soldiers too close. They might kill you. Do not stay here with your horse!"

When I heard those words spoken, I knew the voice. I was convinced that this brave warrior, Teeto Hoonnod,

---

[2] The soldiers Yellow Wolf saw afoot were dismounted troopers on deploy. Doubtless it was visions of the White Bird Canyon and of the Big Hole fiascos that prompted Colonel Sturgis to order the dismounting and the formation of foot troops in a battle line in the rear of the fleeing Nez Perce families and their galloping horse herds.

[3] Corroboration of Teeto Hoonnod's singlehanded exploit is found in J. W. Redington's manuscript, "Scouting in Montana":

"One Indian behind a point of rocks held them [the troops] back for ten minutes, and when the point was taken, I counted forty empty shells on the ground where he had crouched. And they were all government cartridges he had been firing at us."

Teeto Hoonnod, a forty-year-old warrior of Chief Joseph's band, was noted for his courage and strategic ability. He was conspicuous for his fleet-footed bobtailed charger. Immediately after Yellow Wolf's departure, he was joined by Swan Necklace (John Minthon), whose name is already familiar. These two held their position until the families and the horse herd were safely within the sheltering walls of Canyon Creek. Teeto Hoonnod was later killed by the Assiniboins.

was right. I was drawing the soldiers' fire. I made no answer, but turned my horse from there. Only a few jumps, when I noticed my saddle cinch dangerously loose. Saddle slipping back on my horse. I stopped and got off. There was a big noise in my head. I did not hear anything separate. It was the sound of many guns all roaring at once.

I did not turn, I did not look around anywhere! I was fixing tight my cinch. I knew not how close the soldiers were approaching. When I had fixed my saddle, I mounted. I turned my horse and went. Then I looked back. Soldiers still lined up moving forward slowly. Must be fifty of them I could still see. I was not scared because of their shots. I remembered the promise that bullets would never kill me. I made escape from those soldiers and came to where the warriors were protecting the families as they drove the horse herd into the canyon.

Other soldiers horseback, like cavalry, were off to one side. Away ahead of the walking soldiers. They tried to get the women and children. But some warriors, not many, were too quick. Firing from a bluff, they killed and crippled a few of them, turning them back.[4]

In the fighting here a little later, some soldiers got on higher ground. Firing down, they killed two horses and wounded Silooyelam in the left ankle.[5] Two other men were wounded but not at this time. They were Eeahlokoon, shot through the right leg below the knee, flesh wound. The other warrior, Elaskolatat [Animal Entering

---

[4] Yellow Wolf's reference is to Captain Benteen's unsuccessful battalion charge, which, in attempting a flanking movement, fell into an ambuscade. Benteen's men suffered most of the casualties, for Colonel Sturgis' battle line was retained well beyond the range of the Nez Perce rifles.

[5] According to Yellow Wolf and other warriors, these were the only losses sustained. It would appear from Brady, however, that casualties among the Indians at this point amounted to a veritable shambles—considering numbers engaged (*op. cit.*, p. 218). Elsewhere (p. 34) Brady gives the number of Indians killed as twenty-one, with nine hundred ponies captured!

a Hole], was hit from the rear. Bullet entered left hip and came out front left thigh.[6]

We stayed hidden among the rocks and timber. Watching the soldiers who soon went into camp. Then we left for home, barricading the upper canyon as we went.[7] It was after dark when we reached camp. Staking our horses, we had supper, then lay down to sleep.

Next morning the families moved early. We were on Elk River, and some of us stayed back to watch the enemies. I looked one way and saw strange Indians. I looked good! Then I thought, "They must be either Walk-round Sioux or Snakes. I will go see."

I rode closer. *Eeh!* Crows! A new tribe fighting Chief Joseph. Many snows the Crows had been our friends. But now, like the Bitterroot Salish, turned enemies.

My heart was just like fire.

Chief Ollokot, my uncle, was not far away. He dismounted and I, too, got down from my horse. We both fought from the ground. In short time, Ollokot sprang up, leaped on his horse and galloped away. He hurried with others to drive back Crows now fixing to flank the moving families.

Left alone, Crow Indians tried to surround me. To cut me off from all my people. I was not afraid. I brought myself to be brave. I mounted my horse and went. I did not hurry. Just loped along. I paid no attention to the enemies. Distant soldiers and nearer Crows were firing at me.

I looked back. Two Indians were overtaking me. One

---

[6] Elaskolatat was sent to the Indian Territory after the surrender, but escaped afoot with two other men and two women. "Borrowing" horses at night, they reached Idaho mounted. Elaskolatat died in Idaho about 1929.

[7] "Did the Indians tell you how completely blocked they left the trail up the canyon? It was so choked with rocks, trees and brush that any attempt on our part to have followed them by a night march would have resulted in disaster," wrote Theodore W. Goldin, of Captain Benteen's company, Seventh Cavalry, in a letter to the author.

came as close as that [twelve feet], riding hard. We both fired at same time. It was just like one gun. He missed me, and I did not know if I hit him. As I whirled my horse the better to fight, both Indians rode swiftly away. I thought I must have wounded him.

I now brought my horse facing another way. Other Crows were firing at me as they raced past at a distance. They could not hit me from horseback.

I dismounted to do better shooting. Then came both Crow and Snake Indians. There must have been a hundred.[8] They rode, hanging low on side of horses, doing underneck shooting. They got my right thigh—a hidegraze.

Then I took shots lying flat on the ground, but it was hard to hit fast running horses at distance. A bullet struck my saddle. One went through top of my horse's neck, just within his mane. He went sort of wild. I was holding him with rope around his jaw.

Then I thought: "If my horse is killed, they will get me sure!" I was up! Springing to the saddle, I went rapidly away. Those Crows and Snakes did not follow me.

In order to bring out the Nez Perce reply to the charge that the Crows double-crossed the Government forces by giving secret aid to the enemy, I interposed, "General Howard claimed that the Crows helped you to get out of that country by directing you which way to go."[9] Yellow Wolf's reply was emphatic:

Not true! The Crows fought us. They killed one warrior and two old, unarmed men. They did not act as

---

[8] The number of Crow Indians has been estimated at from fifty to two hundred. The Indians that Yellow Wolf saw were of General Howard's Bannack and Shoshoni scouts.

[9] General Howard, chagrined that the Nez Perces had so adroitly eluded him and Colonel Sturgis in the Canyon Creek region when the two commanders thought they had been trapped, sought balm for his wounded pride by attributing the enemy's escape to the aid of some "treacherous" and "wily" Crow Indians. This claim does not hold under candid scrutiny. The Nez Perces received no assistance from any part of the Crow nation. For General Howard's contention see his *Nez Perce Joseph*, p. 255, and his *My Life and Experiences Among Our Hostile Indians*, p. 295.

guides for us. We had men who knew the country, who scouted far ahead all the time. They found each day the way to go.

"History states," I added, "that the Crows only wanted your horses, and that they cut out about three hundred from your herd and drove them back to their reservation." To this, Yellow Wolf replied:

I never heard that story before. If they took horses, it was those we left along the trail. Too lame with sick [tender] feet to travel fast as we were going. We lost maybe thirty or forty horses not too lame. I know not if anybody got them, or if just lost.

Some Crows told Chief Looking Glass not to travel too fast. Said they would join and help us. But Looking Glass paid no attention. He now knew they were against us. He knew the Crows were lying, that they wanted the soldiers to catch up with us. Although they had been helped in battle,[10] we all knew not to trust the Crows.

Leaving those Indians, I overtook some Nez Perce warriors far back of the moving families. They then knew I was alive. Not killed as they had thought. I joined with these warriors who were acting as guards. They must fight off enemy Indians, also pursuing soldiers, should they overtake us. But when I rode among them, my horse would not be still. Kept stepping about, pawing and plunging. He made a great dust. Chuslum Hihhih [White Bull] got mad and began whipping my

---

[10] Yellow Wolf was alluding to the battle at the mouth of Prior Creek, Montana, a tributary of the Yellowstone. It was fought in July, 1874, between the Crows and the Sioux, and Chief Looking Glass and his followers took an effective part with the Crows. The Sioux were badly worsted. See Thomas B. Marquis, *Memoirs of a White Crow Indian*, pp. 84-94. Tributes of respect to the Nez Perces, especially to Chief Looking Glass, in token of their aid, are found on pp. 97, 98, 128, and 129. Thomas H. Leforge, the "White Crow," did himself honor when he refused to serve as scout against the Nez Perces, his tribe's most faithful allies.

The supposition that the Crow warriors were not earnestly arrayed against the Nez Perces is belied by the frenzied war dance which they staged upon entering Colonel Sturgis' camp the night following the Canyon Creek fight, as pictured by Trooper T. W. Goldin, of the Seventh Cavalry, in a letter to the author. Doubtless the incentive for their treachery was chiefly the hope of loot.

horse. A brother of Charley Moses ordered Chuslum to stop with the whip. He said: "You see the horse has been shot?" My uncle, then noticing the wound, said to me, "Do not stay here. You better go to camp."

I believed him and went. I tried to catch the moving families, but it grew dark before I got halfway. I became lost! My wounded horse made poor travel at night.

After two days without eating, I thought to camp. Nobody to be seen anywhere, I looked for a good camping place. There was a great row of rocks—what you call a "slide." You could see farthest from its top. I went there, lay down watching. I could hear—could see all around—everywhere. No blanket, but must not build fire.

I had left my saddle with my uncle. My wounded horse might go down on me, and I did not want to lose my saddle. With saddle and its blanket, camping not bad, but I was just as I had stripped for the fighting.

Came about sunrise. I was looking away off. Watching what might be seen as light grew wider. I happened to drop my eyes. *Eeh!* It was there—a *takialakin!* What you call antelope. I shot that *takialakin*, killed it!

I sat down and turned towards the west. As far as I could see to a rising ground, was an Indian. Of course that Indian had heard the gun report and was coming straight to me. I did not know the kind of Indian. Maybe a Flathead, Snake, Crow, or Sioux. That would be good. I would kill that Indian! He was coming fast, about as far away as that tepee [600 yards]. Then I recognized him. He was of our tribe, my cousin Hekkik Takkawkaäkon [Charging Hawk]. He came up and said: "I was little afraid to come to you. What you shoot?"

"I killed *takialakin!*" I answered.

"That is good! Come my friend, we will now start fire and have roast meat breakfast," was what he told me.

We soon had a fire and roasted all the meat we wanted. When done eating, I said to him, "Where is the camp? I was lost last night."

"You are off from the place," he told me. "Off about half-hour ride away. West of here. What made you go this way?"

"I have wounded horse. It got dark. I could not see direction I was traveling," I told him.

"We will go now," he said, and I got on my horse. We went, carrying the rest of meat with us. My cousin now asked me, "Were you cold last night?"

"No!" That was my answer. "I had company. I had blanket over me. Of course I was not freezing last night."

When I said that, the warrior laughed. He replied, "You are telling the truth!"

Mystified, I inquired of interpreter Hart what Yellow Wolf meant by saying he had a blanket over him, when he was really practically naked and had no covering. Evincing amusement, Hart replied: "Why, Yellow Wolf was mad! His heart was big and sweatin' with mad! That kept him warm."

"Could he sleep under such conditions?" I asked.

"Yes, he says he slept. Night is for the sleeping."

Hekkik Takkawkaäkon, now my partner, knew where the people were, and we went there. We came first among the women who had the camp packed ready to move. The Crows were watching to attack the horse herd and my partner hurried away to help the warriors on guard.

I saw the women were scared at the Crows and the Snakes, with all the best warriors off guarding the horse herd. It came to me strong, how General Howard took many different tribes to help him in the war. I thought this wrong! But of those Indians on his side I was not afraid. When we met them they ran from us. General Howard's warriors were afraid. Only when we were moving would they come after us. I was told later that two hundred Indians helped the soldiers at that time.

A bunch of Bannack Indians, and maybe some Crows, came closer to the women. This bothered them. I had not time to change my wounded horse. That horse could run strong though shot in top his neck. Teeweeyownah [Over the Point] joined me and we rode for those Bannacks. But his horse, a racer and not trained for battle, ran away with him. We were both then alone. When I drew near those Bannacks, they jumped from their slower horses and ran to hiding. I got from my horse and took one of theirs. Then I took another horse. They did not fire at me from the bushes. I did not follow after them. I had horses and rode back to camp. Left the enemies afoot. These Bannacks, I understood later, were of General Howard's scouts.

We were two, but I have told you how my partner's horse ran away with him. After I took those horses, I heard a shot—several shots—off about half a mile, in the direction he went. Then my partner's horse came running by me. I thought, "They have killed him!"

It was true! I do not know which killed him, Bannacks or Crows. He was the only Nez Perce warrior killed in all the Canyon Creek and trail fighting. I do not know if he killed any of the enemies. He was brave and strong, but the Crows were too many. With a trained horse he would not have been killed.[11]

---

[11] Chief White Hawk verified Yellow Wolf's story with the following remark: "Teeweeyownah was my brother-in-law. A fine-looking man about middle age, he

I do not think any Crows or Bannacks were killed. They were many and we only a few. Our warriors could not chase far to fight them. The moving families must be guarded.

No soldiers were seen in this running fight. They must have been back where the yesterday's fight was, burying one another.[12] I could not tell how many Bannacks. They kept too far away. No more came close to trouble the women after we chased them.

At this point I asked the narrator if he thought General Howard wanted his Indians to attack women and children. He answered vehemently in the affirmative.

I am telling you, my friend! It is so, what I have seen, what I have done. They are facts, my words! I do not want anything not true.

I do not like the lie. If I lie, I will know it when I come to my death. I am telling you what I tell all the people at our celebrations."[13] General Howard had those Bannacks, those Crows, to come against us.

Two old men—not warriors—were killed by the

---

was sort of commander in the war. He rode a high-spirited horse which ran away with him, was how he got killed." Doubtless Teeweeyownah was the warrior that Trooper T. W. Goldin writes (December 4, 1934) of seeing lifeless on the barren mesa, as Colonel Sturgis' command limped in hopeless pursuit of the main Nez Perce band:

"... some time after working our way through the blockaded canyon, and reaching the rolling mesa leading off towards the Missouri River many miles away, I, with a bunch of flankers riding to the right of our advance, came upon the body of a dead Indian, a Nez Perce, we decided. He was not stripped, and I do not think he had been scalped, although I am not quite clear on this point. He was a warrior I should say something over five feet six tall. All arms had been taken by the Crows, we supposed, and the body lying there on the open mesa, was already stiffening when we found it. The weather was cold."

[12] Notwithstanding the fact that Colonel Sturgis' hunger-famished troops and their footsore mounts were hopelessly in the rear at the time that the Nez Perces were having these encounters with the Crows and other Government Indian scouts, the Colonel is credited by General Howard with having participated in a "running fight with them for over 20 miles." ("Report of the General of the Army," 1877, p. 624.)

[13] In tribal gatherings where deeds of personal prowess are recited, it is the custom for anyone who may be acquainted with the facts to correct innocent mistakes or false statements on the part of the narrator. In this way the "Iagos" are discouraged, and oral histories are kept nearer the facts. As a race, the Indians are strong for witnesses, and the writer has known aged warriors of creditable reputations for veracity to be deterred from recounting their early exploits simply beecause of a dearth of corroborative testimony. In my various interviews, no Nez Perce ever talked alone if it were possible to have one or more of his companions in arms present.

Crows. Tookleiks [Fish Trap], and Wetyetmas Hapima [Surrounded Goose] became separated from the families and were caught by the once friendly Crows. Tookleiks turned back looking for a missing horse, and was seen no more. Maybe Wetyetmas Hapima was on like business. I do not know. Both were too old to do fighting. General Howard's Indians killed all our old people they found. The two were not killed by soldiers. No soldiers caught up with us from where we left them at Canyon Creek.

None of the three were buried. We had no time, no chance to do the burying. The killed were too far scattered.

I do not understand how the Crows could think to help the soldiers. They were fighting against their best friends! Some Nez Perces in our band had helped them whip the Sioux who came against them only a few snows before. This was why Chief Looking Glass had advised going to the Crows, to the buffalo country. He thought Crows would help us, if there was more fighting.

YELLOW WOLF:
His Own Story

✪

CHAPTER 15

Northward Across the Missouri

The troops under Colonel Sturgis having been left *hors de combat* following the Canyon Creek engagement, the Nez Perce cavalcade proceeded almost unmolested in a general northerly direction up through Montana, heading toward the Canadian border. On September 23 the Indians reached the south bank of the Missouri River at Cow Island Landing, 120 miles east of Fort Benton. This was the head of navigation during low water in the fall, where all steamboat freight was landed, thence to be bull-trained to the Montana settlements and the frontier posts of Canada. On the north bank Major Guido Ilges had half a dozen soldiers, and perhaps a cannon, from the Seventh Infantry from Fort Shaw.

As Yellow Wolf relates in this chapter, the soldiers tried to stand off the Indians but were forced to retire quickly in the face of such a large force. In this region, where straggling whites might be expected, Yellow Wolf was changed from his previous position as rear guard to that of advance guard. That his warrior companions had great confidence in his ability to deal, singlehanded, with the enemy is brought out in a subsequent episode.

NEXT morning after this last fight with General Howard's Bannack Indian scouts, we moved camp early. For five suns we moved, meeting only little trouble. The Crow tribe was left far behind. It came morning of that fifth night, and the families made packs for moving.

There is a little story. I have said that I was scout to keep watch on the back trail. But this sun I was sent early ahead of the families. I took the lead. I brought myself to be a scout. In the fore part of the morning I ran onto a band of *heyets*, the mountain sheep, the bighorn. I thought to kill one of them. My rifle was swung in case alongside my saddle. I drew the gun, but before I got it clear, it went off. My horse was shot through hind leg. Not broken, but bad flesh wound.

I was half a sun ahead of other Indians. I threw my saddle down for them to pick up, and went on afoot. It was toward evening. I came to a small creek. I heard a horse nicker. It was not too far to a small, open place. I saw four white men. I thought, "I will go to them!"

I started, and one said not to come. I did not understand very well, but I knew he wanted me to stop. I did not mind him. I kept on, and those four men grabbed their guns. I jerked my rifle up, but not fast enough. They all fired. I was shot right across the left arm.[1] I nearly dropped my gun! I yelled, and went after them. One made toward me, and I shot him. I know not which fired first, but he missed me. I was too mad to know where the bullet struck him. The three of them ran. They ran fast, and about sixty steps away I downed one. The two went into the brush, and I hurried to the four staked horses.[2]

I led those horses to where they had a tent. It was about five o'clock. I said to myself, "Where will I find my food?" Then I found it.

I thought of my horses. These white men had a saddle, and I put a packsaddle on one horse. There was a sack and a half of flour. I packed up and went on. I did not know where the other Indians were. I was just going any way.

---

[1] This was another skin-graze, a "bullet burn," painful but not of a serious nature. It was his fifth and last wound of the war.

[2] Before relating the foregoing episode, Yellow Wolf paused and conferred earnestly for a few minutes with the interpreter. Later it was explained that he hesitated to tell of his difficulty with the white men, thinking it unimportant to the main story. Also he feared that even at this late date it might get him into trouble, despite the fact that the white men, so he reasoned, were the aggressors, since the first hostile demonstration came from them.

It grew dark. I was taking all the horses and traveling was slow. About nine o'clock I heard Indians shouting. I said to myself, "Now I am getting to my friends alive!"

I answered them and when I got to camp, my mother gave me some food. They then asked me, "Where have you been?"

"On ahead!"

When I answered that, they told me, "You lie down and rest."

I lay down with my blanket on a buffalo robe and slept until morning. We ate breakfast, and my uncle asked me, "Where you get your horses?"

"Four white men made war on me," I answered.

"Were you afraid?"

"No! The whites are just like those little flies. Sometimes they light on your hand. You can kill them!"

"The gun is danger?"

"No! I think they have those play guns. Just like children."

"Not soldiers? Not scouts?"

When he asked me that I answered, "No, just citizen dress. All was easy for me."

Yellow Wolf laughed softly at the recollection, and when asked why he wanted to go to the white men when they told him not to do so, he answered quickly:

All white men were spies. Enemies to be killed. Those four white men with horses would quickly have brought soldiers. Furthermore, I will tell you. Those men spoke war when they drew their guns. I understood that meaning.

We moved on. It was the sixth sun from fighting the Crows and Bannacks when we came to a large river. Its

197

name at the crossing we struck is Seloselo Wejanwais, a kind of colored paint. There were a few buildings there. The chiefs said, "We will cross this river!"

We were just waiting for one another, for all the families to come up. I heard the voice of a man talking. I understood soldiers were camped across the river. It was the only place to ford. The water was deep elsewhere.

Each of the five chiefs called to his own men. When through with this, they all came together. There were not as many as a hundred warriors. We thought those soldiers might shoot at us crossing, so about twenty warriors went first. The others remained close to the river shore, where we would have more chance to return their fire. But there were no shots, so the rest of the warriors started across to the soldiers' side. Of course I did not remain behind. I heard some Indians say, "If the soldiers do not fire on us, we will do no shooting."

We reached an island.[3] We could not see the soldiers. We went a good way and got on shore. The pack outfit came across, the whole train and the horse herd. To let all this and the families pass, the warriors stopped a short distance from the soldiers. One chief instructed me to take the families about two miles and make camp. It was near one hour from sunset. No tepee poles, camp making was not hard for the women. While this was doing, I heard one man say, "Some warriors now riding towards the soldiers."

I hurried to join in the fight. I heard the guns popping. The fighting had started. I soon reached there. The soldiers had a bank protection. We could not get to them and, darkness falling, we slowed up firing.[4]

---

[3] This was Cow Island Landing, about halfway between Fort Benton and Fort Peck, Montana.

[4] The war records contain only a casual reference to the occurrences attending

No warrior was killed. Only one, Husis Owyeen [Wounded Head], had his scalp cut by bullet-splintered wood. In Big Hole battle his head was bullet-glanced, which gave him his good name. He was a brave warrior.[5]

The soldiers had everything fixed up. I saw food piled high as this house [one story] where the steamboats landed. Lots of other goods as well.

Before night came, we took food as wanted. Each family took maybe two sacks flour, one sack rice, one sack beans, plenty coffee, sugar, hardtack. Some took bacon. Everything to eat.

All this we captured from the soldiers. We did not starve that sun, that night. Whoever wanted them, took pans, cooking pots, cups, buckets. Women all helped themselves. When everybody had what they wanted, some bad boys set fire to the remaining. It was a big fire!

We warriors stayed there all night, watching and exchanging shots with the soldiers. The chiefs who made rulings were at camp. They said, "Let's quit! Soldiers are under bank. We can do nothing. Nobody killed and we have plenty of food."

A man was sent who told us what the chiefs said. The older warriors got together and minded the order. We turned from those soldiers, ending the shooting. It had been nearly like play.[6]

the Nez Perce crossing at Cow Island. They give no adequate description of buildings or quarters for the small guard detailed from the Seventh Infantry, which, at the time, states Major Guido Ilges, consisted of twelve enlisted men from Company B, and four citizens; two of the latter and "several Indians" being wounded in the engagement lasting "18 hours." ("Report of the General of the Army," 1877, p. 557.)

[5] A tribal warrior and buffalo hunter, Wounded Head was reckoned a fierce though cautious fighter. When relating his story of the war to me in 1908, he made no mention of his wounding in the Cow Island crossing episode, but his companions in arms speak of it. Possibly he deemed it of no moment. Of the White Bird contingent, he never surrendered. Escaping from the Bear's Paw Mountain battlefield, he fled to Sitting Bull's camp in Canada. In time he drifted back to the Nez Perce Reservation in Idaho, where he died on the Clearwater River below Spalding, in 1912.

[6] Brady, Northwestern Fights and Fighters, pp. 34-35, speaks of a wagon train

When I reached camp, my pack was already done up. The families and warriors were leaving, and I changed horses. I was staying behind. One hour passed, but those soldiers did not go anywhere.

My horse was loose-saddled. I waited about another hour, keeping good lookout. Then tightening the saddle cinch, I mounted and followed after the camp. It must have been three miles I went. Coming to a narrow canyon, I looked ahead and saw that the wagon road crossed a creek. Then I thought I saw signs of a man. I pretended not to see anything. I got down to fix my stirrup. It needed no fixing. I only played working at it. But all the time I watched the spot where the man-sign had moved.

Then I saw a white face peering out of the brush. In maybe five minutes another face came in sight. Then two more. Yes, they were looking toward me. After taking a good look, I knew. They were white men waiting. Four white men waiting to shoot one Indian riding by!

There was but that one way. I could not go around them. I took my heart and said, "I must take this road!" Approaching the enemies, I still kept as if I had seen nothing. My stirrup fixed, I made my mind what to do. I thought how to get by those men.

Mounting, I walked my horse in a circle. I bent over as if looking for lost horse tracks. In the meantime I rolled one blanket-cloth legging below the knee. I tied

destroyed by Chief Joseph at Cow Island Landing, and of a freight depot of good size, and a small "fort" which the whites defended with the loss of three of its garrison of twelve men and a sergeant. He also says that a troop of the Seventh "Cavalry," conveyed by a river steamer, collided with Joseph, but retreated after sustaining light casualties. When Colonel Redington's attention was called to the foregoing from Brady, he wrote (February 7, 1935):

"As stated, we arrived at the landing after that great stack of freight had been looted and destroyed. If there had been any sheds or building there, they were all burned up. If there had been a wagon or bull train there, it was all burned up. And, there was certainly no fort in sight.

"Major Ilges could not have had a Seventh Cavalry troop. He belonged to Gibbon's Seventh Infantry, at Fort Shaw."

it strong and fast. Then I turned my horse to circle a different way while I rolled and tied the other legging. Of course, the enemies did not see what I was doing, working from blind side of horse.

Rolling the leggings was a custom I always followed when going into battle. I will not have clothing on my body. No leggings, no shirt, only the breechcloth, moccasins, and feathers, or whatever I happen to have with me for obtaining power in battle. For this reason did I strip down for the enemies.

I kept my rifle ready but still pretended I knew not of danger. Heading my horse the right way, I kicked him with my heel. Trained, he sprang to a swift gallop down toward the brush-hidden enemies. I passed from their sight a short moment. *Eeh!* There *was* another way—a small trail. I sent my horse up a sandy place where this trail led. I reached the top—not far—and looked down. I saw those men holding ready to shoot. Waiting for me! I was not coming their way. Had some of them been at the gulch, they would have caught me sure. They must not have known the leading-off trail. Maybe they were just scouts watching the wagon road?

I laughed while circling away.

When I got abreast of them, one looked up and saw me. He pointed and all began firing. But I was now about a quarter mile away. They could not hit me. I did not return their fire. I did not stop. I waved my rifle a "Good-by," and just kept loping along. They did not try following me.

I now hurried along to report what I had seen. I came up with rear warrior guards about noon. They told me, "We thought you would be killed! We left some white men horseless back there."

"No! I am alive," I told them. "It was not dangerous passing those men. Had they not looked around when I was so far away, had they lain low, they would have got me. They showed themselves hiding to shoot me."

The warriors laughed. I did not know until then those white men had been placed afoot by our warriors taking their horses. It stopped them carrying to the soldiers news where to find us.

It was early afternoon when we came to a wagon train hauled by many ox teams. The Indians charged. Three white men were killed, and several got away. Then the warriors went for those wagons. They were loaded with supplies—must have been for stores somewhere. There was lots of whisky. But before Indians got at it, soldiers appeared. Not too close, but approaching, and wagons were set afire. There was some shooting, but no Indian was hurt. We thought we killed one or two soldiers. Those soldiers stopped before getting very near us.[7] No oxen were killed. We traveled on a ways, and made early night camp.

---

[7] Major Ilges, of the Seventh Infantry, in his official report of this occurrence, stated that two of the teamsters were killed, while the remainder (seven) escaped to the hills. Major Ilges' force consisted of but thirty-six mounted volunteers, and he wisely refrained from attacking the raiders of the wagon train. In the ensuing long-distance skirmish he lost one man and one horse killed. "The Indians lost two in wounded," Major Ilges stated. ("Report of the General of the Army," 1877, p. 557.)

YELLOW WOLF:
His Own Story

⊗

CHAPTER 16

Forty-eight Hours from Freedom

After Colonel Sturgis' failure to hold the Nez Perces at Canyon Creek on September 13, General Howard had sent to Colonel Nelson A. Miles, Commander of the District of the Yellowstone, then at Tongue River Cantonment in eastern Montana, a courier dispatch, which the latter received on September 17, in part as follows:

"The Indians are reported going . . . straight toward the Musselshell. . . . I earnestly request you to make every effort in your power to prevent the escape of this hostile band, and at least hold them in check until I can overtake them." ("Report of the General of the Army," 1877, p. 73.)

Thus, while the Nez Perce cavalcade, burdened with women and children, was forging slowly ahead to the Canadian border, Miles hastened by forced marches diagonally northwestward—crossing the Missouri on a steamboat—and arrived in the Bearpaw Mountains at the same time as the fleeing Indians.

Miles's force consisted of a medley of the Second and Seventh Cavalry, the Fifth Infantry, mounted, and some thirty Sioux and Cheyenne warriors—the aggregate number being revealed in Miles's vivid depiction of the charge on the Indian camp, where he says: "The tramp of at least six hundred horses over the prairie fairly shook the ground."

When, therefore, the Nez Perce patriots pitched camp on September 29 by Snake Creek near the Bearpaw Mountains, it marked the end of the trail for them. The leaders, and many others of the Nez Perces, well knew their location, knew that two suns' travel should place them in safety. But Lean Elk (Poker Joe), who counseled haste, had been deprived of leadership. Upon Chief Looking Glass's dilatory policy, as at the Big Hole disaster, must be laid the blame for the events which Yellow Wolf narrates in this chapter. It is noticeable, however, that Yellow Wolf exhibits no animus in his bare statement of facts.

203

IT WAS early dawn next morning when two men left camp to scout ahead. Started long before the families had packs ready to go. It was cold, and a storm looked gathering. I remained after all had gone—after the rear guards had gone—to watch back on the trail. During that day I saw no white man.

But those two warriors scouting ahead, after crossing the mountain, found Walk-around Sioux Indians camping. The scouts took our camp below them a short way.

There was friendly visiting that night.

Next morning [Sept. 29], not early, the camp moved. No white men were seen by scouts ahead. We guarded the back trail, but saw no signs of soldiers. We knew distance to Canadian line. Knew how long it would take to travel there. But there was no hurrying by Chief Looking Glass, leader since crossing the big river [Missouri].

About noon the families came to where camp was to be made. The scouts knew and had several buffalo killed on the campground. The name of this place is Tsanim Alikos Pah [Place of Manure Fire]. Only scarce brushwood, but buffalo chips in plenty. There are other places in Montana of same name. With horses' feet mostly sick [tender] and lots of grass, the chiefs ordered, "We camp here until tomorrow forenoon."[1]

It was afternoon when I reached camp. Of course some young warriors were out on buttes and ridges watching if enemies might be near. But we expected none. We knew General Howard was more than two suns back on our trail. It was nothing hard to keep ahead of him.

---

[1] The camp chosen by the Nez Perces was about fifty miles north of the Cow Island crossing of the Missouri River, and about forty miles southeast of the present city of Havre, Montana.

Next morning [Sept. 30], not too early, while some were still eating breakfast, two scouts came galloping from the south, from the direction we had come. As they drew near, they called loudly. "Stampeding buffaloes! Soldiers! Soldiers!"

Some families had packs partly ready and horses caught. But Chief Looking Glass, now head of camp, mounted his horse and rode around ordering, "Do not hurry! Go slow! Plenty, plenty time. Let children eat all wanted!"

This slowed the people down.

The two Indians who brought the alarm had been visiting at the Walk-around camp. Did not follow the families until next morning. Coming, they saw a herd of buffalo stampeding and knew soldiers must be near. One of these men was Tom Hill.

Because of Chief Looking Glass, we were caught.

It was about one hour later when a scout was seen coming from the same direction. He was running his horse to its best. On the highest bluff he circled about, and waved the blanket signal: "Enemies right on us! Soon the attack!"[2]

A wild stir hit the people. Great hurrying everywhere. I was still in my uncle's camp, my home. I saw this uncle, Chief Joseph, leap to the open. His voice was above all the noise as he called, "Horses! Horses! Save the horses!"

I grabbed my rifle and cartridge belts and ran with others for our horses. Warriors were hurrying to the bluffs to meet the soldiers. Soon, from the south came a noise—a rumble like stampeding buffaloes. Reaching the

---

[2] The scout who waved the blanket signal was one of a party of ten or twelve buffalo runners. They were all seen by Louis Shambow, scout for Colonel Miles. (Noyes, *In the Land of Chinook*, p. 75.) Viewing them from a distance, Shambow, alert though he was, failed to detect that the best mounted of the hunters slipped away and sped to a hilltop to give the blanket signal. This bluff has since become the site of memorial monuments.

higher ground north of our camp I looked back. Hundreds of soldiers charging in two wide, circling wings. They were surrounding our camp. I saw Sioux or Cheyenne Indians taking lead ahead of soldiers. I ran a short distance, then heard the rifle reports. I stopped. Turning, I saw soldiers firing at everybody. I could get none of the horses. All running from guns.

I grew tired, could run no more. But continuing, I walked where bullets were flying. Then I came nearer the camp. An Indian called to me he had caught one horse. Indians were not shooting much. Soldiers were firing, hurrying to corral us, to hold us in camp.

Other Indians were out among the horses, not trapped by the circling soldiers. I mounted the horse the man gave me and raced to where those Nez Perces were. Maybe we could still catch a few horses.

I saw an Indian riding a swift horse out where some women were helping catch horses. He looked to be one of General Howard's Lemhi [Bannack] scouts.[3] He was bothering those women, trying to kill them. I grew mad and went after that Indian. I could not catch him, but drove him back among the soldiers.

I well knew the Indian sign language. I can talk to all the tribes. I saw, one hundred steps away, a brave Nez Perce warrior, Heyoom Iklakit [Grizzly Bear Lying Down]. He was talking signs with the chief of General Howard's [Miles's] Cheyenne-Sioux scouts. At head of his warriors, that Cheyenne chief rode toward Heyoom Iklakit, who threw him the command, "Stop right there!

---

[3] Yellow Wolf did not at first realize that it was a new army under Colonel Miles that had struck them. But he soon discovered it, not only by the vigor of the troops, but also in the character of the strange Indians opposing them. The Lemhis are not listed as a tribe in the *Handbook of American Indians* (Bureau of American Ethnology, Washington, D. C., 1907). The Lemhis are linguistically the same as the Bannack Shoshoni; their name is purely a local one, derived from the Lemhi Valley, Idaho. The Lemhis, now practically absorbed by intermarriage, today reside on Fort Hall Reservation (Idaho).

You are helping the soldiers. You have a red skin, red blood. You must be crazy! You are fighting your friends. We are Indians. We are humans. Do not help the whites!"

The Cheyenne chief stopped as told. He answered by signs: "Do not talk more. Stop right there! I will never shoot you. I will shoot in the air. There are twenty more of us down below here."

Ending the sign talking, Heyoom Iklakit called to the Nez Perces, "He is our friend and will not shoot us. He will shoot in the air!"

All the Nez Perces knew about this. None of us believed the Cheyennes or Sioux would shoot at us.

Heyoom Iklakit left his horse and came up the canyon towards the camp to help fight the soldiers. He knew he was sure to die! The soldiers killed him about fifty steps from where he dismounted. I saw him killed.

The Cheyenne chief lied to Heyoom. He rode south about forty steps from where he had talked, and met a Nez Perce woman mounted. He caught her bridle and with his six-shooter shot and killed the woman. I saw her fall to the ground. We shot at that Cheyenne from where we were. But he was a wise Indian, and we could not hit him.[4]

We now went up toward the butte, past the soldiers who were right below us. There were about twenty of us who took position on a small ridge. We were only a little way from the soldiers. We had a fight. We stood strong in the battle. We met those soldiers bullet for bullet. We held those soldiers from advancing.

---

[4] By "wise Indian," Yellow Wolf alluded to the occult "Power" of which every Indian warrior, hunter, and medicine man is possessed—the *Wyakin* of the Nez Perces, the *Tah* of the Yakimas, etc. See "*Wyakin* Powers," end of this volume.

We drove them back.[5] One Indian was killed here and a short distance away another Nez Perce was killed.

Then we went out from that hole! We saw that same Cheyenne chief going toward our camp. He had about thirty Indians with him, and we thought he would be killing more women. We held a short council: "We will go back and save our women."

Three of us rode and headed them off. There were several soldiers back of the Cheyennes and Sioux. I was on a bad horse. One I could not manage. He ran away with me, going towards the soldiers. The Cheyennes and soldiers all ran back. The Cheyenne chief who killed the lone woman turned and ran his horse from me. This was the last time I saw him.

Here the narrator paused for a moment, and with a tinge of bitterness, remarked:

In one way I can not see why the calling of the many different tribes to help fight us.[6] We did not call help! We did not ask others to lead us in fight! The way I look at it, we did not make war with any of those tribes. Our war was with the whites. Started by General Howard at our Lapwai council. As I see it, my story can not tell

---

[5] James Snell, scout for Colonel Miles, who was in this battle, confirms Yellow Wolf's description of the "invincible twenty" when he says:

"In all my Indian career, I never was in a standing fight until I struck the Nez Perce tribe. General Miles gave me eight head of ponies and a span of mules for carrying water for the wounded soldiers when nobody else would go. Captain Snider was ordered by Miles to take a certain position and about thirty Nez Perces held this position and fought the company of soldiers from a little ridge, they being about seventy-five yards apart and forcing the soldiers back. If the Indians only knew, they had Miles defeated. . . . I never went up against anything like the Nez Perces in all my life and I have been in lots of scraps." (Noyes, *op. cit.,* pp. 114-15.)

Colonel Miles lauds Captain Snider in this exploit in a misleading manner when he says:

"At the same time the battalion of the Fifth Infantry (mounted) under Captain Snider charged forward up to the very edge of the valley in which the Indian camp was located, threw themselves upon the ground, holding the lariats of their ponies in their left hands, and opened a deadly fire with their long ranged rifles upon the enemy with telling effect. The tactics were somewhat in Indian fashion, and most effective as they presented a small target when lying or kneeling on the ground." (Miles, *Personal Recollections*, p. 271.)

[6] Ten different tribes were drawn on for scout service.

why those Indians were in the battles, why helping the soldiers. Their joining, it became not like war with whites alone. It can not seem right to me.

This battle continued all that sun, mostly around the camp. I did what I could on the outside with other warriors. But we could not charge close on the soldiers. They were too many for us. The big guns, also, the soldiers had.

A bad mistake was made by Husishusis Kute during this sun's fighting. Three brave warriors, Koyehkown, Kowwaspo, and Peopeo Ipsewahk [Lone Bird] were in a washout southeast of camp. They were too far toward the enemy line. Husishusis thought them enemy Indians and killed them all. He had a magazine rifle and was a good shot. With every shot he would say, "I got one!" or "I got him!"

Lean Elk [Poker Joe] was also killed by mistake. A Nez Perce saw him across a small canyon, mistook him for one of the enemies, and shot him.

Four good warriors killed by friends through mistake. Four brave men lost the first day.

The Last Stand: Bear's Paw Battlefield

If Colonel Miles blundered in his first and unsuccessful Balaklava-like charge of his "gallant six hundred," he did not repeat his mistake in the following days, but wisely refrained from a further attempt to storm the Indians' stronghold. He threw a cordon of soldiers around the field, however, which prevented the Indians from escaping and obliged them to entrench themselves for a siege. The extent of the defensive line of shelter pits dug by the Indians during the first night —probably enlarged and augmented in succeeding nights—is astounding and almost beyond comprehension.

In August, 1935, the writer, aided by Chief White Hawk and interpreter Many Wounds, made a historical staking of the battlefield. Even after more than fifty-five years, the traces of the fortifications were so extensive that it required several days to complete the work of staking.

Yellow Wolf in this chapter briefly sketches the preparations that were made on the night of September 30, 1877, for an indefinitely prolonged siege. He then describes the principal events of the second, third, and fourth days of the fighting. He reveals that no white flag was raised by the Nez Perces, but that three times a white flag appeared over the soldiers' encampment.

EVENING came, and the battle grew less. Darkness settled and mostly the guns died away. Only occasional shots. I went up toward our camp. I did not hurry. Soldiers guarding, sitting down, two and two. Soldiers all about the camp, so that none could escape from there. A long time I watched. It was snowing. The wind was cold! Stripped for battle, I had no blanket. I lay close to the ground, crawling nearer the guard line.

It was past middle of night when I went between

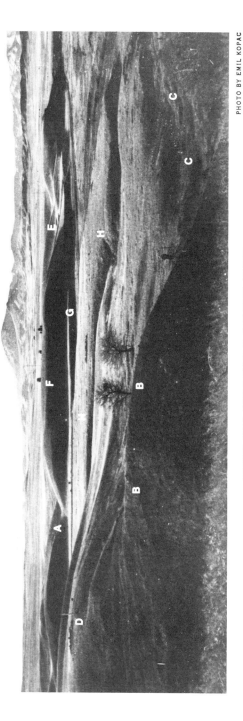

BEAR'S PAW BATTLEFIELD, LOOKING SOUTH

A, break in the bluffs through which the Nez Perces entered on their northward march. B, rifle pits along ridge. C, shelter pits in slough. D, rifle pit where Chief Looking Glass was killed. Monument placed by the Chief Joseph Memorial Association shows as a slender column at this point. E, swalelike canyon which hid General Miles's headquarters and supply train. F, summit with Government and other monumental markers commemorating the Nez Perces' surrender. (Charles A. Smith, who was with Miles's supply train, claims the surrender took place not on the summit but down in the mouth of the swale to the right.) G, line of Snake Creek. H, flat where main Nez Perce camp was pitched.

WHERE OLLOKOT FELL

View taken looking northeast. In background note Chief Joseph memorial shaft and boulder pit marked D in preceding photograph.

NEZ PERCE RIFLE PIT ON BEAR'S PAW BATTLEFIELD

Boulder-constructed rifle pit for Indian defense—Stake No. 131 in survey by McWhorter and Nez Perces, August, 1935.

those guards. I was now back within the camp circle. I went first and drank some water. I did not look for food.

On the bluffs Indians with knives were digging rifle pits. Some had those broad-bladed knives [trowel bayonets] taken from soldiers at the Big Hole. Down in the main camp women with camas hooks were digging shelter pits. All this for tomorrow's coming.

Shelter pits for the old, the women, the children.

Rifle pits for the warriors, the fighters.

You have seen hail, sometimes, leveling the grass. Indians were so leveled by the bullet hail. Most of our few warriors left from the Big Hole had been swept as leaves before the storm. Chief Ollokot, Lone Bird, and Lean Elk were gone.

Outside the camp I had seen men killed. Soldiers ten, Indians ten. That was not so bad. But now, when I saw our remaining warriors gone, my heart grew choked and heavy. Yet the warriors and no-fighting men killed were not all. I looked around.

Some were burying their dead.

A young warrior, wounded, lay on a buffalo robe dying without complaint. Children crying with cold. No fire. There could be no light. Everywhere the crying, the death wail.

My heart became fire. I joined the warriors digging rifle pits. All the rest of night we worked. Just before dawn, I went down among the shelter pits. I looked around. Children no longer crying. In deep shelter pits they were sleeping. Wrapped in a blanket, a still form lay on the buffalo robe. The young warrior was dead. I went back to my rifle pit, my blood hot for war. I felt not the cold.

Morning came, bringing the battle anew. Bullets from everywhere! A big gun throwing bursting shells. From rifle pits, warriors returned shot for shot. Wild and stormy, the cold wind was thick with snow. Air filled with smoke of powder. Flash of guns through it all. As the hidden sun traveled upward, the war did not weaken.

I felt the coming end. All for which we had suffered lost!

Frequent pauses had marked Yellow Wolf's description of the battle thus far, and at this point came a break of several minutes. With no visible emotion, warrior and interpreter sat silent, gazing toward the desert hills beyond the Nez Perce camp at the river's side. When at last Yellow Wolf resumed his story, it was in the same low, evenly modulated tone—generally tinged with sadness, but with an unusual degree of rhetoric.

Thoughts came of the Wallowa where I grew up. Of my own country when only Indians were there. Of tepees along the bending river. Of the blue, clear lake, wide meadows with horse and cattle herds. From the mountain forests, voices seemed calling. I felt as dreaming. Not my living self.

The war deepened. Grew louder with gun reports. I raised up and looked around. Everything was against us. No hope! Only bondage or death! Something screamed in my ear. A blaze flashed before me. I felt as burning! Then with rifle I stood forth, saying to my heart, "Here I will die, fighting for my people and our homes!"

Soldiers could see me. Bullets hummed by me, but I was untouched. The warriors called, "Heinmot! Come back to this pit. You will be killed!"

I did not listen. I did not know if I killed any soldiers. To do well in battle you must see what you want to shoot. You glimpse an enemy in hiding and shoot. If no more shots from there, you know you have succeeded.

I felt not afraid. Soldier rifles from shelters kept popping fast. Their big gun boomed often but not dangerous. The warriors lying close in dugout pits could not be hit. I know not why the shells never struck our rifle pits on the bluffs.

The sun drew on, and about noon the soldiers put up the white flag. The Indians said, "That is good! That means, 'Quit the war.' "

But in short minutes we could see no soldiers. Then we understood.

Soldiers quit the fight to eat dinner!

No Indian warrior thought to eat that noon. He never thinks to eat when in battle or dangerous places. But not so the soldier. Those soldiers could not stand the hunger pain. After dinner they pulled down their white flag.

That flag did not count for peace.

The fight was started again by the soldiers after stopping their hunger. There was shooting all the rest of that second sun's battle. Stronger cold, thicker snow came with darkness. No sleeping in warm tepees. No eating warm food.[1] Only at times was there shooting during the night.

It came morning, third sun of battle. The rifle shooting went on just like play. Nobody being hurt. But soon

---

[1] Cooking facilities in the beseiged camp were piteously meager. The dead brush along the creek—a variety of undersized willow—afforded scant kindling. Buffalo chips, though abundant, became buried the first night of the siege beneath a blanket of snow and were available only under cover of darkness. The women and children, sallying forth would locate the chips by feel of foot and dig them from the freezing snow. Surely their hardy racial training stood them in good stead. Any preparation of warm food, under such conditions and under the enemy guns, was necessarily negligible. One warrior was heard to say that he had had nothing to eat in five days. Nor is it to be supposed that he was alone in the voluntary fasting. Stake No. 71, Bearpaw battlefield, carried the notation, "Three shallow depressions forming a crude triangle, and a large superficial depression near-adjoining on the southeast, comprising the cooking place." This "kitchen" was located in the dry gulch dividing the campsite into two irregular parts.

Chief Looking Glass was killed. Some warriors in same pit with him saw at a distance a horseback Indian. Thinking he must be a Sioux from Sitting Bull, one pointed and called to Looking Glass: "Look! A Sioux!"

Looking Glass stepped quickly from the pit. Stood on the bluff unprotected. It must have been a sharpshooter killed him. A bullet struck his left forehead, and he fell back dead.[2]

That horseback Indian was a Nez Perce.

In the afternoon of this sun we saw the white flag again go up in the soldier camp. Then was heard a voice calling in a strange language, "General [Colonel] Miles would like to see Chief Joseph!"[3]

The chiefs held council and Chief Joseph said, "Yes, I would like to see General Miles."

Tom Hill, interpreter, went to see what General Miles wanted, to tell General Miles, "Yes, Joseph would like to see you!" After some time, we saw Tom Hill with General Miles and a few men come halfway. They stopped and Tom Hill called to Chief Joseph. Chief Joseph with two or three warriors went to meet them.

I did not go where they met. I looked around. There was a hollow place off a distance in the ground. I went there and lay down. I could see General Miles where Chief Joseph met him. I could see all plainly where they

---

[2] Mr. Charles A. Smith, who drove a six-mule team in Colonel Miles's supply train, writes in reply to an inquiry that Milan Tripp, scout, was undisputedly credited with the shot that killed Chief Looking Glass—a single bullet, directly in the left forehead. An unidentified newspaper clipping advances the theory that the chief was recognized by the reflection of a small mirror he was wearing on his forehead, and that the twelve-pound Napoleon gun was turned on him "successfully." At the rifle pit where he fell a small shrapnel was picked up by the transit man while the stake survey of the Bear's Paw field was being made in August, 1935. This find might support this latter claim, but if Looking Glass wore such an ornament, it was on gala days only. Besides, the glass could not have cast any reflection, for, from all accounts, the sun was completely obscured during the entire battle, so dense were the clouds and falling snow.

[3] This call was in Chinook jargon. (Miles, *Personal Recollections*, p. 274.) Yellow Wolf did not understand this form of speech. It was not prevalent among the Nez Perces, and only an occasional member of the war party understood it.

stood. I was saying to myself, "Whenever they shoot Chief Joseph, *I* will shoot from here!"[4]

There was talk for a while, and Chief Joseph and General Miles made peace. Some guns were given up. Then there was a trick. I saw Chief Joseph taken to the soldier camp a prisoner![5]

The white flag was pulled down!

That white flag was a lie!

The warriors came back, and right away a soldier officer [Lieutenant Lovell H. Jerome] rode into our camp. Chief Yellow Bull yelled a warning and grabbed him. I could see them take the officer to the main shelter pit. When I saw all this—Chief Joseph taken away—I ran to where the captured soldier was being held. Held that Chief Joseph might not be hurt. He had on a yellow-colored outside coat to keep off the wet. A strong-looking young man, he did not say much. Looked around, but seemed not much afraid. I do not think he was bad scared.

The chiefs instructed the warriors to guard him. Ordered: "Treat him right! He is one of the commanders."

One man, Chuslum Hihhih [White Bull] got mad at this officer and tried to get the best of him. He said, "I want to kill this soldier!"

The Indians told him, "No, we do not want you to kill him!"

Chuslum Hihhih was mean-minded, had a bad heart. He did no great fighting. Stayed behind where bullets

---

[4] This new position chosen by Yellow Wolf was in closer proximity to the peace conference and far more exposed than the strategically located rifle pit. Doubtless the peace conference was covered by other rifles.

[5] This detention of Chief Joseph by a United States Army commander was in flagrant violation of the hallowed pledge of a flag of truce. It is all the more repugnant because there is no honest statement of the occurrence in Colonel Miles's official report, dated December 27, 1877, at Fort Keogh, Montana. ("Report of the General of the Army," 1877, pp. 527-29.)

could not reach him. Espowyes, my relation, kept telling him, "Do not hurt the prisoner." Scolding, he said, "Don't you know Chief Joseph is prisoner on other side? We have this officer prisoner here on our side. When they turn Chief Joseph loose, we will turn our prisoner loose at the same time. For this we are holding him, to make the trade. We do not want to kill him. He might be headman of the soldiers. Don't you see soldiers on other side with guns? Why do you not shoot them? Not shoot one who is caught! You see all the warriors who do fighting are not mad at him. Why do you, who do little fighting, want to kill him?"

Chuslum Hihhih made no reply. He walked away.

We all thought Chief Joseph was not killed on the other side, so we let this officer soldier keep his own life. You know we were resting a little. Not after the soldiers, nor soldiers after us. We wanted to remain quiet a few moments.

Two men you already have names of, Wottolen and Yellow Bull, took good care of the prisoner officer. Night drew on, and he was given food. We gave him water and a safe place to sleep in. He was given plenty of blankets.

A buffalo robe for a bed to keep him warm. Nothing was taken from him. Guards watched his shelter pit all night. This, that he might not escape nor be hurt by mad Indians.

But we did not know how our Chief Joseph was being treated over there. He might be alive, or he might be killed.

When morning broke, we did not wake that officer. We let him sleep if he wanted. When he woke, he was brought water to wash hands and face. He was given breakfast and water to drink. As far as that [indicating two hundred feet], that officer could go if he liked. Walk there and back often as he pleased. The chiefs gave strong words that he must not be harmed.

It was about noon of the fourth sun when the officer took paper from his pocket and wrote. I know what he wrote. One Nez Perce understood English very well, and the officer said to him, "You must take my letter to the soldier chief!"

The officer read what he wrote on the paper, and when the Indian interpreted it to the chiefs, they said, "All right!"

This is what the interpreter said the paper told: "I had good supper, good bed. I had plenty of blankets. This morning I had good breakfast. I am treated like I was at home. I hope you officers are treating Chief Joseph as I am treated. I would like to see him treated as I am treated."

But Chief Joseph was not treated right. Chief Joseph was hobbled hands and feet. They took a double blanket. Soldiers rolled him in it like you roll papoose on cradle board. Chief Joseph could not use arms, could not walk about. He was put where there were mules, and not in soldier tent. That was how Chief Joseph was treated all night.[6]

When soldier officers received that letter, they took hobbles off Chief Joseph. He could then walk around a little where they let him. Those officers wrote a letter to our prisoner officer. When he read it, he said, "I have not been treated like Chief Joseph!"

The officer then read from the letter, "You come

---

[6] While Yellow Wolf gave no further account of the treatment of his chief than this, Wottolen said that Joseph's hands were cuffed behind him, and his feet drawn up and tied to the cuffs. The charge that he was rolled in a blanket and quartered with the mules appears to have gone undisputed.

across to us. When you get here, then Chief Joseph can go."

The chiefs and warriors replied to the officer, "No! If General Miles is speaking true, he will bring Chief Joseph halfway. To same ground we did that other time. It will be that, if he is speaking true words."

This letter was carried to the soldiers by the same interpreter. The soldier officers must have read it, for soon a white flag went up. Then those officers sent a letter to the Indian chiefs. It said, "Yes, we will bring Chief Joseph halfway. You bring the officer to that same place."

The chiefs said, "That is fair enough!"

Then we looked across and saw officers and Chief Joseph. They were coming to halfway ground. A buffalo robe was spread there. The chiefs and a few older warriors took our prisoner to meet them. He shook hands with Joseph and those officers. Then each party returned to its own side, Chief Joseph coming back to our camp.

The soldiers now pulled down their white flag. When the warriors saw that flag come down, they laughed. They said to each other, "Three times those soldiers lie with the white flag. We can not believe them." We younger warriors had not gone to the meeting place marked by buffalo robe.

Chief Joseph now spoke to all headmen: "I was hobbled in the soldier camp. We must fight more. The war is not quit!"

Then the fighting began again. Shot for shot whenever a soldier was seen. All that day we had the war. Those soldiers stayed at long distance. They did not try mixing us up. They did not charge against our rifle pits.

Some warriors talked to charge the soldiers and fight

it out. If we whipped them, we would be free. If we could not whip, we would all be killed, and no more trouble. But others said, "No! The soldiers are too strong. There are the big guns, the cannon guns. If we are killed, we leave women and children, old people, and many wounded. We can not charge the soldiers."

It was slowed-up fighting. Cloudy, snowy, we did not see the sun set. Full darkness coming, the fighting mostly stopped. Some shooting in darkness by soldiers, but less by Indians. The gun sounds died down as night went on.

All night we remained in those pits. The cold grew stronger. The wind was filled with snow. Only a little sleep. There might be a charge by the soldiers. The warriors watched by turns. A long night.

YELLOW WOLF:

His Own Story

✪

CHAPTER 18

The Last Day: The Surrender

It would be impossible to portray the pathos in Yellow Wolf's voice as he related the events of that cold, blustery day of October 5, 1877, when Chief Joseph, on behalf of his own band, laid down his arms.

Yellow Wolf did not attend the peace negotiations and had no part in them. His status as a warrior was not, according to tribal practices, of sufficiently long standing. The end of the trail had been reached. What could there be, he asked himself, in the promises of a commander who, under cover of a white flag of truce, had seized and held Chief Joseph prisoner? Yellow Wolf was free, by the ancient laws of his nation, to hold aloof from the surrender pact.

This was his decision, then—not to surrender!

FINALLY the fifth morning of the battle drew on, but no sun could be seen. With first light, the battle began again. It was bad that cannon guns should be turned on the shelter pits where were no fighters. Only women and children, old and wounded men in those pits. General Miles and his men handling the big gun surely knew no warriors were in that part of camp. The officer we had held prisoner well knew no fighting warriors were where he sheltered. Of course his business was to carry back all news he could spy out in our camp.

It was towards noon that a bursting shell struck and broke in a shelter pit, burying four women, a little boy, and a girl of about twelve snows. This girl, Atsipeeten, and her grandmother, Intetah, were both killed. The other three women and the boy were rescued. The two dead were left in the caved-in pit.[1]

----

[1] This pit, Stake No. 53, is located in the bank of the dry gulch near the northern extremity of the lower-level shelter-pit section. Its contour is badly

When a few Indians, mad and wild on white man's whisky, killed mean settlers on Indian lands on the Salmon River, along with one or two women and maybe one child, that was very bad.

Soldiers did not need whisky to kill a great many women and children throughout this war.

This woman and child, and Chief Looking Glass, were only ones killed in this battle after the first sun's fighting. None even wounded. All those not fighting were in the shelter pits. The warriors in rifle pits could not be seen by the soldiers. Indians are not seen in the fighting. They are hid.[2]

The fight went on, but we did not fire continually. We thought the soldiers would get tired, maybe freeze out and charge us. We wanted plenty of ammunition for them if they did.

Darkness again settled down, and only occasional shots were heard. These came mostly from soldiers, as if afraid we might slip up on them in their dugout forts.

That night, General Howard arrived with two of his scouts, men of our tribe. He did not see much fighting of this battle, and I think maybe he put it wrong in history. Towards noon next day we saw those two Indians coming with a white flag. Heard them calling and I understood. One of them said, "All my brothers, I am glad to see you alive this sun!"

Then the same bad man, Chuslum Hihhih, came and

---

defaced from the shell explosion. Owing to the loamy nature of the soil, these pits are not nearly so well preserved as those on the stony bluffs. Wetatonmi, wife of Chief Ollokot, stated that two women and a girl were killed in the pit by the shell. Perhaps a careful excavation would verify one or the other of the claims as to the number of victims, and also bring to light some fragments of the shell and other relics of the tragedy.

[2] James Smith, known as "Blockhouse" Smith, member of Captain Henniss' company of volunteers during the Yakima War, 1855-56, informed the writer of a fight near the present site of La Grande, Oregon, which lasted the greater part of a day without an Indian being seen. The volunteers were in the open, while the Indians occupied a skirt of timber.

wanted to shoot this Indian messenger from General Howard. Chuslum Hahlap Kanoot [Naked-footed Bull] took his gun from him. Another fellow said, "Let him alone! Let him kill him!"

Hahlap Kanoot asked Chuslum Hihhih, "Why are you mad? While we were warring, fighting, you lay on the ground, afraid! You are mean! I will take a whip after you!"

Chuslum Hihhih was again ordered to leave. He walked away.

The two Indians he was trying to kill, now speaking again, said, "We have traveled a long ways trying to catch you folks. We are glad to hear you want no more war, do not want to fight. We are all glad. I am glad because all my sons are glad to be alive. Not to go in battle any more." This speaker's name was Chojykies [Lazy]. He had a daughter with Chief Joseph's warriors, was why he followed us.

The other man[3] said, "We have come far from home. You now see many soldiers lying down side by side. We see Indians too, lying dead. I am glad today we are shaking hands. We are all not mad. We all think of Chief Joseph and these others as brothers. We see your sons and relations lying dead, but we are glad to shake hands with you today. I am glad to catch up with you and find my daughter, too, alive.

"You, my brothers, have your ears open to me. General Miles and Chief Joseph will make friends and not let each other go today. General Miles is honest-looking

---

[3] The first of these peace emissaries sent into the beseiged camp by General Howard was Captain John, whose tribal cognomen, Jokais (Block, or Worthless), is identified with Chojykies (Lazy). As a signer to the 1863 treaty, his name appears as "Ip-she-wish-kin (Cap. John) X." (Kappler, *Indian Affairs, Laws and Treaties*, Vol. II, p. 847.) His companion, Captain George, better known as Old George, was Meopkowit (Baby, or Know Nothing). Both of these "captains" had daughters with the war party, and their reason for accompanying General Howard's expedition had been the hope that they might persuade their daughters to return.

man. I have been with General Howard. I was afraid myself. I have been in wars and am no longer a warrior.

"Listen well what I say. I heard General Howard telling, 'When I catch Chief Joseph, I will bring him back to his own home.'

"Do not be afraid! General Miles said, 'Tell Joseph we do not have any more war!' "

Chief Joseph sent those two Indians back where they belonged. Then there was a council. Some of us said to Chief Joseph, "We are afraid if you go with General Howard he will hang you. You know how he destroyed our property, our homes."

Then Espowyes spoke, "I understand every word. If General Howard tries to take us, we will not go with him. All you farmers who had property destroyed feel bad over it. Feel bad because the whites may talk to General Howard, and he will hang us. We should get something out of our destroyed property. Get pay for our homes and lands taken from us."

We heard and believed the words of Espowyes to be true. It must be that we get some pay for our property lost and destroyed.

All feared to trust General Howard and his soldiers.

General Howard we now saw standing, calling loud to know why the Indians were not coming.

All Indians said, "General Howard does not look good. He is mean acting!"

Then came again those two Indians from the soldier camp. They carried a white flag, and General Miles had told them to say to us: "I want to speak to Chief Joseph."

I heard this message, and I heard Chief Joseph make reply, "We will have council over this. We will decide what to do!"

There was a council, and the main messenger talked this way: "Those generals said tell you: 'We will have no more fighting. Your chiefs and some of you warriors are not seeing the truth. We sent our officer to appear before your Indians—sent all our messengers to say to them, "We will have no more war!" ' "

Then our man, Chief Joseph, spoke, "You see, it is true. I did not say 'Let's quit!'

"General Miles said, 'Let's quit.'

"And now General Howard says, 'Let's quit.'

"You see, it is true enough! I did not say 'Let's quit!' "

When the warriors heard those words from Chief Joseph, they answered, "Yes, we believe you now."

So when General Miles's messengers reported back to him, the answer was, "Yes."

Then Chief Joseph and other chiefs met General Miles on halfway ground. Chief Joseph and General Miles were talking good and friendly when General Howard came speaking loud, commanding words. When General Miles saw this, he held the Indians back from him a little. He said, "I think soon General Howard will forget all this. I will take you to a place for this winter; then you can go to your old home."

Chief Joseph said, "Now we all understand these words, and we will go with General Miles. He is a head-man, and we will go with him."

General Miles spoke to Chief Joseph, "No more battles and blood! From this sun, we will have good time on both sides, your band and mine. We will have plenty time for sleep, for good rest. We will drink good water from this time on where the war is stopped."

"Same is here," General Howard said. "I will have time from now on, like you, to rest. The war is all quit."

He was in a better humor. General Howard spoke to Chief Joseph, "You have your life. I am living. I have lost my brothers. Many of you have lost brothers, maybe more than on our side. I do not know. Do not worry any more. While you see this many soldiers living from the war, you think of them as your brothers. Many brothers of yours—they are my brothers—living from the war.

"Do not worry about starving. It is plenty of food we have left from this war. Any one who needs a sack of flour, anything the people want, come get it. All is yours."

The chiefs and officers crossed among themselves and shook hands all around. The Indians lifted their hands towards the sky, where the sun was then standing. This said: "No more battles! No more war!"

That was all I saw and heard of chiefs' and generals' ending the war.

General Miles was good to the surrendered Indians with food. The little boys and girls loved him for that. They could now have hot food and fires to warm by.

What I heard those generals and chiefs say, I have always remembered. But those generals soon forgot their promises. Chief Joseph and his people were not permitted to return to their own homes.

We were not captured. It was a draw battle. We did not expect being sent to Eeikish Pah [Hot Place]. Had we known this we never would have surrendered. We expected to be returned to our own homes. This was promised us by General Miles. That was how he got our rifles from us. It was the only way he could get them.

The fighting was done. All who wanted to surrender took their guns to General Miles and gave them up. Those who did not want to surrender, kept their guns.

The surrender was just for those who did not longer want to fight. Joseph spoke only for his own band, what they wanted to do.[4] Of the other bands, they surrendered who wanted to.

Chief White Bird did not surrender.[5]

When Chief Joseph surrendered, war was quit, everything was quit, for those who surrendered their guns.

One side of war story is that told by the white man.

The story I have given you is the Indian side. You now have it all, as concerned the war.

I did not surrender my rifle.

---

[4] It is a well-established fact that in Indian governments, no chief could speak for other than his own individual following, whatever the emergency. Different bands, whether composing one tribe or a confederation, might join against a common foe and choose a commander, or war chief. He, however, was governed by council deliberations only, and any band was privileged to sever connections at will. Joseph surrendered 87 men, 184 women, and 147 children.

[5] It is known that fewer than six of Chief White Bird's warriors surrendered at the capitulation of Joseph. Aside from Yellow Bull and his two brothers there were possibly two or three others.

PART TWO:
The Fugitive

✪

YELLOW WOLF:
His Own Story

✪

CHAPTER 19

Flight to the Sioux

Yellow Wolf considered that in his narrative embracing the actualities of the war, from its inception to its tragic ending, was contained all that could be of historic moment, and that the postwar experiences of the Nez Perces who did not surrender would be of little moment to anyone.

But his reluctance to speak of the aftermath of the war was overcome, and the reader may judge of the worth of this and succeeding chapters.

YOU ask me to tell what I know after the war, the things that I have done. It is nothing but the facts —what I have seen, what I have done—that I will tell you. It is of my own hands, my own eyes, that I will tell you.

After Chief Joseph surrendered, all warriors who wanted to go with him gave up their guns, or cached them. Soldiers issued rations. When deep darkness came, Chief White Bird and his people walked out from that camp. They made for Chief Sitting Bull's Camp.[1]

Chief White Bird and his band did not surrender!

Near morning came, and Chief Joseph said to me: "You better go find your mother and my daughter. Bring them here!"

That would be good, I thought, seeing my mother. The first sun of the fighting, my mother and my uncle's

---

[1] As for General Howard's accusation that Chief Joseph broke the terms of the peace covenant by permitting Chief White Bird and his followers to "treacherously" escape subsequent to the surrender (Brady, *Northwestern Fights and Fighters*, p. 89), the most charitable explanation is that the General, despite his years of Indian experience, was still deficient in his knowledge of even the primary elements of Indian government.

[Chief Joseph's] daughter made escape. Yes, I would go find them.

I stood with blanket about me, with rifle inside my legging. Not a long rifle, this that I fought with. I had both cartridge belts under my shirt. I would not stay! I would not go with the people, wherever the soldiers took them. Nor would I hide myself about that battlefield.

During the night soldier guards were all about us. Only the guards; all other soldiers sleeping. I waited until just breaking morning. My mind was made up what to do. I would not hide myself. I would walk out past those guards. They would see me, and if they tried stopping me, that would be good. I would kill them both.

I watched but pretended not seeing them. They did not bother me. Maybe just thought, "Damn Injun going after something. He will be back!" But I went out from everybody. Away from everybody!

There was some inches snow. With my moccasins bad worn, I thought, "This will kill me!" I kept going. Headed for a canyon where one horse was hid. A lot of Nez Perces were somewhere ahead of me. I must find them! I got the horse and went on.

Came full morning, but I saw no one anywhere. Later, I noticed signs of people. I came to the half bloods on Milk River. They treated me fine. Boys watched my horse while he grazed. Knowing I was hungry, they gave me food aplenty. They gave me new moccasins, for my feet were part naked. They directed me how to find my people.

I traveled on, but saw no trace of my friends. If they had passed that way their trail was buried in the blizzard's snow. Came the sunset, but that sun had not been shining. I thought to find some sheltered place to camp. I went on. But my tired horse was slow. Soon I saw Indians in the distance. They were camping! I could not tell if Walk-around Sioux. But those Indians, they knew what kind they were. I got scared! I hid from them!

Then I looked at my magazine rifle. It was loaded. I knew I had two belts well filled with cartridges. One around my waist, one across my shoulder, just as in war. Those cartridges about me, I thought, "I am the same as ten men!" I found myself and came out from hiding. In good view of those Indians I rode towards them. They did nothing. Only watched me, about a quarter mile distant. Then I saw plainly.

They were Nez Perces, my friends! I drew closer and saw women and children among them. I saw my brother [cousin], Lahpeealoot [Two Flocks on Water]. There must have been forty, maybe fifty, Nez Perces there.

My mother came to me and said, "Somebody told me you were dead!"

Then I saw my mother, that she had been crying. I answered her, "It is not true! I will sometime get sick and die. The rifle will never kill me. I am saying to you *three times*, I will not die of the gun."

My mother answered me, "When I heard that you lay killed, I had painful feelings about you. My heart grew heavy, but you are alive and with me."

Then my mother laughed. I was happy. Chief Joseph's daugher was also there.[2]

These Nez Perces with horses they could get were

---

[2] The case of Chief Joseph's daughter Kapkap Ponmi (Noise of Running Feet) will be traced later in Yellow Wolf's narrative.

headed for Chief Sitting Bull in Canada. Gathered where they were just a few at a time. While catching horses at beginning of battle they had been trapped by soldiers. Cut out from the camp. Many had no blankets. Barefooted, half naked. The Milk River half bloods had helped them out. Gave them moccasins and clothes.

Next morning my mother said to me, "Your horse is here." That raised my feelings. My mother said my horse was tied to a tree, and I went. There was my horse that I took from the soldiers. Chestnut-sorrel horse. I laughed over my horse! I put the bridle on him. I felt just as if flying! My mother told me, "Here is your blanket!" That blanket the half bloods had given her.

We all then went. I would not take my mother and Chief Joseph's daughter back to the soldiers. I said nothing. Traveling that day, we kept scouts back on trail guarding against pursuing soldiers. Night drawing on, we stopped to camp. We hobbled our horses. We built a fire, for it was cold and snowy. We were not through supper, when the horses suddenly stampeded.

All the people jumped and ran from the firelight. I leaped out and lay down in the darkness. I threw a cartridge into the firing chamber of my rifle. I held ready. Whoever showed at that fire would be killed. I heard nothing. Lying still for a while, I called to the people, "Come on! Nothing here!"

Of course it was dark where they were hidden, and after a little while they returned to the fire. When they reached the light and could see, they laughed at each other. One of the boys said, "This kid is hungry!"

When we ran from the fire, the little supper we had was left there. A boy, maybe of twelve snows, did not leave the fire. Nobody had had anything to eat for about three suns, and that child ate everything up. That was why the people laughed when they saw what he had done. That boy was hungry.[3]

From this place we moved each sun for two suns. Stormy dark, we could not tell direction to go. Often traveled wrong way. It was the second sun, a little past noon, we crossed the border into Canada. In the evening we camped, and next morning, the third sun, we had not gone far when we saw Indians coming. At quite a distance one of those Indians threw a sign:

"What Indians are you?"

"Nez Perce," one of our men answered. Then he signed, "Who are you?"

"Sioux," was the reply.

"Come on," one of our men signed. "We will have smoke ready!"

We knew that some time ago we had trouble with the Sioux, so we must smoke. The Sioux rode up to where we sat on the ground. They got off their horses and sat around as we did. When they sat down, I noticed one to be a woman. Her hair was parted in the center.[4]

All smoked but me. In sign language we asked, "How far to your camp?"

"Must be about one quarter sun ride," was answered.

We got on our horses and followed the Sioux. They rode fast, horses loping all the way. One Sioux rode ahead, fast as his horse would go. He was taking news

---

[3] Both Yellow Wolf and interpreter evinced amusement at the recital of this incident and regarded it as a huge joke on the hungry crowd, frightened from its meal by a false alarm. That the starving lad was able to "clean the platter" during the few moments that the diners absented themselves from the fireside was owing chiefly, of course, to the woeful scantness of the "supper."

[4] Among certain tribes, perhaps very generally, it was not uncommon for women to accompany warlike expeditions, thus earning the right to sit in councils and participate in the war dance along with the most renowned warriors. It has been seen that one Nez Perce woman did fighting in the Big Hole battle. For other historic instances, see P. J. De Smet, *Oregon Missions and Travels over the Rocky Mountains;* also McWhorter, *Border Settlers of Northwestern Virginia.*

to the other Sioux. The Sioux came to meet us, maybe halfway. We could see them coming, and we made a mount [line of defense].

But the Sioux mixed us up. They took us one by one.[5] The women and children were separated from the men. I knew we never were friends to the Sioux Indians, and it must be they meant to kill us. This I well understood, and I had my rifle ready.

When we came only a little ways from the camp, we saw smoke from many tepees of the Sioux. For eight or ten miles they seemed strung. I thought to myself, "There is quite a number of Sioux Indians!" Going closer, I could see down the canyon. Nothing but Sioux tepees.

It was yet early morning when they took us scattering, in different tepees. When I was brought to one tepee, I saw Lahpeealoot was there. We sat down. Nice place fixed up! Then I looked at one Sioux. He was making a smoke. He got up with pipe in hand, and I said in sign, "No!"

He threw a sign at me, "What is the reason you do not want to smoke?"

I answered back, "When I was little, I did not smoke."

"You must have something in you, you do not smoke?"

I answered him, "No! It is bad habit!"

He said to me again, "You must smoke!"

"No!" I answered him.

"What you want, you do not smoke? Maybe you want fight?"

I threw the sign, "Sioux Indian, I will tell you what!"

---

[5] This band of Nez Perces to which Yellow Wolf was the last accession was perhaps the largest to reach the Sioux camp. Chief White Bird's party, on foot and encumbered with children and wounded, was the last to reach that haven.

He answered, "Yes, I know what you going tell me! It is good!"

I signed, "When I was little my mother used to say to me, 'Your father is dead.' Then I would go out in night time, about middle of night, and cry. I would cry until morning! When it grew light, sun was up, I did not know how I came so. I would think to myself, 'Grizzly bear or wolf might kill me.'

"One of the men came to me and said: 'Do not be afraid.'[6]

"I looked at him. A very fine man. He told me, 'It is nothing here dangerous.'

"I felt very good. He instructed me: 'Look at me! I whipped all the tribes around! With what I am giving you, you can do the same things I have done.'

"I do as he instructed me. Everything as directed. I am afraid of nothing in war. One of the things he told me: 'Do not smoke! If you smoke, you will find yourself dead!'

"You are a Sioux. I am a Nez Perce. You do not know me. Take a good look at me. I am telling you, Sioux, three times, I will not smoke!"[7]

The Sioux Indian answered me, "I know now the reason you do not smoke. There are many Sioux Indians same way as you."

Quite a number of Sioux were present, and they laughed at him. After a few minutes he again spoke to me, "Nez Perce Indian, you are now my friend. From this time on. What have you, mother or father? You

---

[6] Yellow Wolf was alluding to his *Wyakin*. The "very fine man" was a guardian spirit, a "*shadow*" warrior of other snows, returned to guide the fearful lad to a trail of safety, even through the most deadly dangers. Any disregard of rules laid down was sure to be attended with dire results.

[7] It will be seen that Yellow Wolf ran the risk of losing his life at the hands of the hot-tempered Sioux for his refusal to smoke; but he preferred death to a violation of the principles of his *Wyakin*.

can go hunt them up. Wherever they are, you can stay with them."

Then my heart felt good. I hunted for my mother and found her in one Sioux tepee. They gave me everything I asked, just as if I were one of their children.

In spring, one Sioux made himself as a brother to me. Of course it was the sign language we talked. He said to me, "We will go to the Flatheads!"

"I have no moccasins to go there!"

When I spoke that, he replied, "My brother, I have lots of moccasins. You must go with me!"

My Sioux brother was Yakaussioo [Hawk]. After six days, one hundred and thirty-two Sioux, myself, and a smaller cousin of mine, making one hundred and thirty-four, were ready to start. You know the Indians, that they always sing when leaving to go somewhere. We were going through the village camp singing, when I heard someone shouting, "One of our chiefs right now is going to head us off!"

Then I heard the chief calling, "Boys, you better not go! You are not enough!"

He told us many times not to go. Finally one of our leaders agreed, "Well, we better not go!"

We were all afoot. There were two of us always behind, my cousin and I. We saw where they camped, and one of my friends said, "That is good, we are now getting to camp!"

I was dry for water. We came to a draw with a little water showing. I drank from that water. Not long until I felt that I had swallowed something. I could hardly speak. I thought to myself, "I have swallowed an *immel* [black waterbug] in the water!"

Then I said to my cousin, "I think I am going to die."

He answered me, "What is wrong with you? You are not going to die with that little thing!"

"I am going to die!"

When I answered him that, my cousin said, "No, you are not going to die. You have something inside you stronger than that!"

I felt my heart was in my throat. I said to him, "I am going to die, I tell you!"

That was three times I answered him that way.

"No! You will not die!" That was three times he told me "No!"

I was on the ground. I could not lie still. I heard, off towards the right, something calling, "You know I have told you, nothing will kill you!"

I said to my cousin, "Throw me in the pond!"

He threw me in the pond. I lay there a short while, when the water I had swallowed poured out. About the size of my little finger came some blood. I felt like it was lead or something in my mouth, and blood ran just like bleeding lungs.

Then I felt better. My cousin broke open the roll of blood. The *immel* was inside.

My cousin made fun of me. He said, "You were going to die with that little bug?"

"You were saying true! This little bug, you die with it."

I soon felt very fine and went on to camp. When we got there, my cousin told the Sioux Indians, "A brave man like him dying with a little bug! Very short time ago he was being dead, and now he is alive."

The Sioux laughed.

Turning Back to the Old Home

After spending from October, 1877, to June, 1878, among Sitting Bull's Sioux in Canada, Yellow Wolf and a number of the other Nez Perce refugees were mistakenly informed, or mistakenly believed, that it would be safe for them to return to their ancestral camping grounds.

Because of the somber colorings given by partisan pens to the events attending their return, Yellow Wolf was induced to give, from the Indian angle, an account of happenings on the way. While it is true that there were instances of lawlessness (which Yellow Wolf makes no attempt to conceal), there is also revealed an honest effort on the part of these outlawed patriots to live up to a council-formed agreement made before leaving Canada: "Trouble will not be sought," to which was added a proviso for self-defense, "but trouble will be found for any who may seek it."

Foraging on the trail for necessary food was regarded by them as legitimate, particularly in view of all that had been taken from them when they were driven out of the Wallowa and Salmon River valleys.

WE GOT along fine with the Sioux, who remained camped in the same place all the time we were there.[1] We stayed with them until the first part of June [1878]. It was then that one Nez Perce made announcement, "Now is about time we go back to our homeland."

Chief Joseph had sent word from bondage for all of his escaped followers to surrender and come to him. We would obey our leader. It was about thirteen men, some nine women and few children that got ready to travel.[2]

---

[1] Sitting Bull's camp was said to be about five hundred miles within the Canadian border. See Appendix D, "Report of Captain Falck," end of this volume.

[2] The following count of those who returned, compiled by Black Eagle, one of their younger members, lists 28 persons. Chief Joseph's daughter is not listed by name, but she is one of the "nieces" of Yahyow (Geese)—another name of

We were informed that we would be safe because belonging to Joseph's band. But not all of us were of Joseph's band.

We left the Sioux camp all mounted, and the warriors had guns. A few old men and one or two not quite man age, so only five or six could be counted on to fight. Unarmed, we would soon be killed. Our ammunition was about ten cartridges to each rifle.

We came about three camps when we had first trouble with another tribe of Indians. They were the Walk-arounds. There must have been twenty of them. The women got afraid, but one of the men told them not to be scared. He took my arm and said to them, "Look at this boy! He will be in front of us. I am not afraid!"

We then all dismounted and sat down, ready for a peace smoke. One of the enemy rode toward us a little way. My friends said to me, "That Indian will not bother us!"

I said nothing. Soon I got up and went forward. That Walk-around was armed, and I took my rifle. I came closer to him, and he threw me the sign, "You see that sun? This is your last day!"

I answered him, "I am not a woman. I am a man. I am a warrior!"

He made reply, "Take a good look at the sun!"

I threw him the sign, "You are nothing!" Then one of the Walk-arounds got mad. He threw me the sign, "You are nothing but a woman!"

Yellow Wolf's mother, Yiyik Wasumwah. It will be remembered that she and Chief Joseph were first cousins—in tribal parlance, brother and sister. Men: Wottolen; Black Eagle, son of Wottolen; Peopeo Tholekt; Wewass Pahkalatkeikt; Iskeloom; Kootskoots Tsomyowhet; Ipnamatwekin; Wahseenwes Sawhohtsoht; Seeloo Wahyakt; Pauh Wahyakt; Weyooseeka Tsakown; Kowtoliks; Hemene Moxmox (Yellow Wolf). Women and children: Niktseewhy, with two children; Ipnatsubah Loolussonmi; Yahyow, with two nieces; Heyoom Telelbinmi; Tommi Yohonmi; Heyoom Yoyikt; Whepwheponmi; Bellutsoo, with two children; Weyadooldipat.

I answered him, "This is good! I will show you what a woman can do with you. Come on!"

All the Walk-arounds got off their horses. They aimed at me, and I yelled. I was a little afraid, and yelled. I came to myself and made my heart as a brave man. I said, "There is nothing here dangerous!"

They then fired. One brave Indian ran at me. I met him, and we fired at each other. Both missed, and I said to myself, "I will not kill him with the gun. I will kill him with the war club!"

I ran up against his gun muzzle. He missed me and jumped back. I struck and missed him. He was so far from his friends, he turned and ran back to them, leaving his horse.

I took his horse and led it away. I threw the sign at him, "A little while ago you said I was a woman. See what a woman can do! Woman can take horse away from you! Come on now! We will have a little war of our own. You have bothered me a long time!"

He answered me the sign, "No! You have your life. You better go ahead, the way you are traveling!"

I answered, "Yes, you go on toward your home. You are still alive!"

I thought they would get mad, the way I spoke. They rode on the top of a small butte, and we went on. Those Walk-arounds were afraid. They bothered us no more. My friend took my arm again, saying to the people, "Now look what he has done. I told you we have one boy who can do a little fighting. He is the same as a thousand soldiers!"[3]

We moved for two suns, camping nights. Another

---

[3] In war or other desperate undertakings, it was conceded that the warrior boasting the strongest *Wyakin* should be honored with the leadership.

tribe of Indians saw us. We saw them coming, where they stopped about a quarter mile away. One man threw the sign, "What tribe are you?"

We answered, "Nez Perce."

He signed, "Come on!"

I went to him, where he came to meet me. When I got there, he signed, "You better come on! We have seven tepees only short ways. You can eat anything you want!"

I told my people, "Let's follow them!"

We followed the direction they went. When we reached the camp, the Nez Perces unpacked and unsaddled. I did not dismount. One of our Indians came and said to me, "Come down to the chief's tepee."

"No," I answered, "go on down!"

The Nez Perce went, and I stayed in the saddle. In a little while my mother came running. She spoke, "One old man told me how one of his people is taking the news to the soldiers!"

"Do not tell me. Go tell them where they are eating bread!" was my reply.

My mother ran. Several Nez Perces came out of the tepees. They said, "We will go see the old man who told your mother." It was true enough, the words of the old man. We packed our things and moved from that place.

They were Lemhi Indians who trapped us.

It was about middle afternoon, and we traveled fast. We all understood signs. We knew what it meant when we saw the buffaloes running, stampeding. One man called out, "Soldiers meeting us!"

We had come to a washout, a gully. We all dropped in

there, and I stood down a ways to one side. One man called to me, "We will die this sun!"

I never answered him. He was a little mad, and called again, "We will now die! Just this sun!"

Then I told him, "Shut up! Do not say a word to me! I am a man, a warrior. I will die. That is good! I will make no council!"

That man said no more to me. I thought that was good. I now cleaned my rifle. Soon an old man, Pauh Wahyakt, spoke, "Now I can see!"

That Nez Perce took his pipe and smoked. A little while and came a fog. All over, just like he was wide smoking. You could not see any distance. Then we went. It was not many steps from the soldiers, where we passed each other.[4] We traveled all night.

We got to a place called Mehtottipmachim [Three Double Mountains] in that country. Coming daylight, sun was up when we reached there. We did not stay long. We went a little ways and saw a buffalo. One man remarked, "We are out of meat. We ought to have meat."

"Yes, we ought to have meat," I answered him.

He was standing on a little bench of the hillside, that buffalo. Three of us went after him. When we got near him, it was not a buffalo. It was a *hohots* [grizzly bear].

---

[4] Commenting on the suddenly arisen fog which enabled the Nez Perces to escape, interpreter Hart explained, "In a dense fog sounds are deadened. A horse may pass within a few feet of you and not be heard. I have often observed this myself when in the mountains. Yes, it was the prayer-smoking that brought the fog to save those people from death or capture. In days gone by there were strong-minded men who could do such things."

Another remarkable instance of apparent Indian occultism, very similar to that given by Yellow Wolf, is related of the battle of Lava Beds, Oregon, fought January 17, 1873. The medicine man assured the fifty-three Modoc warriors he had the promise that they in their stronghold would be effectively hidden from the enemy by a cloud of fog on the coming morning. The cloud appeared only after the sun was shooting its rays across the dreary waste and the beseiging army of four hundred men was moving to the attack from every quarter. Its appearance was so sudden and so adverse to the movements of the troops that it is mentioned by Colonel Wheaton in his official report. While the loss among the attacking force was heavy, not one Indian was hurt in the fight. (Meacham, *Wi-ne-ma and Her People*, Chapter 19.)

When that *hohots* saw us, he made for us. He ran us
down the hill a ways. He must have been four feet high
standing on all his feet. I did not want to tackle with
him.

We split up when running our horses. One man ran
straight ahead. The *hohots* took after the other hunter.
This man turned his horse and circled towards me. That
hohots was close after him. He called to me, "Get off
your horse! We will fight the *hohots!*"

I jumped off my horse and the man came up to me.
He sprang from his horse, for the *hohots* was coming
fast. He drew his rifle, and I thought, "He will shoot,
but we will never kill him with the gun. I will kill him
with my war club."

I drew my club and stepped to meet that *hohots*.
When close, he raised up. The man fired, but the aim was
not to the right place. The bullet struck that *hohot's*
nose. As he dropped down to his front feet, I jumped
and struck him behind the ear. That *hohots* dropped.
He did not get up. I thought, "We have killed him, but
we have no use for him. He is one of the brave men
we have killed."[5]

We moved two suns, and then the same tribe of Lemhi
Indians surrounded us. It was early morning while we
were yet in camp. We were not many. There must have
been a hundred of them. They threw the usual sign,
"What tribe are you?"

"Nez Perce," we answered.

They did not believe us. We knew they wanted to
kill us. Then the Lemhi spoke the sign, "Follow us! Let
us go to camp!"

---

[5] *Interpreter Hart:* "That grizzly had eaten a dead person, maybe one he had
killed. They will eat dead bodies that have laid for days, and when killed they have
the same odor. That is why the Nez Perces—though hungry—would not use the
meat. The grizzly is a brave man, a hard fighter, and it is good for an Indian to
kill him in battle."

That was another lie the Lemhi told us. We answered, "Go ahead. We will follow you!"

The Lemhi then went, riding fast. The Nez Perce who saved us the other time said, "I will do the same thing! I will smoke!"

Then came—after the smoking—in the the same way, a heavy fog. The Lemhi Indians went one way, we took another direction. Maybe the Lemhis looked for us. I do not know, but they never found us. We left our little food right there where we saw the Lemhi Indians. We packed from that camp in a big hurry.

We now moved three suns without anything to eat. We hunted and hunted. Nothing could we find. No birds to kill! No deer, no rabbits! Nothing anywhere!

The fourth sun came, and no food. Two men went ahead looking for game. I was lying down quite a ways from camp. A man came to me as I lay there. He had a whip, and struck me with it. He said, "You, a brave man! You are going to starve to death? Stand up! Look for something to eat!"

I stood up and threw my blanket down. I took my rifle and went up the hill. I went about three miles. There was nothing over that way. No game, no white man's stock.

Changing direction, I came to the top of a ridge. Down below must have been fifty cattle. When I saw those cattle, just as fast as I could, I went for camp. I was not the size I am now. I was a slim fellow. I could go swiftly—could go for a long time. When a little way from camp, I heard one man telling the women, "We are going to starve to death!"

He was not one of two men who had hunted for game. I went on where my blanket was and sat down. The same man who whipped me came and asked, "Did you find anything to eat?"

"Yes," I answered him.

"He has found food," this man told the women.

We got our horses, saddled, and went, all of us. We passed the two men who were looking for game. They told the women, "He is lying! There is nothing around close."

The same man who struck me with the whip then asked me, "Did you find anything to eat?"

"Yes," I answered him.

Then we went fast. When we came to where we could see, I said, "Look! What is that? I never tell the lie to anyone. You know yourself we are starving!"

When they saw the cattle they were ashamed. But they were glad for those cattle. We went down near the herd and unpacked. I had found them, so I shot the first steer. Then another man shot one.

That was the time we had meat.

Next morning we left that place. White people do not know the ways of our tribe. We can dry meat in one night. A whole steer, or two. Whatever it is, we can dry it all. Everything was packed up and ready. The camp went on ahead, but I stayed behind as most always. After about one hour I got on my horse and went. I rode fast. When I could see the Nez Perces, they threw a blanket up.

That told me, "Hurry!"

I ran my horse fast. When I reached them they told me some white men were coming, but quite a little distance away. We agreed that we would meet them, but not fight or kill them. They might have a sack of flour to give us. After a council we said, "We will go see them."

We then went to their camp. Nobody around. Those white men had not arrived. One man said, "Let us wait for them."

That would be good, so we dismounted. While we sat around, our horses were eating. In a short while, I saw three white men coming. When they saw us, they called in rough voice, "Get out from there!"

They brought down their guns, working the levers, ready to shoot. I thought to myself, "Well, I guess they want a little trouble!"

They were calling us all names they could think.[6] One of them came close as that [indicating twenty feet]. He might shoot, and one Nez Perce said to me, "Grab your gun!"

I took my gun and set it off to one side. I had my war club all the time with me. I stepped to meet the white man, and he yelled something I did not understand at me. I dodged under his gun and knocked him over. He was getting up when I struck him on the head. He fell back and did not move.

One white man cried when he saw his friend not living. He raised his hands, and I told him, speaking Nez Perce, "Yes, my friend, you are alive. When calling me, it was just giving yourself to death. I did not want to kill this man. I do not want to kill you."

I went up to him and took his gun. One Nez Perce boy spoke some English. I said to him, "Tell this white man to give us flour, what he has got."

---

[6] Yellow Wolf evinced amusement when recalling the rage of the three white men on this occasion, and showed regret that the Indians' own friendly intentions were misconstrued with such tragic result.

When this was interpreted to him, the man replied, "Yes, lots of flour. Come on!"

He opened the door and asked how much flour we wanted. The sacks weighed one hundred pounds. We told him we would take one sack.

Those men had two soldier saddles, and I thought, "They are soldiers!" When they yelled at me, I noticed the saddles. Then I knew they were soldiers. That was why I struck the man. I asked them, "You soldiers, or just white men?"

They did not answer what they were. After short time I said again, "I am asking you, what? You soldiers? Where is your army?" When I spoke that, one of them replied, "Yes, I have been in the army. I just quit lately. That is the reason for those saddles."

We left the two white men there. It was eight of us came to see them about flour.

YELLOW WOLF:
His Own Story

⊗

CHAPTER 21

A Sanguinary Trail

The majority of the incidents in this chapter are of historic record, but they have never been related from the Indian viewpoint. To hear Yellow Wolf was to be impressed by the unquestionable candor of his conviction that he and his associates were fully justified in all their actions. The returning Nez Perces approached in friendship the various groups of whites encountered on their way, only to meet with rebuffs and threatenings. Inasmuch as this attitude on the part of the whites left no other avenue open to them, they invoked the imperative laws of self-preservation in their own accustomed way.

FROM where we got flour, we kept moving for three suns. About middle of afternoon, we came to a town. We could not go around; only one road. No way to go round. Mountains and woods. When we came to the edge of town, a white man called to us, "Hold on! What tribe are you?"

"We belong to this place!" the interpreter replied.

"No, you are Nez Perces!" he answered, showing a little mad.

"No, we belong to this country!"

I now told the interpreter, "Come on! Do not wait for him!"

We rode on. Some people on the streets, on sidewalks. They ran in the houses. Then I saw one man with a gun coming out of the house. We went, turning off the road. The same old man, Pauh Wahyakt, took his pipe and smoked. It was the same way! A thick fog came and covered everything around us. We, ourselves, could not see. We went up the mountain, over a ridge, to a small creek and camped. I thought to go down the creek a way, afoot. Going, I came to the same town where we had the trouble. In blind fog, we had turned back when above the town. I returned to camp. When I told the people we were again near the town, they got scared. But we stayed at that place all night.

Next morning we got ready, and again traveled the trail we had doubled on. Then we got down from that mountain—back where we had turned off, blinded by the deep fog. Passing over a hill, we stopped at one place. We could not get by there. White men were on the road. We stayed hidden.

At dusk we got ready to move. As we crossed the prairie, one man, listening, said to me, "Soldiers coming after us now." We two were the rear guard.

"We will get off our horses right here," I told him. We did this, and it was not long till the horses we heard came running by. I felt very good that it was not soldiers. It was nothing but a band of wild horses running. My horse got loose, and there I was afoot.

It was dark by now, and my partner helped hunt for my horse. We shouted, calling to the other Indians. They answered from away off. Told us, "Here is your horse!"

When we got to them, we made camp for the night. Morning coming, we packed up and moved. Just after noon, we came to a house. We knocked on the door. The door was locked! I said to the Indians, "I guess they are prospecting around here somewhere."

Everybody went on but myself and one other man. We looked about. We found white men mining, a place dug out. An oldlike man down there digging. He did not see us. I stooped over the hole and called, "Hello!"

That white man jumped! He dropped his shovel, threw his hands up, and yelled, "We-ou-u-u-u!"[1] He was surely scared. He looked up and saw us. He reached his hand to me, but I could not touch it. Too far down. Then he went a little ways, and came up where we were. We shook hands and he asked, "You fellers hungry?"

"Yes!" answered my partner, who could speak a little English. The white man took us in the house and cooked anything he could see to cook. When he got it ready, he fixed the table, and we ate. When through that eating, the old man said, "I am going to tell you what I believe."

"That is right. Tell us," I answered by interpreter.

"You are Nez Perces?"

"Yes, we are Nez Perces."

When I told him that, the old man said to me, "I am a very good feller! Some white men are mean, if they see you. You must travel in nighttime."

"Yes, we will do that," I answered him.

Just then we saw a white man coming, passing by the house. We called him, and he shook his head, "*Weta!* [No!]."

"That feller is mad," said the old man.

I ran to him, caught him on the arm, and jerked him around. He would not let me keep hold of him. I grabbed him again, and he reached for his belt. About the same time I drew my war club. He pulled his gun, and I knocked him on the head. I did not like to do this, only he had the gun.

---

[1] This drama at the prospector's pit was enacted by Yellow Wolf in pantomime with manifest enjoyment. The celerity with which the startled miner hastened to evince his friendship for his callers was not at all misunderstood by them, but was accepted as born of duress.

The old man got scared. I called him to come. When he came, I said, by interpreter, "Now watch!"

I put my hand in the dead man's pocket, and pulled out a long purse. I said to the old man, "Did you see that?"

"Yes," the old man answered.

"Get hold of him! Drag him down somewhere you can bury him," I told the old man, and he did so. I now said to the Nez Perce, "We will leave him."

I asked the old man for a handshake. I said to him, "Look at the sun!"

After that I took the purse. There was lots of money in it. I handed the purse to the white man, but he refused. I said to him, "We did not want to kill that man. You can say it was Indians that killed him."

The white man took the purse and put it in his pocket. We then left him. That white man stood there, looking around. We do not know what he did after we rode away. He might have run away from the house with that amount of money.

At this point in the story, I said to Yellow Wolf, "Were you afraid after you had killed the white man?" He replied:

I was not afraid of anything. Nothing there dangerous. I was mad because he would not stop when I called him. I wanted to be friends. He might be going with alarm.

We rode for about one sun. It was a big creek we came to, and we crossed and camped. Next morning we left the camp, and while moving, looked down a ways. There was a barn, and good horses. Some of our horses were lame with sick feet. I said to my friend, Putim

Soklahtomah [Ten Owl],[2] a young man who always stayed with me, "We can get those horses!"

"Yes, we will take those horses," Soklahtomah replied.

We tore down the board fence. It was a large barn. We got around above the horses. We saw no white man anywhere. It might have been forty steps we drove those horses, when they ran, playing. Could do nothing with them. All ran back to the barn, racing around the barn.

I saw one white man looking at me. Then they came out with rifles and shot at us. The horses ran away from the barn, scared of guns. We took the horses. We looked back. The men had one saddle horse and came after the horses. When we got to the top of the hill in the woods, the white men did not follow us.

We caught up with the other Indians, and waited for any white men coming. No, they never came! We moved on, going over mountains. We camped, and moved again. Next morning we came to a house, a small one. When the people there saw us, they motioned to us, just like calling, "Come on, friends! Come on!"

So we went, just like friends. They said, "Get off! Tie your horses!"

They asked us to go in the house. They were laughing, having lots of fun. One white man asked, "You got flour? We will give you one sack of flour."

Half side of bacon—anything they could think of—they gave us. Then we thanked them. I said by the interpreter, "Will you show me the trail?"

---

[2] The name Putim Soklahtomah should be rendered Fifteen Owl, rather than Ten Owl, it is contended by some Nez Perces. The name has reference to the following well-known legend: There were once five owls who had war clubs, while the other ten owls of the band were unarmed. The five wanted to go to war, but the ten were for peace. The five grew clamorous, and the dispute waxed warm. Black Eagle, soaring aloft in the sky, observed the growing trouble. Swooping down, he compelled the warlike five to agree to peace, on the score that the majority should rule. To honor the moral involved in this legend, the numbers five and ten are often incorporated in Indian cognomens.

"Yes, I know the trail," the white man told me. "It is the creek. Then go right over the hill, over the mountain."

Name of creek is Eeslummineema [Many Trout][3] We saw nobody over the way traveled. The trail was as the white man told us. We got to the top of the mountain and camped.

Next morning the people all got ready and went. I thought to stay a time and watch on our back trail. We had passed several white people coming up the creek of Many Trout. Soldiers might be following us.

But no soldiers appeared. It was near noon when I mounted and followed after the camp. I came to a house. The door was open and I went inside. The floor was all blood! I looked around. Nobody there. I saw no one dead. I thought, "Must have been somebody killing one another here!"

I went outside, around the house. Could find nothing! I saw it was a mining place, and maybe they killed each other for the gold?

I went back inside and took the best gun of some lying on the floor. Took one six-shooter hanging on the wall. Then I left, and after a time overtook the camp. Just then we saw white men, four of them. Seeing us, they ran into a near house. When they did that it came to my mind, "Maybe they killed the men in that other house?"

Those men came out with guns and hung around as if to shoot. I said to the man who talked English, "What is wrong with them? They are mad?"

He interpreted, asking them. They made no answer. Only held their rifles closer. This was just telling us, "Come on! We want trouble!"

---

[3] This is a creek near present Missoula, Montana.

We did not like that. Everybody against us, we seemed to find no real friends. We would make no first trouble.

I now set my rifle against a tree. I said to one of my friends, "I am going to take one of those guns! Just stand and watch what they do with me."

I walked fast towards those white men. They yelled, "Do not come near!"

But I ran at one of them. He drew his rifle to his face. I was too quick, and struck him on the arm with my war club. He dropped his gun and grabbed his arm. The other three white men did not come to help their friend. They ran away. I did not strike him again. It was just taking his gun I was doing.[4]

The Indians watching me laughed. Laughed at the way the white man yelled, "Do not come near!"—at the noise he made. I picked up the white man's rifle and said to my friends, "We will go off and leave them. Let them go where they want. I see no horses, none they can ride to bring soldiers."

Traveling on, we came to a small open place and camped, for it was getting dark. After we had eaten something, I told the men what I saw at the house back on the trail. Where miners had killed one another. They laughed and said it was Heinmot Tosinlikt [Tabador] who had made the floor bloody. They had stopped there, thinking to get something to eat. One white man had got mad, and Heinmot struck his head and killed him. They carried him out in the brush.

Before this man was killed in the house, there had been shooting outside. One white man had started to run

---

[4] When asked why Yellow Wolf displayed such reckless impetuosity, interpreter Hart gravely explained: "Why, he was making himself a brave man in presence of his brother warriors. Anybody could kill at a distance with the gun, but only the bravest would dare lay aside his rifle to rush an armed enemy. Such deeds made a warrior looked up to by his own and other tribes. He was reckoned most powerful, and feared by enemy tribes. His bravery traveled before him."

away. Then the man doing the cooking went out of the door. He ran fast for the brush, somewhere to tell the soldiers. So Peopeo Tholekt, Tabador, and Tipyah-lahna Kikt [Alighting Eagle] chased after him. Geh-wahaikt watched below and kept calling which way the man was running up the mountain. They shot at him but he escaped. They did not spend much time hunting for him. Afoot, and long ways from anywhere, he could not hurry to bring soldiers.[5]

Next morning we packed and got ready to go early. This time two other boys thought to stay as scouts to watch the back trail. They would follow when the sun reached about ten o'clock. The camp started, Ten Owl and I going maybe a half mile ahead. We came down where we could see houses—must be six or seven. We stopped and held a little council. We decided what to do. Waiting until the other people came up, I said to them, "Some of you men go on with the women and children. A few of us will go see the white people, what about their minds."

We thought to be friendly with those people at the houses, and five of us went. They were Tabador, Peopeo Tholekt, Ooyekun [Sliding from Cliff], Putim Soklah-tomah, and I, Yellow Wolf. When the white men saw us coming, they made for the brush. We did not want any fight, only to be friends. I said to the others, "We better not go there."

The camp was now gone quite a way ahead. We started to follow, when we saw eight white men with

---

[5] This episode occurred at a mining camp on Rock Creek, a score or more miles from Philipsburg, Montana. The man whom the Indians chased so unsuccessfully was J. H. Jones, who was ever afterwards known as "Nez Perce" Jones. As Yellow Wolf relates, the Indians stopped at the cabin primarily for food, but it was also their intention to take whatever horses or mules could be found, in order to set the miners afoot and thus delay the spreading of a report of their presence in the vicinity.

many horses. We spoke among ourselves and decided best not to let them think we were bad, afraid to come to them. Peopeo and Ooyekun both said, "We will talk to the whites. Maybe we can find out what is going on."

But when those white men saw us coming, they all ran for the brush. We came up where they had stood and saw an *aparejo* [Mexican packsaddle]. I told the other Indians, "We will go. We will not take anything from that pack outfit. We do not want such things as that."

"We will take all the horses," Soklahtomah said.

"Yes, leave those white men afoot, so they cannot tell the soldiers."

Fifty-two horses we took.

Passing over a little ridge, we came to a big creek. I was dry, and got off to drink. The others had gone some distance when I got in the saddle to go. I followed, not hurrying. I heard shouting on ahead. I did not know what was wrong. I did not know if the calling was to come, or to go away. I did not hear that voice very good. Then I heard plainly. "Get out of here!"

Some white people were mad at the Indians. I heard Soklahtomah calling, "Come on! Come on!"

I ran my horse. They heard me, for I came fast. When I passed a curve, I saw three white men, rifles pointing at Skoloom. One other white man had no gun. Skoloom called to me: "My brother-in-law, come quick! They are going to kill me!"

I jumped to the ground. The white men were just inside from the road, and I sprang over the fence. Soklahtomah said, "Get the guns from them!"

I set my rifle to the fence, when Putim Soklahtomah warned, "You hold on your gun!"

I walked fast towards the white men, only a few steps

away. First man gave back—told me not to come near. Then I made for him. I nearly knocked him over in getting his gun. I think he was a little nervous. He called his companions to do something as I scuffled the gun from him. I pitched this gun to the fence, and went after nearest white man. I took his gun the same way. One white fellow was a good-looking man. Tall, and had a Springfield rifle. Skoloom called, "Brother-in-law, get that gun!"

I ran quickly to this man, grabbing his gunstock near the barrel. He was a strong man. We both held to the gun, but I did not get it from him. He walked away with that gun. My gun lay quite a distance from me. Soklahtomah yelled to Ooyekun, "Shoot him! Shoot him!"

Ooyekun was about fifteen steps away. He shot and missed. He did not hit that white man. His body was good. A bullet might not enter his flesh. That white man jumped over the fence. I was looking on. I did not go for my gun. Soklahtomah ordered, "Shoot again!"

Ooyekun again shot, but missed. When he missed the second time, the white man turned and fired, but missed. That man with the Springfield rifle then ran like a white-tailed deer. Jumped brush and logs, going fast.

We saw him no more.

We did not get mad at those white men. Only robbed them of their guns. I did not want to kill any of them. That good-looking man must have run and told the soldiers on the Missouri River.

One other white man held his gun under his arm. I did not try to take it, for one of the whites put up his hands. I called for the interpreter, and this white man spoke, "You people hungry?"

I turned to my people, and they answered, "Yes, we are hungry."

A house was there, and that man went inside and began cooking fast as he could. Some of us went and watched the man cook. He might put poison in the food.

The white man with gun stayed off outside. Soon there was a rifle shot. It was the old Indian's gun, and I ran out from the house. He had shot at the white man, but missed him. The white man ran about twenty steps, when the Indian shot and missed again. That white man jumped fast to the brush, got away. We told the other white men, "That white man is bad, reason we tried to kill him. We do not want to kill you. You are good!"

Then we sat and ate. It must have been middle of afternoon, we got ready and went. The guns and little ammunition the white men had, we took with us. Going up the gulch, we crossed and went about three miles. Came the dusk. Then dark was on us, and we could not see to go farther. We did not know where camp was. Then I heard a woman laugh. I said to the others, "They are close."

We went to them, and I told the other boys, "We will camp right here," and we went to bed.

Next morning we were saddling horses and packing ready to go. Soklahtomah said to me, "Brother-in-law, I am hungry. We will go back where the white men are, and butcher a steer. We two will go, but if one man goes with us, we will pack the meat. The others can keep going."

I was willing for this. I spoke to Putim Soklahtomah, "We will go back to the white man's place, and kill one yearling calf. We have a long ways yet to go. We must have meat."

"Yes, you are telling true," Soklahtomah answered.

"You will go with us and kill one beef?" I asked the other men.

They were willing, and eight of us went. I told the camp, "Just keep going! We may come quick, maybe a long time."

The camp went on, leaving the fifty-two horses we had captured. We did not want them.[6]

---

[6] Yellow Wolf later explained that before turning the captured horses loose to wander back to their accustomed range, they first took out fresh mounts for themselves, leaving behind, however, an equal number of their own worn and lamed horses in substitution.

YELLOW WOLF:

His Own Story

✪

CHAPTER 22

Soldiers Against Indians

For the first time during the course of their return from Canada, the little band of refugees found themselves pursued by soldiers. News of their passage through Montana had reached several army posts, and though various detachments had been sent in pursuit of them ("Report of the Secretary of War," 1878, p. 68), none had yet caught up. If the Indians, after the capture and release of the fifty-two horses, as related in the preceding chapter, had not delayed, they might have reached their destination unhindered.

I DO NOT know if that good-looking man who ran like a deer took word to the soldiers. Maybe the soldiers just followed us.[1] This very morning when we were going after beef, they were where we had taken guns from the two men the evening before. Only about two and one-half miles from us.

But we did not know this. We went back on the trail. Tomamo [not Tabador, but another Indian of the same name] was about fifteen steps in the lead. We ran our horses to the creek. We crossed and followed Tomamo through the brush. We could hear his horse running. Then I heard a gun report. I thought someone was killing the beef. Tomamo called, "Where are you boys?"

----

[1] One writer, who places the number of the Indians at "about twenty," gives the following explanation of the presence of the soldiers: "When passing through the upper valley they [the Nez Perce refugees] came across Jerry Fahey and his pack train, which they appropriated to their own use. Word was sent to Fort Missoula and a small squad of soldiers, accompanied by a number of settlers, started out in pursuit, with the intention of regaining Jerry's pack train for him and administering some chastisement to the marauding Indians. The Indians ... got careless, supposing that all their pursuers had returned.... [The] soldiers overtook them and surprising them, recovered Jerry's pack train without the loss of a man." (Amos Buck, in *Contributions to the Historical Society of Montana*, Vol. VII, pp. 128-29.) Needless to say, the only animals "recovered" by these soldiers were those which the Nez Perces had turned loose, as Yellow Wolf has related in the preceding chapter.

260

He came back to us and said, "I just ran my horse through the brush and saw dust. I thought cattle were running. When dust settled, it was a bunch of soldiers. They are close enough to shoot us."

All of us rode through the brush where we could see the house. We watched the soldiers, a troop of cavalry. Tabador said, "Let's have a war right now!"

We missed Tomamo. He had gone aside a way, making a little war of his own. When the soldiers saw us, they fired. I did not dodge, as, putting my rifle by a tree, I fired. Rifles from the soldiers were popping fast. Short of ammunition, we made only a few replies. We did not fight much. It was only a short time of shooting.

One soldier drew near us—ran his horse toward us. He must have gone crazy or something. I stepped to meet him. When only a little ways from me, he jumped from his horse. Afoot, he turned and ran back to the other soldiers. Left his horse there standing. Maybe he was hit by one of our bullets. I took his horse.

What I am telling you are facts. What happened in those days of trouble. I am telling no other than facts, what I saw and did. I think now that soldier could not manage his horse.

Four of us went to have Indian fight. Soldiers began digging the ground, burying themselves. We held council. I said, "If soldiers bury themselves, we can do nothing. We better let them alone."

"No use troubling them! They have trenches. We will get killed," Tabador told us.

We quit. We left the soldiers to finish burying themselves.

A little farther than a rifle shot, we went up a hill. Cattle there feeding in open place. I directed the boys,

"Drive the cattle out from that ground. No protection from danger there."

They brought the cattle where it was not quite so open. Those cattle were about two years old. We picked a fat one and killed it. The soldiers were watching us, and we watching them.

Earlier, a soldier who shot at Tabador but missed him, was thrown by his horse, which ran away. Ooyekun now saw this horse on the hillside below us, its foot on the bridle rein. Soldiers were watching the horse and, seeing us looking, one came afoot towards it. He did not get far. A shot sent him running for his dugout shelter.

Tomamo now said, "I am going to get that horse!"

He walked towards the horse. It was just the same. Soldiers fired at him, and he got not near that horse. He ran back from the bullets. Left the horse with foot still on its bridle rein. Tabador now said to everybody, "Whoever wants that horse, go get him!"

Nobody wanted to go. No one cared for that horse. I, too, was scared. Skoloom said, "Brother-in-law, you better get that horse!"

I got ashamed to refuse. I had to go! I stripped my clothes, getting ready. I ran a little, then trotted down the hill slowly. No use hurrying into danger. The soldiers shot at me. I kept going; they kept shooting. I did not get small heart. I became as not afraid. My heart now believed, and I did not get scared. I found my *Wyakin*—just the air. Soldiers could hit nothing of the air.[2] I came to the horse, raised his foot and got the hoof off the bridle. Soldiers did not fire at me after I got there. Maybe they did not like to shoot the horse. I led my

---

[2] Yellow Wolf's *Wyakin*, because imbued with the properties of the air, was able, he believed, to render his body invulnerable to bullets.

prize up where Indians were butchering. Skoloom said to me, "Thank you, my brother-in-law. We are going to pack that soldier horse with meat."

We did pack that soldier horse, and we led him away.[3] Soldiers still in their trenches, we left them. Only eight of us, but the soldiers did not try stopping us. They did not leave their shelter to take their horse or fight us. We did not think much of those soldiers.

We went on the trail and came up with the others in about six or seven miles. Before joining them, I told them, "Do not tell the women about seeing soldiers. They will be scared and eat no dinner. After eating, we can tell them our story."

We stopped for dinner. One man not with us for the beef talked to me. I told him, "We did not come till we have a little trouble."

The women got excited. I said to them, "Let us eat first. Then we will talk!"

They did as I said. The women laughed as they cooked the meat. After dinner the order was called, "Pack up!"

Everything was soon packed, ready to ride. The women told me, "We are all ready."

"Soldiers just back of us. We had a little war."

When I told them that, my mother laughed. She said, "I do not get excited if you tell it before dinner. When they claim to get best of you men, and I am alone, then I get scared!"

We moved camp, coming to the summit of a mountain as the sun went down. We could look back on the trail where we had come. We saw one soldier's horse standing on the trail. Only one trail, and he could go nowhere

---

[3] In thus degrading the trained charger of a uniformed trooper, by imposing on it the burdens of a menial pack animal—and this in full sight of a numerically stronger foe—the Indians expressed their contemptuous defiance.

else. We said, "We will wait for him here. If he comes, we will fire on him."

We stayed there, waiting for the soldiers. We listened, if we could hear them coming in the night. I think they were scared. They never came near us.

Morning came, and after breakfast we traveled till noon. We stopped and after eating something, went on. We found a white man who showed us a trail. A very little trail, over a kind of mountain. It was middle of afternoon when we dropped down into a big canyon. Wottolen, the leader, said, "We will camp here. We will stay all afternoon and watch if soldiers come."

The sun went down. No soldiers had come. That night we watched again for soldiers. Next morning, we wanted sleep, so we stayed another night. We waited on the trail for soldiers, if they showed up.

Came another morning, and we went. It was a zigzag trail, and steep for the horses. Tomamo called: "Look back!"

Looking, we saw dust about one mile away. Everybody said, "Soldiers coming!"

Women and men laughed. Nobody got excited. We finished climbing the trail to the top of the mountain. We went down a small creek, heading up on the mountain. From where we saw the dust, we went about two miles and camped at a spring. It was nine or ten o'clock when we stopped there. At noon one old man told us, "Lots of salmon here. We will look for salmon. We will eat!"

Every man, and some women, went looking for salmon. Only six women and seven children left in camp. We did not think well. We forgot that soldiers might be following behind. We acted as not knowing anything. Those women and children in camp! It was just like giving them to the soldiers. All this came to me, and I thought, "No use that I go looking for salmon. Not good that I go fishing. Soldiers may now be in our camp. I will go back to our camp!"

I returned quickly to camp. I found the women in the shade, patching worn moccasins. A good shade, and I lay down to rest. I was not scared at all. I went to sleep. I do not know what the white man calls that sight which came to me. I went into that sleep we call *kahauto weyakakaun* [short life]. I slept sound. I was sleeping a good rest! Then something pushed on my shoulder, and I heard a voice calling:

"Wake up! You are dead! Look!"

Then after that voice I saw it! Like a cloudy sun—I saw it: full clouds all over! No open places! Nothing clear anywhere!

But it was not clouds. It was smoke from guns in battle, as when soldiers try to kill. I could see it—smoke rolling and curling around. The voice said, "Look back to your own country. Your own Wallowa."

I looked that way. A small opening formed in that smoke. Through that break I saw my Wallowa. The prairies, the mountains, the streams, the lake. The voice now told me, "Your life has escaped through where you are looking. You will not die!"

I awoke, found I was on my feet. I sat down. My mother said to me, "You were dreaming?"

I replied to my mother, "Make your heart strong. Do not get excited. We are now surrounded. Maybe in a few minutes you will hear the guns. While we have been coming slow, soldiers have been crowding us close."

Some way off, I saw strange Indian boys driving our

horses. Six good horses—good horses gone. The Salish had picked our best horses. Those Salish Indians were helping the soldiers.

I now painted my hair with white earth, preparing for war. That smoke-cloud was still over me. I did not try to move from it. Nothing could now go through my body. No bullets from the enemy could hurt me. For this purpose did I paint. I understood the voice.[4]

Mounting a horse, I hurried back over the trail. It was to try finding the six horses the Salish took. Riding a quarter mile, maybe half mile, I ran into a bunch of soldiers. Those soldiers had seen me coming. They had fixed a trap.

Some small fir trees growing there stood thick. I rode through them and, passing on a short ways, I saw a soldier sitting on a fallen tree. What was he doing there? I knew not, and did not bother him.

There were scattered pine trees, and I went around one of the biggest. I passed one soldier close. He was aiming his gun at me. It was leveled at my ear, as I could well see. That soldier was not four steps from me. That soldier was not alone. I did not see all, but four or five guns were leveled. They fired, and it was just as thunder in my ears. So close, smoke fogged all through my clothes. I could see nothing! I grew excited. Knew not anything, because of the noise. I did not know I was yelling as a drunk man. All like fire, I was out of sense. I had thought my heart right, but I lost myself.

It was just like dreaming! Twice I yelled. Third

---

[4] The foregoing episode was related to me by Yellow Wolf in 1909. An instance of his remarkable memory is found in the fact that seventeen years later I happened to ask, without reference to this particular incident, the significance of hair painting. Yellow Wolf immediately replied, "You must understand that this was after the war, when we were on our way back to our old home. I was so directed to paint by a Spirit voice." From this it may be inferred that Yellow Wolf painted his hair but this one time in his entire war career.

time I yelled I found myself. My *Wyakin* had come to aid me. It was as waking from sleep, from dreaming. I felt fine. I am telling you true. I was no longer afraid. I did not care how many soldiers there were. Understanding, I now knew they could not hurt me.

They could be nothing to me.

I gave the war whoop. Whirling my horse, down the steep hill, over logs I went. Soldiers were ahead of me. Blocking the way! They fired from all around. I did not stop for anything. Only changed to a little different direction.

Again I was close to the enemy. It was more of the soldiers waiting for me, and I heard shooting at the camp. I did not know which way was best to go, but I still aimed for camp. Soldiers saw me and must have thought, "Another Injun crazy."

They were not soldiers with cannon. Wearing white shirts, some soldiers [citizens] ran toward me. They thought to kill me first. But I was not stopping for them. I did not try shooting. Only I must get away.

A soldier was ahead of me, just to one side. He was waiting to shoot as soon as I came up. As I passed that soldier, he nearly poked me with his gun. He shot my horse through the withers. I did not fall with my horse. I lit on my feet and went out from there. That soldier got no other shot at me. They were all calling, but I knew not their words.

I could see down to camp, surrounded on my side by soldiers. I did not run, could not run. Too much fallen timber. I passed other soldiers who fired at me. I dodged on down the way. Among tangled logs I thought only of getting to camp. Escaping through the fallen trees, I reached camp. Nobody there![5] Tabador called from where he was sheltered, then came out and said, "Brother-in-law, we are going to die. We will not run away!"

I knew Tabador a brave man, and I answered him, "All right. We can die right here. The soldiers shall not drive us from our last blankets!"

Tabador did not give a small heart. It was like he was giving me a big heart, for I was going to die with him.

But those soldiers made no more attack.

It was sunset. I sat down just as I am now. No blanket, no saddle, no horse. We were afoot. A little way from me just across the canyon, soldiers had all our horses. I was thinking hard. Soldiers still over there, fixing to camp.

Came the dusk. We heard the soldiers chopping wood. We did not know if cutting firewood, or for trench-protection from our bullets.

Full dark settled. The other Indians all came from safe hiding. We still heard the chopping. Henry Tabador, the half-blood Indian, called, "Why are you making trenches? Come over! We will have a war!"

They never answered. We were not mad at them. We only wanted to get back to Lapwai. But we acted right with them. We could not turn them down if they wanted to be friendly. It was near the end. We only had a little way more to travel, but all our horses were gone. Skoloom said to me, "Let us get back our horses!"

"I can hardly walk," I answered him.

"What is wrong with your leg?" he asked me.

---

[5] Black Eagle, then sixteen years old, gave this explanation of the emptiness of the camp: "A few minutes before Yellow Wolf came breaking through the timber, only my father [Wottolen], Peopeo Tholekt, and myself had returned from looking for salmon, and were with the women. The whites fired on us, and all broke for the brush. In crossing the creek which was thigh deep, I saw Peo stagger and nearly fall. I called to him, 'Brother, are you hit?' 'No! I stumbled on a rock!' he replied. We reached the brush and there was firing from both sides. But the Indians were saving of cartridges. I could not tell if any enemies were killed or wounded. None of us were touched."

"I dragged my leg," I told him. "Knee bone stiff."

I did not think I could go with anybody. But there were only us two, and Tabador spoke again: "I can not go alone. You must go with me."

"If you say that, I will go with you," I told him.

Skoloom told the plan to the other men, and said: "I do not want to force any of you, my friends, but if you want to go I will be glad. When there we will see how to recover our horses."

Peopeo Tholekt, Ooyekun, Tabador, and Soklahtomah, five of us would go. It must have been near middle of night, and we could hear soldiers still chopping. They had a fire, and I told the men, "We must go there and see."

We crossed the creek and came opposite the soldiers' fire. It was a big fire and soldiers were standing around in the light. Skoloom told his plans to Peopeo Tholekt, "My brother-in-law will go with me up above the soldiers' camp. You men circle the other way. If you hear us shoot, you do the same. We will try getting our horses some way."

Skoloom and I went up the hill, circling to far side of soldiers. They were moving about the fire. We crawled closer, but it was still long shooting through brush. We fired and heard the guns of the other three Indians. We all gave loud war whoops. We shot only one time. Too much woods and no soldiers now seen. They dodged down among the logs.

After we went away, the soldiers commenced shooting. We could not tell direction of their shots. We took everything they had, food and packsaddles. Their horses were tied up. We drove our own horses towards our camp, and got them all.

Next morning Tabador called across to the soldiers, "What you doing over there? You followed us a long ways. Come over if you want to have a talk!"

The soldiers never answered. We thought they were afraid. We asked the interpreter to tell them again, so he called, "Do you want trouble?"

There came no answer. Maybe they had left during the darkness. We did not go see if they were still there. We now had our horses, and nobody hurt. That was all we wanted.

Those soldiers and citizens we could not count. They appeared more than of us. They got first advantage, but they killed no Indians, got no horses. We recovered all our horses.[6]

We saw no more of those soldiers, so we packed and left. We came to a small stream [Clear Creek] where we camped.[7] While in this camp some Nez Perces came to us, three of General Howard's "good" men—Lawyer and two policemen. One used the bad language to us. Soklahtomah got up and said, "I will get my whip and whip that man."

---

[6] Its mendacity matched by its absurdity, the following is the "official" version of this clash between the military and the Nez Perce refugees, as given by Colonel Gibbon: " . . . Lieut. Thomas S. Wallace, Third Infantry, from Fort Missoula, made a rapid pursuit after a party which was making its way from the valley of the Bitter Root toward the Clearwater in Idaho, after committing additional murders on Bear Gulch and Rock Creek. After a very rapid pursuit, Lieutenant Wallace overtook the party at 1:30 p. m. on the 21st of July, on the middle work of the Clearwater, I.T. [Idaho Territory], and with his small party of 13 soldiers and 3 citizens immediately opened fire on the Indians, completely surprising them. He killed 6 of their number and wounded 3, besides killing in the fight 23 mules and ponies and capturing 31 which he successfully brought off. For the energy and pluck displayed in this handsome affair, Lieutenant Wallace and his party deserve the highest commendation, and whilst he reports his whole party as behaving within the greatest gallantry, he especially mentions First Sert. Edwin Phoenix, Company H, Third Infantry, as particularly conspicuous for his brave conduct. This successful punishment of this band of murderers and marauders produced a most salutary effect upon the Indians, and constitutes another brilliant example for the imitation of our other troops." ("Report of the Secretary of War," 1878, p. 68.) Notwithstanding the "official" assertion that six of the Indians were killed in "this handsome affair, . . . this brilliant example," every member of the group was still alive at their disbanding, some days later, within the bounds of the Nez Perce Reservation.

[7] The refugees' camp on Clear Creek was brought to the notice of the Agency officials when Peopeo Tholekt and Tabador, while acting as sentinels at a considerable distance from the main rendezvous, were seen by two Christian Nez Perce women, who immediately relayed the news to the Agency.

He then took his quirt and whipped him. One of our men stopped him from striking more. Soklahtomah said to this whipped man, "You are the *religious* man! Why do you use the bad language? You are one of *Christian* men helping Agent Monteith and General Howard! All you Christian people joined to make the war! You caused the trouble! You made a *thief* treaty! Chiefs have been killed! Good men have been killed! Good women and little children have been killed! Babies too small to walk, crippled and killed! All this because of you Christians! Many of our people taken prisoners will never see this country again.

"Many good white people did not want war, but could not help themselves. They got killed because you Christian people helped Agent Monteith and old General Howard. I could kill you right now!"

"Do not kill us! Do not kill us!" begged General Howard's good men.

Soklahtomah was mad. All the Indians were mad. During this time one of Lawyer's policemen, Kipkip Elwhekin said to Wottolen, "You come with me to the Agency!"

"No! I will not go with you to the Agency!" replied Wottolen.

Kip again said, "Yes, you are coming to the Agency. You will not be hurt."

Wottolen, more mad, answered: "No! Kip, you are not headman! You do not know what they can do to me. Not headman, you could not help me. You would not help me if you could. I am doing no harm. I do not steal anything. Only traveling around to find some of my own property, my own cache."

Kip was silent for short moments. Then he said, "You

are going with me and have a talk with the Agent! You hear me?"

Wottolen was now full mad. He was holding his rifle by its muzzle, the butt resting on the ground. Partly lifting it, he told Kip, "I hear what you say. Kip, you better go! I am telling you three times, I am not going with you! Kip, you better go now. Go before you get in trouble! If any women want to go with you, take them. Any not wanting to go will stay with me. Go, Kip! Be quick with your going!"

Kip answered, "Yes, I will go right now!"

I, Yellow Wolf, made no council with those Christian Nez Perces. I did not want any talk with them. My heart felt poor. Everything was against us. I considered, and then said to my mother:

"You and the other women better go with these, General Howard's men. For me, I will stay in the prairie like a coyote. I have no home!"

My mother did not cry. She spoke to some women, then made answer to me: "Yes, we will go with General Howard's men." A few of the women and my mother then went with Kip and his Christian policemen.[8]

Our party now separated. Wottolen, leader of those from White Bird's band, had talked strong to the men

---

[8] None of the five women who surrendered at this time belonged to Chief White Bird's band, as asserted in the following military dispatch ("Report of the Secretary of War," 1878, p. 184) :

FORT VANCOUVER, WASH.
August 6, 1878
ADJUTANT GENERAL DIVISION PACIFIC,
San Francisco, Cal.

Commanding officer Lapwai is informed through Agent Monteith that on 28th ultimo small band of Indians appeared at Scott's place on South Fork Clearwater. Indians recognized them as White Bird's band and some Sioux. Commanding officer Camp Howard confirms report. Agent Monteith had head chief Lawyer send some of his warriors to induce or force them to surrender. Five squaws of White Bird's band surrendered and say remainder of party consisted of thirteen bucks and some squaws, who have gone to Salmon River to open some caches and then join Snakes, and that White Bird himself is still with Sitting Bull. Lapwai dispatch dated August first.

NICKERSON
Assistant Adutant General

It is needless to say that there were no Sioux among the refugees, notwithstanding that the "commanding officer Camp Howard confirms report"!

from the Agency who came to us. His heart was heavy, but he would not surrender. Wottolen and most of the others headed for old camping grounds in the White Bird country. Going over a mountain, there was no timber, no way to hide themselves from being seen. Police from the Agency were watching everywhere.

Wottolen, an *inatsinpun* [prophet], said, "Do not be afraid! Something will help us!" Soon the sun was covered over. It grew dark. Wottolen declared, "This is what I was telling you would happen for us! No enemy can now see us passing through the open land! I asked for this!"

They all reached the Salmon River without being seen. The women with Wottolen afterwards surrendered.[9] Some of the men also surrendered.[10]

---

[9] Homeless, outlawed, beggared, and disheartened, with every hand raised against them, the women and children had but one alternative—surrender. But they surrendered wholly voluntarily; it can not be shown that there was a forcible capture of a solitary individual among the band.

[10] The charge that the remnant of this band joined the hostile Indians in Idaho and Oregon to participate in the Bannock Indian War (see, for example, Hawley, *History of Idaho*, p. 547) contains no element of truth. However, the known presence of roaming Nez Perces had by this time sufficed to throw the settlers of the vicinity into a hysteria of fear. The following dispatch ("Report of the Secretary of War," 1878, pp. 181-82) shows how little there was in the actual conduct of the Nez Perces to excite alarm:

Camp Howard, Idaho, August 2, 1878

[Assistant Inspector General
Department of the Columbia
Vancouver, Wn.]

Considerable excitement prevailed during the month in vicinity of the post, the citizens anticipating a raid of hostiles to Camas Prairie. These fears so far have been found groundless, none of my scouts, which I have employed to scour the country and watch the trails, having seen any signs of Indians, with the exception of 34 warriors, supposed to be members of White Bird's band of Nez Perces, returning from Sitting Bull's camp, who were encamped several days on the Clearwater and vicinity.

These Indians abstained from open hostilities and I sent a dispatch to the commanding officer of Fort Lapwai, requesting him to consult with the Indian agent and to send some influential men to the camp of the Indians to induce them to surrender to the agent. As yet I have not heard from the commanding officer of Fort Lapwai. The Indians left their former camp and have, as far as I can learn, crossed Craig's Mountains. I do not apprehend any trouble here and the people are gradually calming down, unless there are more return. . . .

I am respectfully, your obedient servant,

D. P. Hancock,
Major Second Infantry, Commanding

A Voluntary Surrender

Yellow Wolf in this chapter shows that he realized the sunset to his free roving had fallen. As a warrior he had rendered a good account, but now he had no place to spread his blanket, no place to go that was not encircled by enemies. It was while riding through scenes of other and happy times that he resolved to turn back to the Nez Perce Indian Agency and surrender himself.

TABADOR, Putim Soklahtomah, two others, and I, Yellow Wolf, stayed together. We hid around for about three suns, until we came to Lahmotta. When we reached there, when I saw that place, it broke my heart.[1] I thought to myself, "These white people—they did not start the trouble. It was only General Howard and the Indian Agent. In council, our Chief Toohoolhoolzote, talking for us, was mistreated. We did not try stopping them, what they wanted to say. We did not try stopping their Christian prayer at council openings. We were not given such privilege with *our* religion."

All this came before me and I made myself that I was a good-hearted man. I would make no trouble. But if any white man got mad about me—if he troubled me— I would kill him with my war club.

There had been a cache where we buried some buckskins and other things before going to war. We went to open it, but dusk drawing on, missed it. Not finding

---

[1] It will be recalled that Lahmotta was the ancient tribal gathering place of the Nez Perces. It was there the patriots had been camped when they were aroused from slumber to meet, for the first time, the white man in battle. Immediately afterwards the tepees were folded, never again to be erected there.

it, we went on. Soon we came to a house where white men were milking cows. We tied our horses and went there. Could see nothing of them! They had run away!

I told Tabador, who spoke English, to call them, that we were friends. He did so. Called several times. Nowhere was there an answer. Nobody showed up.

We had tied our horses at the house. The other Indians got their horses and were leaving. I was still afoot when the white men must have seen me alone. Below the house, corn was planted. It was through this corn patch they came. It was growing dusk, almost dark. Only a few steps away a white man took a shot at me. I knew only by the flash of the gun the direction of shooting. He was so close, I saw smoke all over myself, covering my shirt. My partner, a short distance away, shot at the man as he sprang to the brush. I heard the noise of his running. He must have been scared, missing me.

I now heard a voice quite a little ways from me. Putim Soklahtomah was making a roar. He came running his horse through the corn patch fast as he could. But the white man was then well gone. His name was Charley Wood.

About forty steps down from the house a horse was tied at the edge of a willow thicket. That horse was already saddled. A buckskin horse, fine looking. I pointed and said to my partners, "Look, a good horse! These white men do not come from hiding, only one to take a shot at me. They do not want to be friends. They must want trouble! We will take that horse!"

When dark, the five of us went. Two stopped halfway to watch. Horse was not tied short. The long rope lay across the brush, leading back among thick bushes. Noting all, I thought to myself, "Those white men, hiding, may be holding that rope. Waiting for me to grab the horse, they will shoot me down. If the rope is moved they will know."

I told Soklahtomah what was on my mind. With six-shooter ready, I took hold of the rope but did not pull or jerk. I then said to Soklahtomah, "Cut the rope and let it stay on the brush!" Of course we talked only by whisper.

When he did that I led the horse away. Reaching a short distance I took the bridle hanging on the saddle-horn and bridled the horse. I then gave the reins to Soklahtomah, and told him to mount. He did so, and that buckskin got to dancing. He was lively! But Sok-lahtomah knew how to ride all hidden from the enemy, hanging to the side of his horse. We rode away, not bothering there any more. Those white men milking—we would never have taken their horse had they come out and been friends.

We camped that night, and early next morning got to Tahmonmah [Salmon River] just above Lahmotta. We looked across. One of the Chinamen[2] came with a boat from the other side. Soklahtomah and I crossed over with him.

One man stayed with our horses. Two men stood back on a butte as scouts, watching for danger. After we landed, one scout called to us, "White man coming up the river trail!"

We waited for the man on the narrow trail. When his horse got wind of us, it did not want to go. When he drew near to pass, I caught his bridle rein. I stopped the horse. That man's eyes were turned up. We could see nothing of his eyes. Then Soklahtomah spoke, "Do not

---

[2] The ferry at this point was operated by some Chinese.

be afraid! We are just asking you a question? We heard
Bannacks and soldiers are in trouble. Having a war!"

That man's eyes came back down, but he looked
scared. He answered, "Yes, Bannacks and soldiers are
fighting. Now I want to know. What tribe are you?
Not my business, but I like to know."

Then I talked to him, through Soklahtomah. I told
him, "We are from Lapwai, hunting our cattle. Out
three weeks, we hear no straight news. We could not
know. We turn home now. We have no trouble with
you."

That man shook hands with us, and rode on. When a
little ways from us, he whipped his horse and rode fast
out of sight. We laughed to see him go.

We recrossed to our partners, and traveled on down
the Tahmonmah. We were now in Chief Toohoolhoolzote's country, where he lived below Lahmotta when war
was brought to us. Two white men came meeting us.
When the foremost one was a little distance away, I got
off my horse and sat down.[3] I spoke friendly: "Hello!"

When he would not speak, I stepped ahead of him.
I grabbed his bridle and told him by interpreter, "Get
off!" He answered, "No!"

I held his horse and he yelled at me. I said to him, "Get
off!"

When Soklahtomah interpreted my words, the man
replied quickly, "This is my horse. I am not getting off!"

I drew my war club, and cracked him on the ankle,
and told him, "Get off!" He made a cry and got off. He
just crawled on hands and knees, and cried with pain. I
did not strike hard. Just a light tap on the bone. I said

---

[3] To dismount was preliminary to declaring friendly intentions when meeting
members of an alien tribe.

to Soklahtomah, "Take the other fellow. Let him get off too."

He told the man to get down, who did so. It was nearly a black horse. Bridle of hair, a brand-new saddle.

It was soon I parted from my four friends of many hardships. I gave Soklahtomah[4] my six-shooter. The horses I left with them all. I kept only the buckskin captured from the man who shot and covered my clothes with powder smoke.

There is nothing more to tell of my tricks, of my danger deeds. All these are now behind me. It is not as a warrior that I now talk.

I was riding alone, knowing what was ahead of me. Then the places through which I was riding came to my heart. It drew memories of old times, of my friends, when they were living on this river. My friends, my brothers, my sisters! All were gone! No tepees anywhere along the river. I was alone. No difference if I was hanged. I did not think I would die by the gun. The only way I could be killed was by hanging. That church Agent! That brave General Howard! They would see how I could die! I, a warrior, who knew the fighting! Keeping the religion of my ancestors, I knew not to fear.[5]

I was heading for the Reservation. That Indian Agent who helped General Howard make trouble was there. I would see him, he would see me. I had told Soklahtomah

---

[4] Putim Soklahtomah was of Chief White Bird's band. With his wife and two other Nez Perces, he went to the Umatilla Reservation (northeastern Oregon). After some difficulty with the Agent there he left and went to the Palouse country. His wife died about 1925 between Lapwai and Spalding.

Yellow Wolf's procedure against the two horsemen may strike the reader as inexcusable outlawry. But it should be remembered that—through ignorance or otherwise—his overture of peace and friendliness had been ignored, proclaiming, in the only parlance that he knew, an enemy. Mounted, the strangers would soon have the military or citizen guardians hot on their trail. Self-protection demanded that they be set afoot.

[5] Yellow Wolf's surrender was prompted by a dual purpose. First, he wished to be loyal to Joseph's call that all of his band should come in to him, in accordance with the terms of capitulation at the Bearpaw field. But secondly, Yellow Wolf considered that, if condemned to be hanged, he would take a fierce joy in showing his contempt for death in the presence of Monteith, the hated Agency head.

and others nothing of what I was to do. I thought to let no one know what I was going to do. I traveled all day. I did not stop to camp overnight. I came first to Amos Chely's place. It must have been middle of night when I got there. When I told him my mind, he said, "You have done no wrong coming here. Tomorrow I will take you to the Agency."

He gave me some food and showed me where I could sleep. Next morning he called, "You awake in there, brother? A good stream runs here. Take a swim and you will feel better!"

I went out and took a good swim. When I returned to the house, Amos said to me, "I think best to put your gun upstairs. Soldiers might take it!"

I told him all right. We ate breakfast, and I said to Amos, "I am going to rest up for a while. I will lie here on the floor."

The kitchen door was open and Atpahlatkikt came in. He stepped straight to me and spoke friendly, "I am glad, brother, you are alive and safe from war. I am going to shake hands with you!" Then he asked, "You will be down there to the Agency?"

"Yes, that is who I want to see," I answered. "Who is the Agent? Is it the same man who made the war?"

"Yes, that is the one!"

When they told me that, I knew him to be a bad man, that Agent.

Next man came was James Reuben. He did not offer to shake hands. He said, "You warriors so proud! Too proud to listen! Lots of you killed on the trail. Lots of you rotted on the trail!"

That was all the talk for me. He went out. I was feeling mad. Would have killed him had I my gun. He did not stay. I heard his horse gallop away. That was James Reuben, Christian!

In a little while a boy brought horses for the riding. Amos told me, "Leave the horse you got at Lahmotta. Leave the saddle. Boys have saddles, and horse is saddled for you."

We started and reached Lapwai, which is now Spalding, about noon. We stopped at the store. An Indian policeman took me to the Agency. The Agent instructed this policeman, "Sit around until one o'clock. I will see him and talk to him then."

While waiting, three men came and shook hands with me. One was Charles Monteith, brother to the Agent. Many Indians gathered around me. They were saying to me, "If you make any mistake, they will hang you. Tell nothing but the truth, the facts."

They kept telling that to me. Told it many times. I got mad when they talked that so much, and I spoke the order, "Shut up! Say no more! If the old Agent makes his mind to hang me, I will take it. It is all right. He will get fat off me when he hangs me. That is reason I come to this Reservation!"

They said no more. They did not want me to get hanged or killed. The Indian policeman came and told me, "About noon, about half an hour, the Agent will see you and talk to you."

I never answered. Then the policeman asked me, "Do you hear?"

That policeman was one of the Christian Indians.

I replied, "I do not want to listen to anyone. If I belonged here, you could talk. If I was raising anything, whatever stock I might raise, then I would come and see the Agent, who might help me. When the Agent comes

will be time if I want to talk. I am one of the warriors!
I never belonged here. I am a stranger! You will all know
if the Agent hangs me, without saying anything. If he
hangs me, that will be good. I no longer have a home!"

That Indian policeman said no more to me.

I stayed a long time in the office, waiting. Finally the
policeman came to me again and said, "I am just letting
you know that the Agent will see you in short minutes."

"Mr. Monteith is still the Agent?" I asked him.

"Yes, he is the Agent," he told me.

"Do not tell me anything about him. If some of the
good men come to me, I will listen."

That is all the reply I made the Indian policeman. I
did not want to know when the Agent was coming. Then
I heard his steps in the other room. I knew those steps!
He opened the door and came in. I did not look around,
but I knew who it was. The same man! I felt him—as
with a needle he pierced the hearts of our chiefs—our
chiefs killed! He stood looking at me. I did not look at
him. I did not want to see his face. I just turned to one
side.[6] Then the Agent spoke, through an interpreter.

"Look at me!"

No, I did not look at him at all! He spoke again, "I
know you. You are a very good boy. I would not bother
you!"

---

[6] Yellow Wolf's hatred for Indian Agent John B. Monteith is easily understood.
Because there had been so much strife among the various church "isms" in their
efforts to carry the soul-saving Gospel to the benighted heathen, President Grant—
under an 1869 Act of Congress which violated the Constitutional assurance of
religious liberty—had in 1870 parceled out the Indian reservations to the different
Christian denominations. Exclusive authority over each reservation was given
to a single sect. The Indians, of course, had no voice in the choosing of their
overseers. The Nez Perce Reservation was awarded to the Presbyterians.
As each denominational diocese was empowered to select—subject to easy
Government confirmation—its own Agent, the Presbyterians chose Monteith, son of
a Presbyterian minister, "for his piety and Christian ideals." According to
missionary Spalding, however, Monteith was far from being a model Christian,
and some of his employees were profane and intemperate. (*Whitman College
Quarterly*, Vol. III, No. 3, pp. 10-11.) A sectarian zealot, Monteith wielded the
Gospel lash as a part of his official duty, and found an ardent supporter in
General Howard. Yellow Wolf and other Nez Perces, brought up in the Dreamer
credence, saw the cosmic faith of their ancestral heritage scorned, reviled, and
suppressed as a thing of evil by both missionary and Government official.

He walked up to me and shook hands with me. I thought not to touch his hand, but I did. He said, commandingly, "You must tell what you know. You were fighting General Howard. Four days ago you had a battle with the soldiers. They killed six Indians of you, and captured two women."

That was what the Agent said to me. I answered, "No!" I thought, "Why is the old Agent asking me?"

"You are a pretty good boy."

When the Agent said that, I replied, "No! I do not want to speak about such things as that. Everything is over! The war is quit! I do not want it brought back as new. I do not want to talk, for everything is quit. Look at me [standing in demonstration, both arms lifted]! I have no weapons about me! I do not want to speak about war any more. It is gone! It is like you taking the gun and shooting me again, the way you are speaking."

Eeikish Pah: The Hot Place

It appears evident that Yellow Wolf's notoriety as an outstanding warrior, and especially his connection with the recent sanguinary happenings on Rock Creek and Bear Gulch, had reached the ears of the Nez Perce Agency. This, because of the vindictive antipathy of Agent Monteith towards the "heathen hostiles," would have boded ill for the self-surrendered Yellow Wolf.

But his investigation by that worthy was not to be. Captain Falck, by authority of his office as Post Commander at Fort Lapwai, took the friendless young warrior under his own charge, and his handling of the case, as told by Yellow Wolf, reveals a regard for justice too often lacking in the breast back of a gold-embroidered uniform during the Indian wars.

THE Agent showed some mad. He walked around a little. But before he could make answer, whatever was his mind, a noise outside came fast. The door opened, and there came in an officer, a sergeant, and a few soldiers. The officer made request, "Where is that Indian who came and wanted interpreter?"

"There he is," and they pointed to me.

Those soldiers shook hands with me. They told me to stand up and come with them. I went as they said. They put me in the jail [guard house]. They did not stay there fifteen or twenty minutes, but went right away.

In a short while I heard steps outside. Then the door opened, and quickly entered Lieutenant or Captain, named, I think, Fellis.[1] He shook hands with me, and asked, "Who is your chief?"

---

[1] Yellow Wolf's pronunciation of Falck. Captain William Falck, Second Infantry, was Post Commander at Fort Lapwai, Idaho Territory, at the time.

"My chief was Joseph," I told him.

Of course we talked through an army interpreter. When I said, "Chief Joseph," that officer replied, "Yes, I understand. That is why I sent the lieutenant and sergeant. I sent them because I know the Agent. He will never help you. The white men are mad about you Indians, and if they found you on the Reservation, they would kill you. The Agent can do nothing. He would do nothing. The white men will not bother you, so long as you are in here. Our soldiers will protect you. But do not think you are prisoner. We put you here just to be away from the whites."

That was what the captain told me all the way through. Then he began asking questions. He said, "I am glad you came to your home country. You tell us the story true what you did as you came. Swear to it. If you lie, the Government will punish you."

I gave him the answer, "Yes, I thought you a good man. I came over to see you, if all right. I can not swear anything [*i.e.*, the Christian oath]!"

That captain looked strong at me. Then he spoke, "I am going to ask you. Did you take a horse, kill a cow, or something? I want you to tell all."

"Yes," I replied. "I am glad you asked me that. War

The following dispatch ("Report of the Secretary of War," 1878, p. 182) sent by Falck undoubtedly refers to Yellow Wolf, though he is mistakenly classed as a member of Chief White Bird's band:

Fort Lapwai, Idaho
August 4, 1878

Assistant Adjutant General
Headquarters Department of the Columbia
Fort Vancouver, Washington Territory.

Sir: I have the honor to inform you that yesterday one of the hostile Nez Perces, belonging to White Bird's band, surrendered to the Indian agent and is now in confinement at the post guard-house; the remainder of the band, 13 in all, crossed the Snake River on the night of the 2nd near Craig's, and are doubtless making for the Umatilla Reservation. The agent there has been notified, also the commanding officer at Camp Howard, in case this band should go to the Salmon River country.

Very respectfully, your
obedient servant,
Wm. Falck,
Captain Second Infantry, Commanding Post.

was quit. Chiefs on both sides shook hands. Since I was in a strange country, and all had been settled, I thought to come back to my own country. We made no trouble as we came along. But some took shots at us. Would that make you mad? What would you think? Would you shoot, or just say, 'I am going to die?' "

"I want you to tell only truth so the Government will protect you," the officer made reply. "Anybody will shoot in self-protection. I would do that."

"Yes," I told him, "I am telling truth. When anybody takes the gun to me, I will take his horse. Will shoot him, or he may get away. They bring the gun on themselves."

The officer said, "That is so." He then took a rolled paper, and looking at it, continued speaking, "This is White Bird's country. Why were you there?"

"I did not go there for trouble. We went to get cached stuff. Charley Wood took a shot at us, and of course we took his horse."

"Report is you took Charley Wood's horse?"

"Yes. He took a shot at me. I made my mind to take his horse and did so. Not for nothing did we take that horse. We saw another man's brand on the buckskin. Wood did not own him. Must have stolen him."

"You are telling truth?"

"Yes."

"You had no right taking that horse. You should have witness. You might get in prison three or four years."

That would be all right if they wanted to send me there. The officer looked at more papers, then spoke again, "You tell the truth. In the mountains you found a horse with saddle on?"

"Yes."

"Good horse? Did you take it?"

"I do not deny it."

"You had a fight with soldiers. Those soldiers killed six men and captured two women from you."

"Yes," I said, "it was about two suns before the real fight. The soldiers fired on some of us when we went to get beef. That made us mad, and we had a little fight. I took one soldier's horse which got away from us. We found one horse saddled and took it. Afterwards came the fight, but nobody was killed, nobody wounded. No women captured."

"Is horse you got with saddle here?" the officer asked.

"No, I gave that horse to Skoloom," I answered.

"Yes, you are the party soldiers took women, children, and horses from."

"No! We got all our horses back. No women, no children captured."

"You are telling lies?"

"No! They killed none of us."

"You are telling truth?"

It was three times this officer asked that question. I answered him, "Yes, I am telling true. If that had happened, any killed, any captured, I would not deny it."

The officer made no more questions. He now said, "I am glad you tell the truth. If Skoloom will bring in that horse, and the man [owner] comes along within a year, we will give it to him.[2] Since you left Canada, and killed some people on the trail, somebody will trail you here. For this reason you must stay with soldiers for protection. You were making a new war, but other parties, whites, started it first. I am glad you told everything. If they trail you here and make complaint, we will have

---

[2] This was the cavalry horse captured by Yellow Wolf as told in Chapter 22. It is evident that Captain Falck was not aware it was a Government-owned animal.

this, your story, as evidence for you. We will also take good care of other Indians coming from Canada."

Then he asked, "Who is this with you?"

"My cousin. I slept in his house last night. He brought me to the Agent this noon," I told him.

When I answered him that, he wrote on a paper that I was from Canada and turned me over to the sergeant of the soldier guards, with instructions to keep me from trouble. He then shook hands with me, and told me I was to go to that place [Indian Territory]. Said he was glad I was now back from Canada, and advised, "Do no wrong, and all will be well for you."

That was what the captain told me all the way through. After that I was treated right while prisoner there. I had no more trouble with anyone. From that time, I have come through safe to this night [May, 1935].

I went with the sergeant. When the soldiers saw us coming, they waited for us. They took me to a building, their room. Then we went to the next room. They asked, "You starving?" They divided crackers with all.

After four or five suns, Tabador came of his own will. A few nights after, we heard a calling to soldiers, wanting to "leave somebody in jail." Then soon I heard horses running up the road. Whoever did that calling to leave somebody in jail, escaped from the soldier guards. Whites had come to kill us but they did not fool the soldiers. After that we were watched carefully. No white men could pass who did not look good.

A band of eleven men and one woman of White Bird's band had come through from the Sioux camp to the Salmon River about fifteen days ahead of us. The leader,

Tahmiteahkun, was a brave warrior. The woman with them was his wife. This band never was captured.

A few days after Tabador came, five more came and surrendered of their own mind. The Agent was glad to see them, but he must take them to the soldiers. He told the soldier captain how they had escaped from Canada. That they must be protected from whites mad at them. Must stay close around and sleep in jail nights. The Indians were told not to go too far away in daytime. Whites might kill them. They were kept around there, but were not made to work. Never were sent to the Territory, but remained on the Nez Perce Reservation.[3]

Tahmiteahkun, his wife, and the other four men stayed in the mountains for some time. Never were captured.

There were four others at this jail, all running loose. Four women, among them my mother. They came in with the Kamiah Indians, Lawyer, and the policemen after we parted. Chief Joseph's daughter was among them. But she was not brought to the jail, was not sent to the Indian Territory.[4]

I was not permitted liberty, but kept locked inside. Another man in the Spokane jail was under lock all the time he was there. We were never fed heavy, but did not go hungry.

I was sent to the Territory with these people—nine others—of Chief Joseph's band. There we united with our old friends and relations—those left of them.

The horse and saddle I rode to the Agency, I took

---

[3] See Appendix I, this chapter.

[4] The reason why Joseph's daughter was separated from her parents and not permitted to join them in exile is palpably manifest: Joseph was to be made to feel to the last degree the bitter sting of isolation. Kapkap Ponmi was turned over to her aunt and placed in the Lapwai Agency school. In 1879 she was married to George Moses, a full-blood Nez Perce, at Spalding, on the Nez Perce Reservation. She died at Lapwai some years later. Her mother, Heyoom Yoyikt, Chief Joseph's "old" wife, was permitted, upon her return from exile, to take residence on the Reservation.

from an unfriendly white man [Charley Wood]. The Government got them. Government kept all horses and saddles that General Miles got from us at the last battle. We lost everything. Many horses, many cattle on Snake and Salmon rivers. Only the few clothes I had on and my blanket were left me.

My war club which I had carried all through the war, I held onto. Keeping it concealed in my legging, I had it while in prison. I carried it when being taken to bondage. Kept it all the snows, the same club I gave you.

We were not badly treated in captivity. We were free so long as we did not come this way, towards Idaho and Wallowa. We had schools. Only the climate killed many of us. All the newborn babies died, and many of the old people too. It was the climate. Everything so different from our old homes. No mountains, no springs, no clear running rivers. We called where we were held Eeikish Pah [Hot Place]. All the time, night and day, we suffered from the climate. For the first year, they kept us all where many got shaking sickness, chills, hot fever.

We were always lonely for our old-time homes.[5]

Chapman was there during entire years of our captivity as interpreter. He lived with a Modoc woman as his wife, but left her there when he came back with us in 1885. Of course Chapman was Government employed. Andy Davenport was also interpreter, but Chapman was the main one. James Reuben sometimes did interpreting.

When finally released from bondage [1885], brought back to this country, religion had to do with where they

[5] For a description of the inexcusable maltreatment accorded the Nez Perce patriots in exile, with a complete enumeration of Indians received, and a statement of the appalling mortality suffered because of climatic conditions, see *Report of the Commissioner of Indian Affairs*, 1878 (E. A. Hayt, Commissioner), pp. 32-35.

placed us. We believed in our own Hunyewat [God, or Deity]. We had our own Ahkunkenekoo [Land Above]. Hunyewat gives us food, clothing, everything. Because we respected our religion, we were not allowed to go on the Nez Perce Reservation. When we reached Wallula, the interpreter asked us, "Where you want to go? Lapwai and be Christian, or Colville and just be yourself?"[6]

No other question was asked us. That same had been said to us in our bondage after knowing we were to be returned from there. We answered to go to Colville Reservation.

Chief Joseph was not given choice where to go. But he had the promise that as soon as the Government got Wallowa straightened out, he could go there with his band. That was never to be.

On the Colville we found wild game aplenty. Fish, berries, and all kinds of roots. Everything so fine many wanted to remain there, after learning that Wallowa was not to be returned to us. Chief Moses advised Joseph to stay. The Indians were good to us.[7] Gave us horses, and other useful property and goods. Deer everywhere, and good salmon at Keller. It was better than Idaho, where all Christian Nez Perces and whites were against us.

I have two sons,[8] but have never told them of my warday fighting. I want them to see this story, all that I have given you. It is a true story, all as I have told you. It is a true history, what I have seen and done.

---

[6] This was a continuance of the same religious persecution that was a large factor in the inception of the Nez Perce War. As Yellow Wolf shows, a home on the Nez Perce Reservation at Lapwai was to be had only at the price of abrogation of the Dreamer faith in favor of that of "Spalding's God."

[7] Chief Moses was the leader of the band of Sinkiuse Indians resident on the Colville Reservation.

[8] Yellow Wolf's younger son, Jasper, was of delicate constitution and died several years before his father. The older son, Billy, is still living on the Colville Reservation (1940).

EXCLUSIVE PHOTO FOR THIS VOLUME BY ALONZO V. LEWIS

YELLOW WOLF AT CHIEF JOSEPH'S GRAVE

Taken at Nespelem, Washington (Colville Indian Reservation), July, 1926.

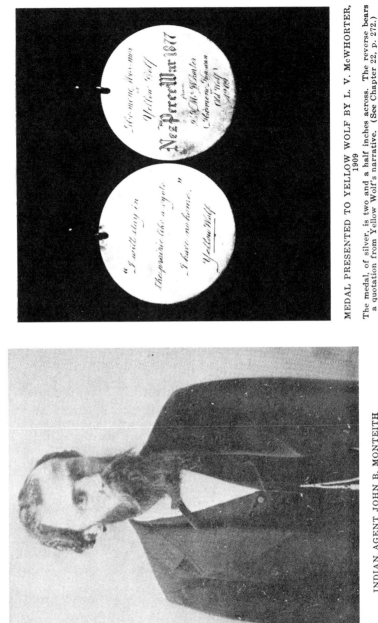

MEDAL PRESENTED TO YELLOW WOLF BY L. V. McWHORTER, 1909

The medal, of silver, is two and a half inches across. The reverse bears a quotation from Yellow Wolf's narrative. (See Chapter 22, p. 272.)

INDIAN AGENT JOHN B. MONTEITH

This is all for me to tell of the war, and of our after hardships. The story will be for people who come after us. For them to see, to know what was done here. Reasons for the war, never before told. Nobody to help us tell our side—the whites told only one side. Told it to please themselves. Told much that is not true. Only his own best deeds, only the worst deeds of the Indians, has the white man told.

❈　❈　❈

APPENDIX I

It is difficult to believe that Agent John B. Monteith, with his diocesan antipathy for the Dreamer war party, could have shown such benign favor to the White Bird refugees as attributed to him by Yellow Wolf. It is far more likely that there was some other humanely inclined Agency official who smuggled the unfortunates into the Reservation, unknown to the Agent proper, of which Yellow Wolf would not have been cognizant. Apropos is the following material obtained in a personal interview with Mr. G. D. Fleming, who said in part:

"I was head clerk at the Nez Perce Indian Agency in the early eighties, when Charles D. Warner was agent. He was supposed to handle cases touching Reservation governmental affairs, but practically all the petty offences, real or fancied, came before me for settlement. We held regular court, ofttimes empaneling a jury of six to twelve men. At such times I have heard pleadings by blanketed Indians, long-haired and uneducated—acting in the capacity of attorney—truly remarkable for logic, deep thought, and eloquence of oratorical deliverance.

"During my incumbency, many of the Nez Perce war band who escaped from General Miles at the last battle and made their homes with the Sioux, Blackfeet, and other tribes, drifted back to the Nez Perce Reservation. These 'hostiles,' as so termed, were all known to the Indian police, who arrested and brought them into the Agency as soon as discovered. Coming before me, I was supposed to turn them over to the Agent, whose duty was to deliver them to the military post commander, to be transported to the Indian Territory.

"I have always been glad that in no instance did I ever do this. I would talk to the prisoner, who never failed to show anxiety to be accorded a chance to prove a sincerity of intentions to be law-abiding and peaceable. I would then turn to the Indian police, pointing to the fact that the refugee had suffered enough; that there was nothing to be gained by holding him (or her) prisoner, to be sent so far from their old home and people; that they were full willing to abide by the laws of the Reservation as prescribed by the Government; and I requested that the brother or sister be turned loose, which was invariably done.

"Not once did any of these forlorn outcasts prove recreant to the trust placed in their promises. They had fought and lost! Returning broken in spirit and in purse, they stoically accepted the inevitable, burying the dead past.

"I had gone to the Agency holding an adverse opinion of the Indian in general. But I soon changed my notion as to his worth and possibilities under proper treatment and environment. That he has been woefully wronged goes unchallenged, to the lasting shame of the Caucasian race.

"You ask concerning the disposal of Chief Joseph. He was not permitted to reside on the Nez Perce Reservation.* All influences possible were bent to that end. Not only the citizens in general, but the missionaries and the Christian Nez Perces united against all thought of such measure."

---

* Maj. C. T. Stranahan, former Superintendent of the Nez Perce Indian Agency, responding to an inquiry, confirms Yellow Wolf's testimony that residence on the Nez Perce Reservation by the returned exiles could be had only by a declared abrogation of their Dreamer religion tenets.

APPENDICES

❀

A. *Wyakin Powers*
B. *Yellow Wolf's War Club and War Whistle*
C. *Henry Tabador*
D. *Report of Captain William Falck*
E. *Chief Red Heart's Band*

Wyakin Powers

A STUDY of anthropology reveals that the mind of man has advanced along the same channel the world over. The idea of a personal deity has been a comparatively late growth, for in primitive cultures, particularly those in primeval surroundings, the first and dominant form of theism has been belief in a multiplicity of gods.

The majestic and awe-inspiring environment of the North American Indian made him peculiarly prone to deify the manifold forces, or intelligences, of which Nature in the wild state is redolent. That he came to believe in a living consciousness residing not only in the animal kingdom but also in all components of the mineral and vegetable kingdoms is amply attested by his legendary lore.

This pervasive spirituality forbade the wanton destruction of game and plant life: the Indian exacted only so much as was necessary for his actual sustenance. Even the nonedible remains were guarded from debasement. The hunter never left offal (scant as it was) exposed for others of its kind to "see and feel bad," nor would he place a green fir bough on his campfire. This sentiment likewise impelled him to pick up, for instance, fragments of deer antler and drop them into a rosebush, safe from tramping feet. He believed in the immortality of all life.

With the earth thus infinitely peopled with spirits, the Indian believed that he could invoke them to be peculiarly his own, in the role of guide or protector. This relationship is that which is known as *Wyakin*. *Wyakin* is a generic term; it may be a sngle force, or it may embrace a combination of mystic forces acting in unison. It is a grave error to confuse this medium of the supernatural with God or Deity outright, as some writers have done. On this score, Many Wounds, who had a profound knowledge of his native religion, and who had, moreover, once taught a Methodist Bible class, wrote in reply to an inquiry: "It is this way. You have faith, and ask maybe some saint to help with something where you probably are stalled. It is the same way climbing a mountain. You ask *Wyakin* to help you." Thus, metaphorically, *Wyakin* is placed in the category of mediator.

Although Yellow Wolf was reticent about his own sources of occult aid, he thus explained in a general sense the acquisition of such powers:

"I will tell you! Beginning with the forefathers of all Indians, they had such a Power given them. Different spirits coming out of once living animals. Also from the thunder, the wind, the sun, the earth, rocks, or whatever it might be. This Power descends from one person to another, and I inherited it to live through all engagements of the war. All the dangers and hardships of that war. It came to me from my father, and perhaps he inherited it from his father, and perhaps that grandfather from his father. The Wolf-Power I was given made me a great hunter, a sure scout."

The secrecy with which these occult rites are surrounded may be inferred from Yellow Wolf's remarks on one occasion:

"No one has ever told—I will not tell—just how this Power is received. Only when approaching the enemy ready to fight life for life can you hear and learn from fellow warriors. Only then are these things told—what Power has been given the warrior, what Power he must use. It is at such time the guardian Spirit enters into the warrior's head. Enters that he may defend himself, escaping bullets, arrows, spears, clubs, or knives. To escape with life through the battle.

"Therefore no one must ever tell anywhere outside of the war, only when the war happens. I will not tell just how I obtained that Power. I should not express it. I can not, I must not tell."

However, it may be said that, in general, relationship with these elemental powers was chiefly contingent upon the observance in early childhood of certain practices, learned either through rigorous parental training, or, more often, through the tutelage of some renowned warrior, hunter, or medicine man, whose word from that hour became law. If the votary was a girl, an elderly woman of reputed power would be selected as tutor.

At the proper age—in general, from nine to fifteen years—the child candidate was sent, unarmed and without food, to spend a given time—perhaps only one night, or possibly a week—in fasting and silent contemplation in the solitude of mountain or desert. The more fearful and awe-inspiring the surroundings, the more readily would the child mind become spiritually endowed. However long the votive period, the fasting could not be broken, nor could a fire at night be built. Water in strictly limited amount was permissible in case of intolerable thirst. Night and day the mind must be kept steadily fixed on the object of the quest.

In time the candidate would fall into a comatose state of mind. It was then that the *Wyakin* revealed itself, sometimes merely as a voice, or at other times as a recognizable apparition. If it was the air—the wind soughing among the trees or over the desert waste—such Power was understood to render the body invulnerable to the passage of bullets or arrows. If the *Wyakin* came as thunder or as lightning, it conferred a terrible potency in battle.

Among the apparitions that might be seen, the deer bestowed fleetness of foot upon the suppliant; the grizzly bear or buffalo bull, strength in battle; the coyote, cunning in approaching enemies; the wolf, excellence both in war and in the hunt; the prairie chicken, ability to hide from danger.

The eagle, the hawk, the raven, and many other denizens of the air have a place in the *Wyakin* category. A rare Power given by the rock wren—that relentless enemy and hunter of the rattlesnake—enabled the recipient to handle the deadly serpent with impunity.

In my last interview with him, Yellow Wolf gave the following explanations:

Wyakin is your faith in some strength to help you in dangers, in battle. A man may have any of three different Powers. First, you see a warrior in front of you in battle. You fire at him only a few steps away. You miss him! You fire again, maybe often. You miss him every shot! He can not be hit.

Second, you shoot a warrior. You wound him two or three places. But bullets will not go through him. He does not feel them. He is not hurt.

Third, you shoot a warrior and the bullets do not penetrate. They will not enter his flesh.

This is the way I understand. I know by my religion. Suppose you are to fight tomorrow. You are told by your *Wyakin* not to do certain things. You have a wife. You tell her of the rules to be observed by her. If she does this, then when the battle comes the enemy bullets will miss, or will not enter your body. If she disobeys, then such bullets will surely enter your body. It is this way:

If your Power is in feathers which you place at a certain height, and your wife throws them down, or they fall down, then the Power you had in those feathers is destroyed for all time. Your prayer has been killed. But if everything is handled right and you are true, your *Wyakin* will surely help you when there is danger.

You know our schooling. Young people sent out into wild, night places without anything, their hands empty. I did that! Often stayed from home three, maybe five, suns and nights. Because my father died when I was young, no living man had sympathy for me. Your father's spirit outside somewhere might recognize you and come to you.

My father had a Power, but a soft body. Bullets entered his body but he did not die. Scars, many scars, on different parts of his body. All these showed his bravery in war.

The life in trees, in grass, might compose your Power. It is impossible to explain. It is against orders of your *Wyakin* to explain, if you could. This is all impossible to be understood by whites. I believe if I now went to war I would be killed by gas. My Power is not against that, only against arrows and bullets.

But I have no more chances to fight. No more wars; and I am growing old. When I come to dissolve, then I will tell my children and grandchildren how I was when young. But they have a different schooling, different beliefs. They have learned the white man's thinking.

In war, *Wyakin* was generally embodied in material objects, such as amulets, charms, or feathers. The war whistle in particular was most conducive of safety and was always blown when in the rage of battle. (See Appendix B, "Yellow Wolf's War Club and War Whistle.") But most exacting were the stipulations of such protection. The slightest infringement of the rigid rules laid down by the guardian Spirit was sure to be followed by dire results.

As a final example of *Wyakin*, the following episode was related by Many Wounds:

It was far up in the wild mountains of the Little Salmon River, Idaho. A small boy, I was camping with my grandparents. Early in the morning I went up the mountain to look after our horses. I looked ahead a short distance to a small hill against the mountain. There, sitting with his back against a stump of a fallen tree, I saw a man. A fine-looking Indian wearing a blanket. Long hair falling about his shoulders. It was splendid hair, yellow or golden. He looked at me but spoke no words.

I saw him sitting there, a light like a rainbow circling above his head. I saw the sun rise off to one side of him. I saw its rays shooting down the mountain slope, saw its rays passing over and by the man, but never striking him. Soon the vision faded, nothing remained to be seen of it.

I think the meaning of this vision was this: the sun rays passing without striking the blanketed person in plain view meant arrows and bullets of battle passing without hurt to me. Should I ever be in war I would be willing to try the danger. That vision man had been some great warrior with that kind of *Wyakin*.

Appendix B

Yellow Wolf's War Club and War Whistle

A T THE close of our 1908 interviews, I asked Yellow Wolf what had become of his war club and was informed that he still had it. I expressed a desire to own it, should he ever care to part with it. After some moments he said simply, "I understand."

Returning to the hop fields the following year, he brought both his war club and war whistle and presented them to me. I well knew that there was interesting mysticism connected with the club's production, but of

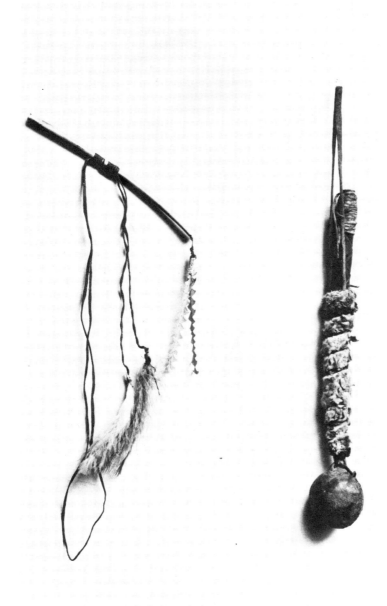

YELLOW WOLF'S AIDS IN BATTLE

Left, his magic war whistle. Right, his *kopluts*, or war club.

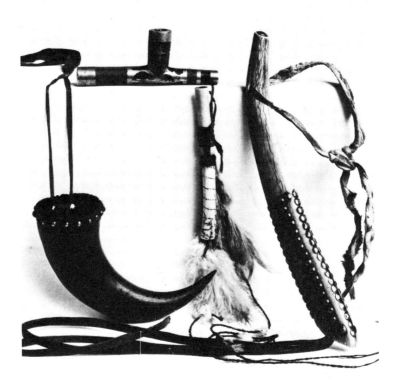

RELICS OF THE NEZ PERCE WAR

Left to right: Husis Owyeen's drinking cup, made from a buffalo horn; on this he tallied the number of dead in the Big Hole fight. Peopeo Tholekt's magic war whistle. Chief Joseph's elkhorn quirt; this passed to his successor, David Williams, at the great chieftain's funeral feast. Joseph's pipe, carried throughout the war.

the occult Yellow Wolf seldom spoke unless the subject was broached, so I requested that he give me whatever details he cared to concerning it. Through interpreter Whitman he gave me the following account, graphically demonstrating with the weapon itself the various phases of his story:

The regular war club is generally short handled, about five or six inches aside from the stone at its end. It must be only five or six inches in length for this reason: because in the battles and fights with another tribe, the warriors do not meet face to face and strike at each other. They grab and scuffle. This *kopluts* hangs on the wrist with a buckskin thong. When the enemy grabs hold of you to throw you down and kill you, if you have a long-handled club to your wrist, he can easily seize it and hold on to it. But if a short handle, you have it well covered with your own hand. You can then club your enemy and you are privileged to break his arm.

I, Yellow Wolf, raised among warriors, made it a study how I should go to war against different tribes and fight from horseback. How I should have the enemy to meet and match when mounted. I would have to strike across from horse to horse, fighting for my life. Trying for the death of my enemy. From all this, I judged I would need a long handle on this club, which you now see as I fashioned it.

At the time I made this *kopluts*, preparing for war, I put this war paint on it which has been there ever since. Not that I did this of myself. It was the belief that I have within me, obtained from the fowls that fly, from the creatures that creep or leap through the wilds, that gave me a Power to be strong in battle, in war, where life is against life. This Power told me to make such a weapon for protecting myself.

It was in this way, by the instructions of this Spirit, that this *kopluts* was made and painted. When I give this weapon to my friend, it is as much as giving my life to him. For this man is near my heart. When I see him, always a friend to me, I, Yellow Wolf, give him this club to keep it always.

I was small, quite young, when I fashioned this *kopluts*. I did not select the stone. Searching around to select, I was given instructions —directions about the rock to pick from—when and how to make it. This stone I rounded myself. You can select a rock from the river and try breaking this one: *Tock! tock! tock!* [Striking imaginary blows.] The other rock will break. This one is a selected stone for war business.

I was instructed to cover the *kopluts* with elk rawhide, then wrap the handle with the fur of the otter.

I am Heinmot Hihhih [White Thunder]. That thunder, when it rolls and strikes anything, it kills. That thunder gave me its Power to be with this *kopluts,* striking as the lightning strikes. This Spirit guided me in making this weapon.

I have a boy. If these Spirits should know him, that he is my boy, like me a warrior, someday he shall have that Power. It will be taken from me when I am old—when I die—and everything be given him. If he is given the same Power, then he shall have a *kopluts* like this.

Not that I will ever promise my boy to make such for him. I will not. He must have instructions direct from that Power—then make it himself. Nobody will know why he made it. Nobody knew when I made mine or why I made it. If he has Power, he will construct it alone. If he has not the Power, then he has no use for the club.

The war whistle carried by Yellow Wolf through the 1877 conflict, although having but one shrill note, was more often referred to as a flute. When requested to blow it, he refused, stating that only in battle or deadly danger was it to sound. Of its use and potency, he explained:

This war whistle which helped me in dangerous places is made from the wingbone of the crane. Spirits guided me in its making. Guided me from what bird the bone must be taken. It is not to be used in sport and amusement. For war only, I always sounded it in battle. The soldiers then could not hit me. Only in battle or other dangerous places did I sound this whistle. Not at any other time was it to be sounded.

I wore it by the buckskin thong still fast to it. This loop was about my neck and left shoulder. The flute hung under my left arm. There it was away from handling the rifle. These two small eagle-down feathers at the end of the thongs were plucked from over the bird's heart. Their fluttering up in the wind was good. Always moving, you could not see that which does it. There was good prayer in the feather movements.

You must not let my flute be wrongly used.

When in April, 1910, a painting of Yellow Wolf in full tribal regalia was being executed from a series of photographs, he was written to for a description of his garb during the war, also for the loan of the streaming feather plumage he sometimes wore on his right arm during gala days.. This was sent, together with this message:

You ask what I wore during the war. My shirt was white, with green stripes running both ways [plaid pattern]. My leggings were dark, striped with green, red, and white. Breechcloth—a shawl without apron straps; such would be in the way of fighting.

The medicine that gave me strength during the war was in my feathers. These were wrapped in red flannel cloth. This bundle I carried on my back. I do not think I will get along well without my feathers. You must care well for my feathers.

When Yellow Wolf was shown the finished painting, he studied it a few minutes and then commented: "Not good fighting picture. Looks nice on wall."

APPENDIX C

Henry Tabador

HENRY TABADOR'S real name was Henry Rivers. He was a half blood. He is the Indian who figures as "Charley" in the account of the Carpenter-Cowan tourist party in Yellowstone National Park as related by Frank Carpenter. (See the reprint edition, Guie and Mc-Whorter, *Adventures in Geyser Land*, pp. 92 ff.) His Nez Perce name, Heinmot Tosinlikt, is apparently subject to a dual interpretation, "Lightning Tied in a Bunch," or "All Pulling Together." Concerning him Mr. Camille Williams writes:

The Indian called "Charley" in Frank Carpenter's story was a half blood, supposedly of the Snake tribe. This belief came about in the following manner. When small, his parents lost him on a trip to the Coast, and the Bannacks found him, and he grew up among them. Then he came to the Nez Perces, where he married. We think Carpenter's story half invented.

The name given him by the Bannacks was Ta-ba-bood-ze: "White Man." Pronunciation of this name in Nez Perce is Tom-memo [Tomamo], as he was known ever after. But the name at the Agency appears as Tababo, his parental name.

Tabador left an unsavory reputation because of some of his deeds, but his courage in the face of danger could not be gainsaid. He was the warmate of Yellow Wolf in divers nerve-testing occasions, particularly as related in Chapter 21. Of the last days of his old-time companion, Yellow Wolf, in our final interview in May, 1935, gave the following account:

In Eeikish Pah [Hot Place] where we were sent prisoners, there was lots of sickness. Heinmot was goodhearted to his friends. A boy had pneumonia, and Heinmot told me one morning he was going after alcohol for him. Alcohol was good for a fever which walked there. Many were cured with it.

Heinmot got ready his horse, but could not go. A Government inspector came, and Heinmot was the only one to do the interpreting. The Agency interpreter was not there. Heinmot took his horse a ways over the hill to pasture, thinking to get back for the meeting. He tried to be fast, but the inspector was ready, and Heinmot returned too late.

Because of a strong wind, the meeting was held inside. They called for Heinmot to interpret. I told them he was gone with his horse to the pasture. No interpreter found, someone said, "Get Reuben, the teacher." A policeman brought James Reuben. The same man who had helped the soldiers against us in the war.

Soon as he entered he called out, "What are you people thinking? You fought the Government! You can not do anything!" That was the way of James Reuben. Always against us, but he was allowed to interpret.

The inspector then said, "I came here to learn if all are doing right. Tell me whatever is on your mind. I will put it on paper and send it to Washington."

Those were the inspector's words. But James Reuben interpreted differently. He made as if the inspector had said: "Joseph, if you or people do anything wrong, I will send it to Washington. Then you will be punished."

Heinmot had returned, and stood at the door. He interpreted correctly, not as had Reuben. Reuben spoke loud: "You can not interpret anything! Where is policeman? Put that man out!"

Heinmot stepped outside. An Indian policeman shot him. There were five Nez Perce policemen among us. All had taken Christian religion. Right away the Agent was sent word of the shooting. He came quick. Heinmot was shot in the hip. The bullet ran down towards his knee.

The Agent asked him, "Why were you shot?"

"I do not know!" was Heinmot's reply.

"Well, you are shot! Don't you know *why?*" The Agent spoke sharply.

"No, I do not know why! Why don't you ask the one who shot me?" was Heinmot's reply. When he said that, the Agent called loudly: "Who shot this man?"

"Tom Hill!" several people answered.

"Did you shoot him?" the Agent asked Tom Hill, standing by.

"Yes!" was Tom Hill's answer.

"Why did you shoot him?"

When the Agent asked that question, Tom Hill answered: "Look at me! I am dressed in Government clothes. I was advised by you to shoot any one bothering me!" Tom Hill pointed to his police star and added: "This was what shot him—the Law!"

"That was not what I appointed you for, to shoot your brother! I appointed you to arrest murderers, and bad men only. This man is wounded. We must care for him. If he dies, there will be trouble for some of us. No use talking any other way!" The Agent showed anger.

Heinmot went off fishing. He did not get sick, did not go to bed. He came out of that wounding all right.

About one week, maybe ten suns later, he went uptown and bought liquor. Returning, he came to one man's house and stopped. Drinking, but not drunk, he sat in a chair, rocking back and forth. He had a cap and ball six-shooter on his belt. Someway the gun fell from its holster. Two shots went off, knocking away all the top of Heinmot's head.

This happened some time in the morning, and he lived until five o'clock that evening. His head must have been bent forward, to be struck in such manner.

That was how Heinmot Tosinlikt died. All this happened soon after we reached Eeikish Pah. It is the last story about him. A brave warrior, a good fighter. Dangerous when mad, he always stood by his friends.

At time of the war Heinmot had seen twenty-six or twenty-seven snows.

APPENDIX D

Report of Captain William Falck

THE little-known report of Captain William Falck (Second Infantry), post commander of Fort Lapwai, Idaho, gives interesting sidelights upon Yellow Wolf's narrative of the Nez Perce refugees' return from Canada, June-August, 1878. While the discrepancies in the two accounts in regard to the number of guns and horses are of moment, the testimony of other members of the band tend to confirm Yellow Wolf's computation.

Although it was—and is still—contended by Black Eagle, the only surviving member of the band, that there was not a "Lucy" among their number, and that, aside from Henry Tabador, there were no English names among them, doubtless Captain Falck did interview a "Lucy." As "Charley" was a common appelation for any Indian man accosted by a white stranger, so was "Lucy" among Indian women.

Many of "Lucy's" statements exhibit a desire to please her interlocutor, as she shrewdly read his mind by the intonation of his queries. This complaisance was characteristic of primitive-minded Indians. They never argued or contradicted a point where no tangible gain was apparent.

Captain Falck's report is found in "Report of the Secretary of War," 1878, pp. 180-81:

Fort Lapwai, Idaho
August 1, 1878

[Assistant Inspector General
Department of the Columbia
Fort Vancouver, Washington Ter.]

Sir: I have already informed you by telegraph of the return of a part of White Bird's band, and the measures taken by me to arrest these Indians. James Lawyer, who went out with a large force of his Indians, found the party had disappeared; he followed the trail to near Mr. Chapman's place, where he was stopped by a party of white men from Camas Prairie, who advised him to return to the reservation, else he might meet with disastrous consequences. He therefore gave up the chase, and it is probable if the whites come across the party they will kill them all. Five squaws with two children left the hostile party and were brought in by Lawyer last night, and during a long and close examination this morning, I elicited some interesting facts regarding White Bird's band and Sitting Bull.

The squaw who gave me the information is named Lucy; was married to one of Joseph's men killed last year; she says, when White Bird saw that Joseph intended to surrender he told him to go in first with his band, and he would follow, but instead of following Joseph, he took all the young men of his band and some women and escaped during the night. They have been living with Sitting Bull ever since, who treated them all very badly, except White Bird; owing to this treatment great discontent had arisen among them, and especially among those who were not members of White Bird's band proper; for that reason many of them had made up their minds to escape and return to their native homes. The first to leave was a party of seven, who are now in confinement at the post; then a party of four more and one squaw left who went to the Pend O'dreille [d'Oreille] country; and lastly, the party to which they belonged, hearing that the Umatillas were about to fight the whites, made up their minds to join them. The entire party consisted of 11 men, 2 boys, 8 women and 3 children. They left Sitting Bull's camp about the 20th of June; in ten days they struck Milk River in a southwesterly direction from the camp; and in five days thereafter the Rocky Mountains. They came through the Blackfeet country and saw no whites until they reached the Bitter Root Mountains; thence they came in by the Elk City trail. The women all had horses when leaving Sitting Bull's camp; some of the men were dismounted till near Helena; north of there they stole two good American horses. When near the Hellgate River in the Flathead country three men of the party left, and the following morning drove in a large band of good horses; after selecting the best and gentlest, the balance were set adrift. The men and women of the party separated every morning and met in camp at night, when the men would bring in blankets, clothing, coffee, sugar and plunder generally.

When in the Bitter Root Valley the women were left in charge of the two men, with directions to take the Elk City trail, while the men were to take the Lo Lo trail, but on the following day the women overtook the men and found the latter in possession of a large and fine band of mules and horses. They went in camp about 90 miles from Elk City, and while resting there the following day were overtaken in the afternoon by a party of thirty white men, who attacked them and fought them at long range till evening. The white men were successful in capturing all the horses and mules, including the horses and saddles of the entire party, excepting six on which they mounted the squaws, the men marching till they reached the reservation, where they again provided themselves with mounts by stealing from the Kamia [sic] Indians. In this fight the squaw says one white man was killed and no Indians. The entire party camped near Clear Creek; when James Lawyer's party first found them they all refused to surrender, and declared their determination to join the Snakes. During the night the five squaws escaped and surrendered to Lawyer. Three women and children are still left with the party, who are probably gone to the Salmon River, there to open some caches left by their people last year, containing money, blankets, provisions, etc., thence they will endeavor to join the hostiles, unless intercepted by the whites, which is probably the case. The Indians are but poorly armed; the whole party had only four guns and one revolver and belts partially filled with ammunition. For one of the guns they had no ammunition; this was a Henry rifle;* the other

* This was Yellow Wolf's gun, but not a Martini Henry rifle, which was a single-shot arm developed in England. Yellow Wolf's gun was a repeating Win-

guns were Springfield rifles. Lucy tells me that as the party leaving Sitting Bull's camp were not all mounted, they only marched about 50 miles a day (marching day and night); it took them ten days before they struck Milk River; consequently Sitting Bull at that time was about 500 miles from the border.

She tells me Sitting Bull has no permanent camp but keeps constantly moving; they always camp on the prairie. During all the time she was here she saw no towns or settlements, only the Canadian police, who have to go a long way north, as she expresses it, to find the camp. Last winter Sitting Bull had plenty of buffalo meat, but nothing else except such articles as he can get from the traders. Sitting Bull has plenty of arms and gets all the ammunition he wants from the traders who bring goods and provisions for sale. There seems to be no restriction placed on the sale of ammunition; it is sold openly to whoever wants to buy it. White Bird is determined to remain with Sitting Bull and help him fight the white men; only a few of his own band are left; one of the young chiefs with him, Huts-e-cut-la-trat, however, says he is coming in shortly to surrender. One of the five squaws is a young daughter of Chief Joseph; she showed me a photograph which had been sent to her by her father from Leavenworth.

I have informed the commanding officer at Mount Idaho of all the facts in my possession regarding this band, his command being in close proximity to Salmon River.

Very respectfully, your obedient servant,

WM. FALCK,
Captain Second Infantry, Commanding.

----

chester. An inquiry to the Winchester Repeating Arms Company elicited the reply: "Dear Mr. WcWhorter:

"Our records show that the gun you mention, No. 126589, is a Model 66 [1866] carbine and it was shipped on April 24, 1876.

"It is regrettable that a record of those early guns was not kept more completely than it was, but at that time we did not record to whom these guns were sold."

(Signed) "EDWIN PUGSLEY."

There seems reason to believe that these early model Winchesters were sometimes called Martini rifles. In the autumn of 1909 Yellow Wolf presented to the writer his war-battered weapon. See illustration in Chapter 6.

Chief Red Heart's Band

THE treatment accorded Chief Red Heart's band of noncombatant Indians makes this one of the most unjust episodes of the Nez Perce War. That this group of peaceful Indians surrendered voluntarily is acknowledged by General Howard in the following field dispatch, sent to Division Headquarters, San Francisco, July 19, 1877:

> Majority of hostile Indians have fled on Lolo Trail to buffalo country; forced to go. Thirty-five men, women, and children, in my hands voluntary surrender.

These prisoners, as attested by every contemporary Nez Perce interviewed, were taken to Kamiah, where their horses and equipment were confiscated. They were forced to march afoot through the blistering July heat and dust, under guard of mounted Government Nez Perce scouts and soldiers, to Fort Lapwai, to be sent to the Vancouver Barracks as prisoners of war.

In a letter from the late Colonel J. W. Redington, who was an active scout for General Howard during the later days of the Nez Perce campaign, he speaks of seeing these prisoners at the barracks, under guard of members of the military band, the regular soldiers being on duty afield.

The following compilation of Chief Red Heart's band is that of Black Eagle, son of warrior Wottolen, as interpreted to me in May, 1930 by his brother, the late Many Wounds.

MEN

"Old" Chief Red Heart

Ne-ne-tsu-kus-ten (son of Red Heart)

Te-me-nah Ilp-pilp (youngest son of Chief Red Heart)

"Old-man" Half Moon

Tsa-lah-e

Nosm

John Reuben

Little Bear

Alex Hayes (still living, 1930)

Te-po-noth

Kai-ye-wich

Ha-ha-tsi He-ke-lan-tsa

"Old" Chief Jacob (signer of treaty of 1855)

A-yok-ka-sie

Pile of Clouds

Wal-we-yes

James Hines (still living, 1930)

Kole-kole-tom

Jim Powers

Pa-cus-la-wat-akth

George Raymond

WOMEN

Tsa-cope

He-ma-kio Aut-way

Pe-tol-we Ta-looth

Hamo-lits-hamo-lits

Pe-to-lack-yoth

We-tah-wee-non-mi

GIRLS

He-yum-ki Yum-mi

Tal-we Nom-mi

BOYS

Il-soo-pop (three years old)

Unnamed son of Little Bear. This child died at Vancouver.

———————

Total: 33

No record of prison commitment of Chief Red Heart's band has yet been found, but after long and diligent search through the Vancouver Barracks Post Headquarters vault, Mr. J. L. Sharon unearthed an order for their transfer, and the reply thereto. These papers he was granted permission by the Adjutant to copy especially for this work. The two documents follow:

WESTERN UNION TELEGRAPH COMPANY
PORTLAND, OREGON

APRIL 20, 1878

TO COMMANDING OFFICER FORT VANCOUVER W T
NOTIFY CAPTAIN BOYLE TO BE READY TO TAKE

INDIAN PRISONERS TO LAPWAI IDAHO MONDAY IN
PLACE OF COLONEL WHEATON VERY ILL.

> ORDER ISSUED TODAY
> (SIGNED)
> SLADEN
> AIDE

> Fort Vancouver, W. T. April 22, 1878

Adjutant:

Sir;

I have the honor to report, in obedience to instructions from Post Headquarters; I have this day transferred to Captain William H. Boyle, 21st U. S. Infantry, all Nez Perce Indian Prisoners of War.

Viz;

23 Twenty-three	Adult Males	)	
9 Nine	Adult Squaws	)	(33)
1 One	Boy	)	

All of which have been borne on general report as Prisoners of War.

> Captain Robert Pollock,
> *21st Infantry*
> *Officer of the day*
> *Order officially stamped and*
> *filed, April 22, 1878*

It is noticeable that there is a difference of but one in these two listings in regard to men, but a difference of two in regard to women. The latter can be accounted for by the absence of the two girls from the releasement tally, Captain Pollock evidently classing them as adults.

These figures attest the astounding memory of Black Eagle, fifty-three years after the transaction. That the individual name of each should be retained, even down to that of a three-year-old child, is truly marvelous.

Publications and Manuscripts

Arnold, R. Ross. *Indian Wars of Idaho.* Caldwell, Caxton, 1932.

Brady, Cyrus Townsend. *Northwestern Fights and Fighters.* Garden City, Doubleday, Page, 1923.

Brosnan, Cornelius J. *History of the State of Idaho.* New York, Scribner's Sons, rev. ed., 1935.

Buck, Amos. "Review of the Battle of the Big Hole," in *Contributions to the Historical Society of Montana,* Vol. VII, 1910.

Cave, Will. *Nez Percé Indian War of 1877 and Battle of the Big Hole.* Missoula, Montana, n.d.

Catlin, J. B. "Battle of the Big Hole," in *Historian's Annual Report, Society of Montana Pioneers,* 1927.

De Smet, P. J. *Oregon Missions and Travels over the Rocky Mountains.* ("Early Western Travels," Vol. XXIX.) Cleveland, Clark, 1906.

Fuller, George W. *History of the Pacific Northwest.* New York, Knopf, 1931.

Gibbon, John. "Battle of the Big Hole," in *Harper's Weekly,* December 28, 1895.

Guie, H. D., and McWhorter, L. V. *Adventures in Geyser Land.* Caldwell, Caxton, 1935.

Hathaway, Ella C. *Battle of the Big Hole* (as told by T. C. Sherrill). No pub., 1919.

Hawley, J. H. *History of Idaho,* Vol. I. Chicago, S. J. Clark Pub. Co., 1920.

Hayt, E. A. *Report of the Commissioner of Indian Affairs.* Washington, D. C., 1878.

Hodge, Frederick W., ed. *Handbook of American Indians.* Washington, D. C., Government Printing Office, 1907.

Howard, O. O. *My Life and Experiences Among our Hostile Indians.* Hartford, Worthington, 1907.

———*Nez Perce Joseph.* Boston, Lee and Shepard, 1881.

Hunt, Garrett B. "Sergeant Sutherland's Ride," in the *Mississippi Valley Historical Review,* Vol. XIV, No. 1, June, 1927.

Kappler, Charles J. *Indian Affairs, Laws, and Treaties.* Washington, D. C., Government Printing Office, 1904-09. 2 vols.

McBeth, Kate C. *The Nez Perces Since Lewis and Clark.* New York, Revell, 1908.

McDonald, Duncan. "Nez Perce War of 1877: Indian History from Indian Sources." (A series of eighteen articles in the *New Northwest*, Deer Lodge, Montana, 1878-79.)

McWhorter, L. V. *Border Settlers of Northwestern Virginia.* Hamilton, Ohio, 1915.

Marquis, Thomas B., ed. *Memoirs of a White Crow Indian.* N. Y., Century, 1928.

Meacham, A. B. *Wi-ne-ma and Her People.* Hartford, American Pub. Co., 1876.

Miles, Nelson A. *Personal Recollections.* Chicago, Riverside Pub. Co., 1897.

Mourning Dove. *Cogewea.* Boston, Four Seas Pub. Co., 1927.

Noyes, Al J. ("Ajax"). *In the Land of Chinook.* Helena, Montana, State Pub. Co., 1917.

Progressive Men of Montana. Chicago, A. W. Bowen, [1901?]

Redington, J. W. "Scouting in Montana" (MS). In Historical Society of Montana.

Report of the General of the Army. Washington, D. C., 1877; 1878.

Scott, Hugh Lenox. *Some Memories of a Soldier.* N. Y., Century, 1928.

Shields, G. O. ("Quoquina"). *Battle of the Big Hole.* Chicago, Rand, McNally, 1889.

U. S. House Doc. No. 552, 56th Congress, 1st Session, 1900. "Claims of the Nez Percé Indians."

Wilmot, Luther. "Nez Perce Campaign" (MS).

Wilson, Eugene T. "The Nez Perce Campaign" (MS). (A paper read before the Tacoma Research Society.)

Correspondence

Army War College, Fort Humphries, D. C.
Bailey, Colonel Harry L., second lieutenant, Twenty-first Infantry.
Bond, Fred G. (He flatboated Nez Perce prisoners to Bismark.)
Brainard, General D. L., Second Cavalry.
Brininstool, E. A., author.

BIBLIOGRAPHY

Brown, General C. W., retired.
Bruce, Robert, author.
Day, Cassius, volunteer, Nez Perce campaign.
Freeman, Dan, courier for Colonel Gibbon.
Goldin, Theodore W., Seventh Cavalry.
Holmes, H. E., of Page's Volunteers, Nez Perce campaign.
Jerome, Lovell H., second lieutenant, Second Cavalry.
Loynes, Charles N., corporal, Company I, Seventh Infantry.
Painter, Rev. Harry M., late lieutenant, Washington National Guard.
Rand, Phillip, Montana pioneer.
Redington, Colonel J. W., Army scout, Nez Perce campaign.
Smedberg, Colonel, W. R. J., Eighth Cavalry.
Wood, Colonel C. E. S., second lieutenant, Twenty-first Infantry.

Interviews

Allen, Frank, volunteer, Nez Perce campaign.
Beall, Thomas, Jr., Nez Perce authority.
Brenner, Mr. and Mrs. Charles, Nez Perce residents of Horse Prairie.
Callaway, Lieuellyn, justice of Supreme Court, Montana.
Cowan, Mrs. George F., Nez Perce captive.
Cullen, John W., Captain of volunteers, Nez Perce campaign.
Darr, Elias, volunteer, Nez Perce campaign.
Fleming, G. D., chief clerk (*circa* 1878), Nez Perce Indian Agency.
Garcia, Andrew, packer for Colonel Sturgis.
Humble, J. L., captain of volunteers, Lolo Trail fiasco.
Lynch, John, First Cavalry.
McDonald, Duncan, pioneer and Indian trader.
Morris, Sam, Nez Perce scout for Army, Nez Perce campaign.
Osterhaut, David B., volunteer, Nez Perce campaign.
Rawton, J. G., volunteer, Nez Perce campaign.
Schorr, John P., sergeant, Troop F, First Cavalry.
Slaper, C. W., Seventh Cavalry.
Slickpoo, Nez Perce scout for Army, Nez Perce campaign.
Stranahan, C. T., former Agent, Nez Perce Reservation.
Wilkinson, Barnett, volunteer, Nez Perce campaign.

YELLOW WOLF:

His Own Story

✪

GLOSSARY

THIS Glossary is not intended to be exhaustive. Its aim, rather, is to include names interesting from an etymological standpoint, and names particularly subject to controversial interpretations. The syllabication is, in numerous instances, uncertain; but it will serve as a guide for pronunciation. Perfect accuracy can not be attained, inasmuch as the Nez Perce tongue has never had a rigid standard of pronunciation.

Ah-kun-ke-ne-koo: Land Above; figuratively, the Hereafter.

Aih-its Pal-o-ja-mi: Fair Land; Of Fair Land.

Al-lez-yah-kon: old-time name of uncertain meaning. Known to whites as Lazzykoon. Father of Phillip Williams.

at-e-mis: dead deer; spirit deer.

At-si-pee-ten; Itsi-pee-ten: Girl Chasing Animal.

A-so-tain: Eel Creek, from *a-so'*, eel.

Chel-loo-yeen: Bow and Arrow Case; Wearing Quiver. Later known as Phillip Evans.

Cho-jy-kies: Lazy.

Chus-lum Hah-lap Ka-noot: Barefooted Bull.

Chus-lum Hih-hih: White Bull.

Chus-lum La-pit-kif Hots-wal: Bull Second Boy.

Chus-lum Mox-mox: Yellow Bull. Also called Weyatanatoo Wahy-akt (Sun Necklace).

Da-koo-pin; Koop-nin: Broken.

Dis-kos-kow: Sun Faded.

Doo-ki-yoon; Doo-ko-yoon: Smoker.

Ee-ah-lo-koon: signifies a flock (of geese) turning to light on water.

Ee-i-kish Pah: Hot Place—the term applied to Indian Territory.

E-las-ko-la-tat: Animal Entering a Hole (?) Later known as Joe Albert.

E-loo-sy-ka-sit: Standing on a Point. Later known as John Pinkham.

Es-pow-yes: Light in the Mountain.

Hein-mot Hih-hih: White Thunder, or White Lightning. The Nez Perces do not have separate words for thunder and lightning. Heinmot Hihhih's more common name was Hemene Moxmox (Yellow Wolf).

Hein-mot Ilp-pilp: Red Thunder.

Hein-mot Too-ya-la-kekt: Thunder Traveling to Loftier (Mountain) Heights. Known to the whites as Chief Joseph.

Hein-mot To-sin-likt: Bunched Lightning. Usually called Henry (Charley) Tabador.

Hein-mot Too-tsi-kon: Speaking Thunder.

Hek-kik Tak-kaw-ka-äkon: Charging Hawk.

He-mene Mox-mox: Yellow Wolf.

He-na-wit: Going Fast.

he-yets: bighorn, or mountain sheep.

He-yoom Yo-yikt: Bear crossing.

ho-hots: grizzly bear.

Hu-sis-hu-sis Kute: Naked Head.

Hu-sis Ow-yeen: Wounded Head.

In-nee-chee-koos-tin; Nin-nee-chee-koos-tin: Yellow Wolf's boyhood name; definition unknown.

it-si-yi-yi: coyote.

It-si-yi-yi Op-seen: Coyote with Flints.

Jee-kun-kun; Jee-kam-kun: Dog. Called by whites John Dog.

Kah-mu-e-nem: Nez Perce name for Snake River as far up as the junction with the forks of Salmon River. Probably named after a "twining vine."

Ka-mi-a-kun; Ka-mi-ah-kin: Human Skeleton. Head chief of Yakimas and other tribes west of the Palouse.

Kam-is-nim Tak-in: Camas Meadows—a place name.

Ke-talk-poos-min: Stripes Turned Down.

Kip-kip El-whe-kin: not a Nez Perce name. One interpreter writes that it may be intended for Kipkip Pahlekin, a Cayuse name.

Kip-kip Ow-yeen: Shot in Breast.

koos: water.

Koos Kap-wel-wen; Kap-is-wel-lah Pah: Swift Water (Yellowstone River).

Koots-koots Tsom-yo-whet (Tsom-yo-kat): Little Man Chief.

kop-luts: a war club, consisting of a rock attached to a stick handle.

kous; kouse: an edible root.

GLOSSARY

Kow-tol-iks: this name implies the "remains of a human body scattered by wild animals."

Lah-pee-a-loot: Two Flocks on Water; Twice Lighting on Water. This man was later known as Phillip Williams.

La-koch-ets Kun-nin: Rattle on Blanket.

Le-loos-kin: said to be a Flathead name meaning Whittling.

Le-peet Hes-sem-dooks: Two Moons.

Me-op-kow-it: Baby.

Moo-sit-sa: Four Blankets; apparently a Salish name.

Nik-tsee-why: definition unknown. Also called Heneenee. She was the mother of Kowtoliks.

Nos-na-ku-het Mox-mox: Yellow Long Nose (literally, Nose Long Yellow).

Ol-lo-kot: supposedly a Cayuse or Umatilla name meaning Frog.

Ots-kai: probably a Flathead name, of undetermined meaning. It has been translated "Wild Oat Moss," but this is uncertain.

Pah-ka Al-ya-nakt: Five Snows; *i.e.,* Five Years.

Pah-ka Pah-ta-hank; Pah-hat Ip-ta-hank: Five Fogs.

Pah-ka-tos Ow-yeen: Five Wounds. Derived his name from an ancestor, not from an actual instance in war.

Pah-ka-tos Wat-ye-kit: Five Times Looking Up.

Pa-uh Wa-hy-akt: Hoof Necklace.

Pe-nah-we-non-mi: Helping Another; also defined as Travel in a Band.

Pee-ta Au-ü-wa: Nez Perce name for Cottonwood Creek.

Pee-tom-ya-non Tee-me-nah: Hawk Heart; Bullet Hawk Heart.

Peo-peo Hih-hih: White Bird.

Peo-peo How-ist-how-it: Curlew.

Peo-peo Ip-se-wahk: Lone Bird.

Peo-peo Thol-ekt: Band of Geese.

Pis-wah Ilp-pilp Pah: Place of Red Rock—name of a spring.

Pit-pil-loo-heen: Calf of Leg; Large Calf of Leg.

Pu-tim Sok-lah-to-mah: Ten Owl.

Sa-pach-es-ap: Drive In—a place name.

Sarp-sis Ilp-pilp: Red Moccasin Tops.

See-kum-ses Kun-nin: Horse Blanket.

See-loo Wa-hy-akt: Eye Necklace.

See-skoom-kee; Es-koom-kee: No Feet.

See-ya-koon Ilp-pilp: Red Spy; Red Scout.

Se-wat-tis Hih-hih: White Cloud; early name of Husis Owyeen (Wounded Head).

Si-wish-ni-mi; Sau-wis-ni-ma: Mussel Creek—a place name.

Si-yi-kow-kown: Lying in Water.

So-ko-li-nim; Jo-ko-li-nim: Antelope—a place name.

Tah-mon-mah: Salmon Waters; *i.e.,* Salmon River.

Tah-wis To-kai-tat: Bighorn Bow; or possibly, Throwing Bighorn.

ta-kia-lak-in: antelope.

Tak-seen: Willows—a place name.

Tee-to Hoon-nod; Te-to Mom-nood: Bare Legs; or possibly, No Leggings.

Tee-wee-yow-nah: Over Point of Hill.

te-kash: cradleboard.

Te-nah-tah-kah We-yun: Dropping from a Cliff.

Te-pah-le-wam: Split Rocks.

Te-wit Toi-toi: definition unknown; probably a Flathead name.

Tip-yah-lah-nah E-las-sa-nin: Roaring (Thundering) Eagle.

Tip-yah-lah-nah Kaps-kaps: Strong Eagle.

Tip-yah-lah-nah Sis-kon: Eagle Robe.

Tip-yah-lah-nah-kikt: Alighting Eagle.

Tis-ku-sia Kowia-kowia: Whittled Buckskin. It has also been defined as Blond Skunk.

Tis-saik-pee: Granite. A name probably derived from Tissaik Pah (Granite), a district southeast of Kamiah Valley.

To-ma Al-wa-win-mi: Springtime (?). This definition is questioned by a Nez Perce interpreter of considerable ability.

Tom-yun-mene; Tom-yan-nin: Struck (by lightning?)

Too-hool-hool-zote: Sound; probably a Flathead name.

Took-leiks: Fish Trap.

To-was-sis; Tee-we-was: Bowstring.

Tsa-ya Tee-me-nah; Te-mi-ni-si-ki: No Heart.

Wah-chum-yus: Rainbow.

Wah-kaw-kaw: Woodpecker.

Wah-li-tits: Shore Ice (?) This name can not be clearly defined; it refers, according to one interpreter, to "ice along the shore, with open channel in center of a river. "Crossing" by another interpreter.

Wah-seen-wes Saw-hoht-soht: Mountain. A Flathead name. One interpreter says this is one of Tabador's names.

Wat-tes Kun-nin: Earth Blanket.

Weippe: English corruption of some unidentified Nez Perce word. It is said by some, and denied by others, that the original was O-yi-pee (Unstrung Beads) (?) One interpreter suggests it may come from O-ya-yap, a meaningless name bestowed on the locality by Grizzly Bear (legendary animal-person).

GLOSSARY

We-mas-tah-tus; We-ne-mas-tah-kis: Elder Deer.

Wetti-wetti Hou-lis: Mean Person (?)

Wet-yet-mas Hap-i-ma: Surrounded Goose.

Wet-yet-mas Lik-lei-nen: Circling Goose (Swan).

Wet-yet-mas Wa-hy-akt: Swan Necklace. Later took the name John Minthon.

We-ya-ta-na-too Lat-pat: Sun Tied.

We-ya-ta-na-too Wa-hy-akt: Sun Necklace. Known to whites chiefly as Yellow Bull.

We-yoo-see-ka Tsa-kown: Geese Flying Above (?)

Wi-yu-kea Koos: Elk Water (River)—a place name.

Wot-tol-en: Hair Combed Over Eyes.

Wy-a-kin: an occult force. See Appendix A.

Yi-yik Wa-sum-wah: Swan Woman. According to one interpretation the name conveys the idea of swans lighting (on water).

Yoom-tis Kunnin; He-yoom-tsi Kunnin: Grizzly Bear Blanket.

YELLOW WOLF:
His Own Story

✪

INDEX

INDEX

324

INDEX

INDEX